SINCE HE WROTE ABOUT ME

JESUS OF NAZARETH SPEAKS IN HIS OWN WORDS ABOUT THE AUTHENTICITY, RELIABILITY, AND ACCURACY OF THE HEBREW SCRIPTURES

By William P. Welty, Ph.D.

Koinonia House

Since He Wrote about Me

Jesus of Nazareth speaks in his own words about the authenticity, reliability, and accuracy of the Hebrew Scriptures

All Scripture quotations are from the *Holy Bible: International Standard Version®* (ISV®), v2.0. Copyright © 1996-2017 by The ISV Foundation. All rights reserved internationally. Used by permission. Visit the ISV Foundation at http://isv.org.

Except for brief quotations in printed reviews, no part of this publication may be reproduced, stored in a retrieval system, or transmitted in any form or by any means (printed, written, photocopying, visual, electronic, audio, video, over the Internet, or otherwise) without the prior written permission of the publisher.

The *Appendix: Evidence from History for Biblical Figures* contains material that cites heavily from Dr. Lawrence Mykytiuk's excellent article entitled "53 People in the Bible Confirmed Archaeologically". The article is Copyright © 2014, 2017 by that author and published by Biblical Archaeology Review (http://www.biblicalarchaeology.org). Used by permission and pursuant to Fair Use. Cited from http://www.biblicalarchaeology.org/daily/people-cultures-in-the-bible/people-in-the-bible/50-people-in-the-bible-confirmed-archaeologically/.

On the Cover: Portion of the *Great Isaiah Scroll* (1QIsa) from Qumran Cave Number One of the Dead Sea Scrolls, (ca. 200 BC) showing Isaiah 52:13-54:4. Cited from http://dss.collections.imj.org.il/isaiah#52:13.

© Copyright 2017 William P. Welty Ph.D.
Published by Koinonia House
P.O. Box D
Coeur d'Alene, ID 83816-0347
www.khouse.org

ISBN: 978-1-57821-731-1

PRINTED IN THE UNITED STATES OF AMERICA

DR. PETER WILLIAM FLINT
21 January 1951 – 3 November 2016

Until his passing, Dr. Flint held the Canada Research Chair in Dead Sea Scrolls Studies and was Professor of Religious Studies at Trinity Western University, Canada. He earned his Ph.D. from the University of Notre Dame. Dr. Flint authored literally dozens of scholarly studies, many of which were on the subject of the Dead Sea Scrolls, including *The Dead Sea Psalms Scrolls and the Book of Psalms* (1997) and *The Meaning of the Dead Sea Scrolls* (2003). He edited over 25 Dead Sea Scrolls for Oxford University Press, and recently completed the official edition of the Great Isaiah Scroll and the *Second Isaiah Scroll* from Cave One (Oxford University Press).

Dr. Flint translated the Book of Isaiah directly from the *Great Isiah Scroll* (1QIsa) from the Dead Sea Scrolls for the *Holy Bible: International Standard Version,* producing the first translation of that book into modern English intended specifically for lay Bible readers. Due to Dr. Flint's contribution to the *ISV Bible*, the 2,200 year old *Great Isaiah Scroll* is now rendered into modern English simple enough that a junior high school student can comprehend it easily, accompanied by a register of scholarly footnotes that graduate students who are expert in biblical languages can appreciate and study.

Dr. Flint's colleague Dr. Martin Abegg summarized Dr. Flint's contribution to conservative biblical scholarship as follows:

Peter was born in Johannesburg, South Africa, on January 21, 1951, to Alwin and Edelweiss Flint. After graduate studies at the University of South Africa, Peter relocated to the United States to pursue doctoral studies in Old Testament and Second Temple Judaism at the University of Notre Dame. His dissertation was titled The Dead Sea Psalms Scrolls and the Book of Psalms (1993) and was directed by Eugene Ulrich. Professor Ulrich himself said that this remains the most comprehensive and right-thinking study of the Psalter as illuminated by the Qumran scrolls.

After a two-year period as Associate Professor of Biblical Studies at Southwestern College in Phoenix, Arizona (1993–1995), Peter moved to Trinity Western University (TWU) in Langley, British Columbia, Canada, in 1995 and continued as a much-beloved member of the TWU faculty until his death.

At TWU, Peter played an integral role in founding the Master of Arts in Biblical Studies program in 1995. He also cofounded and directed the Dead Sea Scrolls Institute with me. In 2004, Peter was awarded the Canada Research Chair in Dead Sea Scroll Studies and Related Literature.

It is an understatement to say that Peter reveled in his career as a Dead Sea Scroll scholar. He was certainly the greatest "evangelist" for the discipline. BAS events were a fertile ground for Peter's persuasive powers. Many participants were at least momentarily convinced that they should change careers and study the Dead Sea Scrolls with Peter. A good number actually did so. Thus Peter's students are clearly what he himself would point to as his greatest legacy—all "reaching for the stars" in the footsteps of their mentor.

> *Peter's contribution to research is no less important. He was a member of the Discoveries in the Judaean Desert editorial team—contributing to volumes 16, 22, 38 and, perhaps the pinnacle of the project, volume 32, Qumran Cave I.II The Isaiah Scrolls (Oxford: Clarendon Press, 2010) with his doktorvater, Eugene Ulrich. The Isaiah volume was granted the award for the "Best Book Relating to the Hebrew Bible" for the years 2009–2010 by BAS.*
> *Peter was also keen to ensure that the hard-won results of Biblical scholarship and Qumran studies did not remain in research papers and monographs. The Dead Sea Scrolls Bible (San Francisco: HarperCollins, 1999) in partnership with Martin Abegg and Eugene Ulrich,*
> *The Meaning of the Dead Sea Scrolls (San Francisco: HarperCollins, 2002) with James VanderKam, and his own The Dead Sea Scrolls (Nashville: Abingdon, 2013) attest to his passion for communicating the importance of the scrolls to the general public.*[1]

Dr. Flint is survived by his wife Amanda, his children Claire, Amy, Abigail (Daniel), Jason (Nadine), Taryn, and Ethan, as well as grandchildren Jacob, Olivia, Andrew and Benjamin.

Dr. Flint was arguably the finest expert in biblical era Hebrew, Aramaic, and Greek that I've met this century, easily on a par with my graduate school mentor, the incomparable Dr. Gleason Archer, the late Professor of Semitic Languages and Old Testament at Trinity Evangelical Divinity School of Deerfield, Illinois. He is already sorely missed, and this work, though vastly inadequate in comparison to Dr. Flint's excellent scholarship, is the best I can do to celebrate, memorialize, and honor with gratitude and respect his contributions to the eternal Kingdom of Jesus the Messiah.

William P. Welty, Ph.D.
Executive Director, The ISV Foundation
Fall 2017

---

1 Martin Abegg, Milestones. (Biblical Archaeology Review: March/April 2017), page 14.

In Remembrance of

CHARLES ROY WELTY
24 October 1952 – 20 April 2016

(http://weltybrothersstudios.com)

My twin brother, whose phenomenal talent at motion picture and radio scriptwriting remains a source of continual amazement to me. May God grant you rest from your labors, after having produced more than 36 full length motion picture screenplays, more than 20 completed radio pilot scripts, and countless television series scripts and production treatments over a 20 year period—and all of them with a God-centered, family values orientation and world view—as we await the sure and certain resurrection from the dead at the end of days, when we are promised that we shall meet again.

> *I heard a voice from heaven say,*
> *"Write this:*
> *'How blessed are the dead,*
> *that is, those who die in the Lord from now on!'"*
> *"Yes," says the Spirit.*
> *"Let them rest from their labors,*
> *for their actions follow them."*

Revelation 14:13

AUTHOR DEDICATIONS

TO DR. GARRY ANSDELL
Senior Pastor, Hosanna Chapel of Bellflower, California

TO DR. BRIAN HUGHES
Senior Pastor, Calvary Chapel of Auckland, New Zealand

TO DR. CHUCK MISSLER
Founder, Koinonia House and Koinonia Institute

Three expositional Bible teachers who believe, as did Jesus the Messiah, that the Scriptures are historically accurate, trustworthy, and reliable records of the activity of God on earth.

FOR DR. MARGIT BRANDL
My elegant, sophisticated, perennially fascinating, and faithfully loyal European telecommunications attorney friend and world class modern art photographer. May you soon meet and become acquainted, both in this life and also in the one to come, with the magnificent and amazing Person whose respect for the Hebrew Scriptures is described so inadequately in this present work.

FOR KRISTIN QUINN
My kind, thoughtful, loving, and drop-dead gorgeous world-class fashion model friend. Her character, courage, fortitude, and life activities remain a perennial source of inspiration and amazement to me.

FOR JOYCE H. TELL
My friend from high school days past, who became a welcome source of encouragement for me following the unexpected passing of my twin brother, Charles, in late April 2016. Her appreciation of our works *I, Jesus: an Autobiography* and *Mary: Ten Test Questions for the World's Finest Woman*, provided a sense of eternal perspective as I was reminded once again that you never know who's watching your life and work, even if it seems sometimes that no one else is doing so…

Table of Contents

Should We Trust the Records? 1
  Jesus' high view of the Hebrew Scriptures 2

1 | The Rabbi Who Believed the Bible 9
  An astonishing claim about Jesus of Nazareth 9
  An astonishing claim by Jesus of Nazareth 10
  Jesus on the integrity of the Scriptures 11
  The Kenosis: a discredited theory to explain away Jesus'
    high view of Scripture 12
    Kenotic Theology 15
    Implications of Kenotic Theology 17
    What is the emptiness of the ***Kenosis?*** 20
  The orthodox view of the Incarnation 21
  The Brilliant ***Simplicity*** of the Hebrew Language 22
  Comparing biblical Hebrew to other ancient alphabets 22

2 | Why Should You Read this Book? 25
  The Emerging Challenge of the Emergent Church 26
    Characteristics of the Emergent Church 27
  What Good can there be in Heresy? 31
  Thoughts on How to Start Fixing the Problem 33
  On the Need for Renewed Emphasis on Systematic Biblical
    Study and Doctrinal Soundness 35
  Background to the New Testament Records 37
    The Gospel of Matthew 37
    The Gospel of Mark 38
    The Gospel of Luke 39
    The Gospel of John 40

3 | Jesus and the Hebrew Scriptures 43
    *Claim #1: Jesus claimed that Moses specifically mentioned him,
    even though the **Torah** had been written about 1,500 years
    before Jesus had been born.* 44

Claim #2: Jesus linked his claim that he would judge the dead at the Day of Resurrection to him having been written about by Moses in the **Torah**. 47

Claim #3: Jesus claimed that the Hebrew Scriptures in general spoke of him, even though the last book of the **Tanakh** had been written about 430 years before he had been born. 48

Claim #4: Jesus endorsed the absolute reliability and enduring nature of the Hebrew Scriptures so emphatically that he claimed not a single letter or portion of a letter would fail. 49

On the Biblical Text of Jesus' Day 55

4 | Jesus and Moses 59

Claim #5: Jesus considered the laws contained in the **Torah** to have been authored by Moses. 59

Claim #6: Jesus considered circumcision to have been handed down from the days of the Patriarchs through the authority of Moses. 64

Jesus on the **Torah**: The singular unity of the text 64

Claim #7: Jesus had little respect for the **traditions** handed down about how to obey the **Torah**, but he had high respect for the authority of the **Torah** itself. 67

Claim #8: Jesus believed that the authority of the **Torah** originated from the earliest days of humanity, not merely from Mount Sinai. 67

Claim #9: Jesus believed that the book of Genesis was written by Moses... 68

Claim #10: Jesus believed that Moses also authored the books of Leviticus, Exodus, and Deuteronomy. 70

Claim #11: Jesus believed that the Ten Commandments were authoritative and binding upon national Israel. 71

Claim #12: Jesus linked his claim to have been the only person to have gone to heaven with the historical reality of the incident of the serpent in the wilderness. 72

Claim #13: Jesus assumed that the claim of ancient Israel that Moses delivered the Law to the nation had historical validity. 74

Claim #14: Jesus assumed that the **Torah** continued in full immutable force and effect through the completion of the life ministry of John the Baptizer. 74

Claim #15: Jesus claimed that throughout the entirety of the Hebrew Scriptures, its writers mentioned him. 76
1. The Coming of Shiloh 78
2. The Star from Jacob 82
3. The Seed of the Woman 82
4. The Prophet like Moses 83

Claim #16: Jesus certified that the feeding of national Israel in the wilderness with manna actually occurred. 84

Claim #17: Jesus believed and stated publicly that the Scripture cannot be disregarded or broken. 86

Claim #18: Jesus believed and stated publicly that the authority of Moses should be respected and obeyed. 87

Claim #19: Jesus believed and stated publicly that the suffering and betrayal that he would undergo was predicted in the Hebrew Scriptures by the Prophets. 87

Hebrew Scripture prophecies fulfilled by Jesus the Messiah .. 88

Claim #20: Jesus held the books of Leviticus and Deuteronomy in such high esteem that he linked the entirety of the Law and the Prophets to their integrity. 103

Claim #21: Jesus held conversations from time to time with Satan, which demonstrated that he believed this creature existed and had influence in the world. 104

Claim #22: Jesus held the book of Deuteronomy in such high esteem that he used it to rebut the temptations of Satan during his time in the wilderness. 105

Claim #23: Jesus held Deuteronomy in such high esteem that he cited it as the basis for Church discipline. 108

Jesus on administration of justice 109
Guidelines from Jesus adjudicating a capital criminal case . 111

5 | Jesus and Bible History 115

Claim #24: Jesus' publicly stated belief that Adam and Eve existed formed the basis of his high view of marriage. 116

Jesus' use of the passive voice to describe his deity 117

Claim #25: Jesus' publicly stated belief that Abel and Zechariah existed formed the basis of his rebuke and warning that judgment was coming to national Israel. 120

Claim #26: Jesus' publicly stated belief that Able and Zechariah existed formed the basis of his warning about how Israel would soon be destroyed as a nation, an event that occurred in 70 AD.................... 120

The Destruction of Jerusalem 121
Chronology of the Siege 131

Claim #27: Jesus' publicly stated belief that Noah existed and that the flood of his day affected the entire world formed the basis of his warning about how his return to earth would affect the entire world.... 142

Claim #28: Jesus' publicly stated belief that Abraham, Isaac, and Jacob actually lived formed the basis of his warning to and rebuke of Israel's leaders about their threatened **exclusion** *from eternal life.*..... 143

Claim #29: Jesus' publicly stated belief that Abraham, Isaac, and Jacob actually lived formed the basis of his defense of the resurrection of the dead.... 144

Claim #30: Jesus' matter-of-fact mention of Abraham in his dialogue with Zacchaeus demonstrated that he took it for granted that Abraham had been a real person.... 145

Claim #31: Jesus publicly stated and believed that the destruction of Sodom and Gomorrah was a real, historical event and referred to it as the foundation of his warning about the coming judgment at the end of the world.... 146

Claim #32: Jesus believed that Moses and Elijah were real figures in the history of Israel, and claimed to have spoken with both of them... 148

Claim #33: Jesus demonstrated that he believed King David existed by affirming the man's existence and by citing many Psalms, all the while attributing their authorship to David.......................... 149

Claim #34: Jesus quoted Psalm 8:2 as a basis for his rebuke to the high priests and scribes of Jerusalem.... 153

Claim #35: Jesus quoted Psalm 35:19 and Psalm 69:4 as referring to himself.... 154

Claim #36: Jesus said that King David authored Psalm 41, using its authority to bolster his claim to be God incarnate............................ 154

Claim #37: Jesus said that King David authored Psalm 110, and used a quotation from it to demonstrate how David's Messiah was also God incarnate.... 155

Claim #38: Jesus demonstrated that his admission to be the Messiah was linked to statements from King David and the prophet Daniel contained in the Hebrew Scriptures of his day.................... 156
Claim #39: Jesus attributed authorship of Psalm 118 to King David....... 158
Claim #40: Jesus cites Psalm 118, claiming that King David's psalm is predictive of his second coming.... 159
Claim #41: Jesus cites Psalm 118, claiming that King David's psalm is predictive of his rejection by Israel and subsequent exaltation......... 160
Claim #42: Jesus believed that King Solomon and the Queen of Sheba were real figures in the history of Israel, and that they both would have a place with him at the resurrection of the dead...................... 160

6 | Jesus and the Biblical Prophets 165

Claim #43: Jesus believed that Jonah existed and was swallowed by a sea creature. He employed that historical fact as a comparative to explain his coming resurrection.... 165

On the historicity of Jonah and Nineveh 167

Claim #44: Jesus' matter-of-fact mention of Jeremiah the prophet and his quote from his book demonstrated that he took it for granted that Jeremiah had been a real person and that his book was authoritative... 170
Claim #45: Jesus' matter-of-fact mention of Isaiah the prophet and his extensive quotes from his book demonstrate that he took it for granted that Isaiah had been a real person and that his written works were authoritative... 172

Jesus' use of ***Targums*** in teaching 174
Jesus' use of paraphrase to highlight his divine nature 176
On the ***unity*** of Isaiah's book: the Apostle John's view 178
Evidence of the Unity of Isaiah from New Testament Quotations 183
New Testament quotes from Isaiah 1-39...............................183

1. Matthew 4:14 cites Isaiah 9:1-2 183
2. Matthew 13:14-15, John 12:39-41, and Acts 28:25-27 cite Isaiah 6:9-10 184
3. Matthew 15:7 and Mark 7:6-7 cite Isaiah 29:13 186
4. Romans 9:29 cite Isaiah 1:9 187
5. Romans 15:12 cites Isaiah 11:10.....................................187

xvii

New Testament quotes from Isaiah 40-60 188
1. Matthew 3:3, Luke 3:4, and John 1:23 cites
   Isaiah 40:3-5 188
2. Matthew 8:16-17, John 12:37-38, Acts 8:28-30,
   and Romans 10:16 cite Isaiah 53:1-17 190
3. Matthew 12:17 cites Isaiah 42:1-3 193
4. Luke 4:16-20 cites Isaiah 61:1, 2 194
5. Romans 10:20 cites Isaiah 65:1-3 195

Claim #46: Jesus cites Isaiah the prophet to link the apostasy of his generation to Isaiah's mention of him. 196

Claim #47: Jesus links the authority of the prophets Isaiah and Joel as predictions relating to his second coming. 197

Claim #48: Jesus cites the prophet Isaiah as applying to the rejection by Israel's first century leaders in their rejection of the righteous requirements of the Law in deference to their oral traditions. 197

Claim #49: Jesus cites the authority of the prophet Isaiah to explain the necessity of all prophecies written about him in the Hebrew Scriptures being fulfilled. 199

Claim #50: Jesus cites the authority of the prophet Isaiah to explain what life will be like under his reign during his Millennial Kingdom. 200

Claim #51: Jesus cites the authority of the prophets Isaiah and Jeremiah to explain why he expelled merchants from the Temple. 201

Claim #52: Jesus quoted the work of the prophet Isaiah, proclaiming to his generation that he was the fulfillment of Isaiah 58:6 and 61:1-2. 205

Claim #53: Jesus' matter-of-fact mention of Daniel the prophet and his quote from his book demonstrated that he took it for granted that Daniel had been a real person and that his book was authoritative. . 207

Claim #54: Jesus' quotation of the prophet Micah from the man's book demonstrate that he took it for granted that Micah had been a real person and that his book was authoritative. 209

Claim #55: Jesus' mention of the prophet Zechariah and his quote from the man's book demonstrate that he took it for granted that Zechariah had been a real person and that his book was authoritative. 211

    Claim #56: Jesus' quotation from the prophet Hosea's book demonstrate that he took it for granted that Hosea had been a real person and that his book was authoritative. 212

    Claim #57: Jesus' mention of the prophet Malachi and his quote from the man's book demonstrate that he took it for granted that Malachi had been a real person and that his book was authoritative. 213

7 | Summary and Conclusions 215
    Jesus' high view of the Hebrew Scriptures 216

Appendix: Evidence for Biblical Figures 223
    The One Faithful Witness of the Scriptural Record 223
    On the Existence of the Historic Figures of Scripture 225
    Lawrence Mykytiuk's List of 53 Biblical Figures 226
        Egypt 226
        Moab 229
        Aram-Damascus 229
        Northern Kingdom of Israel 231
        Southern Kingdom of Judah 234
        Assyria 239
        Babylonia 241
        Persia 244
    "Almost Real" People: The Biblical and Archaeological Evidence 245

Ammon 246

Northern Arabia 248

Southern Kingdom of Judah 248
    Symbols & Abbreviations 256
    References 259

An Invitation to Participate in a Grand Adventure 261
    How to Meet the Most Amazing Man who ever Lived 265
        Step 1: Admit your Spiritual Poverty 265
        Step 2: Begin to Mourn 265
        Step 3: Be Brought to a State of Humility 266
        Step 4: Begin to Hunger to Know Him 266

    Step 5: Treat Others the Way Jesus has Treated You............267
    Step 6: Let your Heart be Transformed from the Inside out......267
    Step 7: Let your Life begin to be Productive for God's Glory......268
    Step 8: Watch Some People Hate you for your New Life ...268
    Step 9: View Yourself in Light of Eternity, not Present Circumstances 268
  How to Begin to Recognize your own Poverty of Spirit 269
    1. All People are Born Sinners..270
    2. All People Sin 271
    3. The Price of Sin is Death...271
    4. Jesus Paid Your Debt..271
    5. You Have Earned Death, not Eternal Life 271
    6. Christ Died in Your Place 272
    7. You Must Confess your Sin and Declare His Lordship.272

An Introduction to the Koinonia Institute............................275
  Mission Statement 276

Index..277

About the author 283
  William P. Welty, Ph.D...283
  About the Holy Bible: International Standard Version 283
  Also by the Author: 284
  As Contributing Author and/or Editor 285

Table of Figures

Figure 1: Proto-Hebrew Alphabet (ca. 8th century BC)..............23
Figure 2: Hebrew Alphabet (ca. 6th century BC) 23
Figure 3: Hittite alphabet (ca. 1800 BC) 24
Figure 4: Model of Pool of Bethesda at the Model of Ancient Jerusalem, Israel Museum..44
Figure 5: Ruins of Byzantine era chapel near the site of the Pool of Bethesda..45
Figure 6: Page from the Aleppo Codex 56
Figure 7: Exodus 15:2-16:3 from Lenin-grad Codex 57
Figure 8: Targum of Onkelos..79
Figure 9: Three pages from Samaritan Pentateuch.....................81
Figure 10: Wilhelm von Kaulbach's The Siege and Destruction of Jerusalem, 1846. 122
Figure 11: The Siege and Destruction of Jerusalem, by David Roberts (1850)..123
Figure 12: Detail of von Kaulbach's work showing suicide of the Jerusalem Temple's High Priest...........................123
Figure 13: The Arch of Titus in Rome. 142
Figure 14: The fragmentary Tel Dan stela inscription 148
Figure 15: Simplified plan of Nineveh ruins, including location of tomb of Jonah (Nebi Yunus)....................167
Figure 16: Tomb of Jonah in 1999 before its destruction by ISIS...168
Figure 17: 11th century Hebrew Bible with Targum, probably from Tunisia originally..............................175

SHOULD WE TRUST THE RECORDS?

Jesus the Messiah trusted the Hebrew Scriptures of his day. That's why Christians have claimed for centuries that the collection of 66 books we call *The Bible* is reliable with respect to what it affirms, correct in its history of God's dealings with his universe and with humanity, historically accurate regarding its doctrinal teachings, and utterly trustworthy as a guide for day-to-day life.

But frankly, *every* generation has had its share of doubters. Maybe you're one of them…

That's why we've provided this book for your reading. We wish to demonstrate to you what Jesus the Messiah believed about the Bible. Specifically, we've counted 57 separate conclusions about the Hebrew Scriptures with which Jesus would have been familiar during the early part of the first century AD.

Since He Wrote about Me

We've gleaned these conclusions by studying every account recorded in the New Testament in which Jesus the Messiah resorted to a quotation or citation of a portion of the Hebrew Scriptures during his discussions with his disciples or in argument with the Jewish leaders of his day. We've also include all references to biblical figures or events to which Jesus alluded in the New Testament.

Here's a summary of each of the 57 claims about the Hebrew Scriptures that Jesus made about the reliability of the Bible that had been recorded current as of his lifetime:

JESUS' HIGH VIEW OF THE HEBREW SCRIPTURES

Claim #1: Jesus claimed that Moses specifically mentioned him, even though the *Torah* had been written about 1,400 years before Jesus had been born.

Claim #2: Jesus linked his claim that he would judge the dead at the Day of Resurrection to him having been written about by Moses in the *Torah*.

Claim #3: Jesus claimed that the Hebrew Scriptures in general spoke of him, even though the last book of the *Tanakh* had been written about 430 years before he had been born.

Claim #4: Jesus endorsed the absolute reliability and enduring nature of the Hebrew Scriptures so emphatically that he claimed not a single letter or portion of a letter would fail.

Claim #5: Jesus considered the laws contained in the *Torah* to have been authored by Moses.

Claim #6: Jesus considered circumcision to have been handed down from the days of the Patriarchs through the authority of Moses.

Claim #7: Jesus had little respect for the traditions handed down about how to obey the *Torah*, but he had high respect for the authority of the *Torah* itself.

Claim #8: Jesus believed that the authority of the *Torah* originated from the earliest days of humanity, not merely from Mount Sinai.

Should We Trust the Records?

Claim #9: Jesus believed that the book of Genesis was written by Moses.

Claim #10: Jesus believed that Moses also authored the books of Leviticus, Exodus, and Deuteronomy.

Claim #11: Jesus believed that the Ten Commandments were authoritative and binding upon national Israel.

Claim #12: Jesus linked his claim to have been the only person to have gone to heaven with the historical reality of the incident of the serpent in the wilderness.

Claim #13: Jesus assumed that the claim of ancient Israel that Moses delivered the Law to the nation had historical validity.

Claim #14: Jesus assumed that the *Torah* continued in full immutable force and effect through the completion of the life ministry of John the Baptizer.

Claim #15: Jesus claimed that throughout the entirety of the Hebrew Scriptures, its writers mentioned him.

Claim #16: Jesus certified that the feeding of national Israel in the wilderness with manna actually occurred.

Claim #17: Jesus believed and stated publicly that the Scripture cannot be disregarded or broken.

Claim #18: Jesus believed and stated publicly that the authority of Moses should be respected and obeyed.

Claim #19: Jesus believed and stated publicly that the suffering and betrayal that he would undergo was predicted in the Hebrew Scriptures by the Prophets.

Claim #20: Jesus held the books of Leviticus and Deuteronomy in such high esteem that he linked the entirety of the Law and the Prophets to their integrity.

Claim #21: Jesus held conversations from time to time with Satan, which demonstrated that he believed this creature existed and had influence in the world.

Claim #22: Jesus held the book of Deuteronomy in such high esteem that he used it to rebut the temptations of Satan during his time in the wilderness.

Claim #23: Jesus held Deuteronomy in such high esteem that he cited it as the basis for Church discipline.

3

Since He Wrote about Me

Claim #24: Jesus' publicly stated belief that Adam and Eve existed formed the basis of his high view of marriage.

Claim #25: Jesus' publicly stated belief that Abel and Zechariah existed formed the basis of his rebuke and warning that judgment was coming to national Israel.

Claim #26: Jesus' publicly stated belief that Able and Zechariah existed formed the basis of his warning about how Israel would soon be destroyed as a nation, an event that occurred in 70 AD.

Claim #27: Jesus' publicly stated belief that Noah existed and that the flood of his day affected the entire world formed the basis of his warning about how his return to earth would affect the entire world.

Claim #28: Jesus' publicly stated belief that Abraham, Isaac, and Jacob actually lived formed the basis of his warning to and rebuke of Israel's leaders about their threatened *exclusion* from eternal life.

Claim #29: Jesus' publicly stated belief that Abraham, Isaac, and Jacob actually lived formed the basis of his defense of the resurrection of the dead.

Claim #30: Jesus' matter-of-fact mention of Abraham in his dialogue with Zacchaeus demonstrated that he took it for granted that Abraham had been a real person.

Claim #31: Jesus publicly stated and believed that the destruction of Sodom and Gomorrah was a real, historical event and referred to it as the foundation of his warning about the coming judgment at the end of the world.

Claim #32: Jesus believed that Moses and Elijah were real figures in the history of Israel, and claimed to have spoken with both of them.

Claim #33: Jesus demonstrated that he believed King David existed by affirming the man's existence and by citing many Psalms, all the while attributing their authorship to David.

Claim #34: Jesus quoted Psalm 8:2 as a basis for his rebuke to the high priests and scribes of Jerusalem.

Claim #35: Jesus quoted Psalm 35:19 and Psalm 69:4 as referring to himself.

Claim #36: Jesus said that King David authored Psalm 41, using its authority to bolster his claim to be God incarnate.

Claim #37: Jesus said that King David authored Psalm 110, and used a quotation from it to demonstrate how David's Messiah was also God incarnate.

Claim #38: Jesus demonstrated that his admission to be the Messiah was linked to statements from King David and the prophet Daniel contained in the Hebrew Scriptures of his day.

Claim #39: Jesus attributed authorship of Psalm 118 to King David.

Claim #40: Jesus cites Psalm 118, claiming that King David's psalm is predictive of his second coming.

Claim #41: Jesus cites Psalm 118, claiming that King David's psalm is predictive of his rejection by Israel and subsequent exaltation.

Claim #42: Jesus believed that King Solomon and the Queen of Sheba were real figures in the history of Israel, and that they both would have a place with him at the resurrection of the dead.

Claim #43: Jesus believed that Jonah existed and was swallowed by a sea creature. He employed that historical fact as a comparative to explain his coming resurrection.

Claim #44: Jesus' matter-of-fact mention of Jeremiah the prophet and his quote from his book demonstrated that he took it for granted that Jeremiah had been a real person and that his book was authoritative.

Claim #45: Jesus' matter-of-fact mention of Isaiah the prophet and his extensive quotes from his book demonstrate that he took it for granted that Isaiah had been a real person and that his written works were authoritative.

Claim #46: Jesus cites Isaiah the prophet to link the apostasy of his generation to Isaiah's mention of him.

Claim #47: Jesus links the authority of the prophets Isaiah and Joel as predictions relating to his second coming.

Claim #48: Jesus cites the prophet Isaiah as applying to the rejection by Israel's first century leaders in their rejection of the righteous requirements of the Law in deference to their oral traditions.

Claim #49: Jesus cites the authority of the prophet Isaiah to explain the necessity of all prophecies written about him in the Hebrew Scriptures being fulfilled.

Claim #50: Jesus cites the authority of the prophet Isaiah to explain what life will be like under his reign during his Millennial Kingdom.

Claim #51: Jesus cites the authority of the prophets Isaiah and Jeremiah to explain why he expelled merchants from the Temple.

Claim #52: Jesus quoted the work of the prophet Isaiah, proclaiming to his generation that he was the fulfillment of Isaiah 58:6 and 61:1-2.

Claim #53: Jesus' matter-of-fact mention of Daniel the prophet and his quote from his book demonstrated that he took it for granted that Daniel had been a real person and that his book was authoritative.

Claim #54: Jesus' quotation of the prophet Micah from the man's book demonstrate that he took it for granted that Micah had been a real person and that his book was authoritative.

Claim #55: Jesus' mention of the prophet Zechariah and his quote from the man's book demonstrate that he took it for granted that Zechariah had been a real person and that his book was authoritative.

Claim #56: Jesus' quotation from the prophet Hosea's book demonstrate that he took it for granted that Hosea had been a real person and that his book was authoritative.

Claim #57: Jesus' mention of the prophet Malachi and his quote from the man's book demonstrate that he took it for granted that Malachi had been a real person and that his book was authoritative.

Jesus of Nazareth trusted the historical validity of the *Tanakh*.[1] Every single person, without exception, who is mentioned by Jesus as having lived during Israel's previous centuries is recorded in the Hebrew Scriptures. Jesus considered those records to be accurate and trustworthy accounts of actual events. As we will demonstrate within this work, Jesus displayed an unwavering confidence in the historical reliability and internal integrity of the Hebrew Scriptures. His respect for the Word of God even extended to the regulations about divorce and Sabbath observance.

Furthermore, when it came time for Jesus to defend his person, nature, and his mission, he cited the Bible of his day to authenticate his own authority and identity. To Jesus, the Hebrew Scriptures were the inerrant, infallible, and plenary inspired Word of God. If Jesus displayed such unwavering confidence in the integrity and inerrancy of the Scriptures, considering every word, letter, and stroke of a letter to be valid and reliable, should not all of us express the very same confidence in the entire record of the completed Old and New Testaments, as well?

---

1   The word *Tanakh* is the traditional Hebrew language word for that collection of books Christians call the Old Testament.

1 | THE RABBI WHO BELIEVED THE BIBLE

AN ASTONISHING CLAIM ABOUT JESUS OF NAZARETH

The Gospel of John records a remarkable statement uttered by one of the first disciples of Jesus the Messiah. In John 1:45, we find this claim made by Philip on the very day the two of them first met, while Jesus was going about calling to himself the twelve individuals who would form the core group of his first followers:

> *Philip found Nathaniel and told him, "We have found the man about whom Moses in the Law and the Prophets wrote—Jesus, the son of Joseph, from Nazareth."*
>
> John 1:45

That this incredible claim could come from the lips of a man who had only moments before met Jesus the Messiah at the very beginning of the man's ministry is remarkable enough to warrant its own special study.

The Apostle John records Philip as saying that national Israel's greatest historical figure wrote about Jesus the Messiah around 1,500 years *before* the rabbi from Nazareth had been born. If we were inclined to do so, we could spend quite some time delving into the implications that come to mind when we ask ourselves just *how* Philip could have reached such a conclusion after talking to the man for only a few moments. The Apostle John also affirmed that the prophet Isaiah wrote about Jesus of Nazareth. In John 12:41, he wrote that Isaiah "saw his glory and spoke about him."

An astonishing claim by Jesus of Nazareth

But there's more at stake than merely asking the questions, "How did Philip know that Moses wrote about Jesus?" or "How did John know that Isaiah wrote about Jesus?" Consider, for example, this statement uttered by Jesus during one of his angry encounters with the theological leaders of Israel who attacked the man and his message. As the Apostle John records the incident in John 5:43-47, Jesus makes this stinging rebuke:

> [43] *I have come in my Father's name, and you do not accept me. Yet if another man comes in his own name, you will accept him.* [44] *How can you believe when you accept each other's praise and do not look for the praise that comes from the only God?* [45] *Do not suppose that I will be the one to accuse you before the Father. Your accuser is Moses, on whom you have set your hope,* [46] *because if you believed Moses, you would believe me, since he wrote about me.* [47] *But if you do not believe what he wrote, how will you believe my words?"*
>
> John 5:43-47

In this remarkable statement, Jesus of Nazareth *confirmed* Philip's comments that Moses wrote about Jesus. "If you believed Moses, you would believe me, since he wrote about me." The simplicity of this seemingly matter-of-fact statement is astonishing in its implications. Speaking about 1,500 years *after* Moses led the early nation of Israel out of Egyptian slavery, not only does Jesus affirm the historic authenticity of the existence and work of Moses as he confirms the essential validity of Philip's comment, but he also boldly asserts that Moses wrote about himself!

JESUS ON THE INTEGRITY OF THE SCRIPTURES

The late Dr. Robert Dick Wilson, professor of Semitic Philology and Old Testament Criticism at Western Theological Seminary and Princeton Theological Seminary (back in the early 1900's when these schools had an evangelical heritage), was arguably one of the foremost conservative ancient Semitic language experts of the nineteen century. He summarized the importance of gaining an accurate understanding of—and agreeing with (!)—the view that Jesus the Messiah held regarding the reliability of the Scriptures. About a century ago, Professor Wilson observed:

> *Objection has frequently been made to the use of the testimony of Jesus in corroboration of the historicity of the persons and events of the Old Testament to which the Gospels tell us that He referred, apparently in full belief in the accuracy and veracity of the Old Testament accounts of these persons and events. These objections are based fundamentally upon the supposition that Jesus in these references was merely conforming to the opinions and beliefs common among the Jews of His time, or that He really did not know enough to perceive that these opinions of His contemporaries were false and their beliefs groundless. For myself, I have always been of the belief and am today, that Jesus knew more about the Old Testament than the Jews of His day than any, or all, of the wise men of all time; and this belief is based upon the conviction that God hath demonstrated Him to be the Son of God by His resurrection from the dead. And, if He is the Son of God, I can believe that He was conceived by*

the Holy Ghost, born of the Virgin Mary, crucified for my sins, and that He has ascended up on high, having brought life and immortality to light in His gospel.[1]

Dr. Wilson was correct: His conclusion that Jesus held the Hebrew Scriptures in very high regard, that he considered the entire canon of the *Tanakh* to be reliable with respect to what it affirms regarding the history of God's dealings with humanity, and that the Scriptures were trustworthy regarding its doctrinal teachings has never been successfully refuted. Professor Wilson also suggested that anyone who studies the life and claims of Jesus should address themselves:

> *To answering the questions, What did Jesus say with regard to the Old Testament? And, Can anyone show that what He said is not true? In view of the character of Jesus as portrayed in the New Testament, it seems to me that all Christians at least should accept His opinion as to the facts of the Old Testament, unless it can be proved beyond controversy that what He thought and said about these facts is false. When it shall have been shown that Jesus was wrong in His treatment of the Old Testament, it will be time to resort to the theory of kenosis, in order to retain at least a remnant of our faith.*[2]

THE KENOSIS: A DISCREDITED THEORY TO EXPLAIN AWAY JESUS' HIGH VIEW OF SCRIPTURE

Starting about 200 years ago, a school of biblical studies called *the higher critics* began to influence Christian thought. This school of "scholarly" study assumed that the religious heritage of ancient Israel was *evolutionary* in its growth and development. Many higher critics were heavily influenced by German theologians, who denied the deity of Jesus and the historical reliability of the Scriptures.

To these people, the recorded history of ancient Israel was largely mythological in nature. The stories recorded in the ancient texts

---

1 Robert Dick Wilson. *Jesus and the Old Testament*. Princeton Theological Review Vol. 24 No. 4 (1926), p. 632.
2 *Ibid.*, pp. 632-633.

that told of miracles were, in their view, largely only *hagiography*, that is, idealized religious stories intended to lend an atmosphere of the supernatural to what in the higher critics' view was only a set of myths to begin with that had the effect of making the story seem more divine than it really was.

The higher critics also held the view that Jesus believed in the ancient traditions only because he was a product of the religious mythology and ethos of his day. In short, these deniers of all things evangelical and supernatural believed that Jesus believed that the Scriptures should be taken as reliable historical records simply because he didn't know any better!

These higher critics believed—without *any* substantiating evidence—that Jesus' views about the Hebrew Scriptures were a by-product of his backward era, cultural milieu, and religious heritage. Jesus held a high view of Scripture, these critics claimed, only because *he was raised that way!*

In an attempt to provide an "answer" of sorts to these critics, the now largely *discredited* theory of *kenosis* posited that in his incarnation, God the Son *divested himself* temporarily of a portion of his divine attributes, knowledge, form, and glory. These kenoticists, as they were called, claimed that Jesus could be mistaken about the reliability of the Hebrew Scriptures because he grew up in a culture that naively thought that the scriptural record could be trusted as reliable.

The word *kenosis* (based on the Greek verb κενόω, *kenóō*) is derived from a reference to the incarnation of Jesus the Messiah in Philippians 2:7, which is rendered by the *Holy Bible: International Standard Version* as "emptiness." The result was that Jesus was indistinguishable in outward appearance from generic human beings. Accordingly, due to the *kenosis*, Jesus could be mistaken about the literalness of Israel's ancient history as recorded in the Hebrew Scriptures.

But this view contains significant problems. Dan Musick, M.A. (Theology: Wheaton Graduate School, 1978) explains these problems with the following thoughts:

It is not uncommon to hear godly radio and television speakers, pastors and teachers teach that Jesus "emptied Himself of His divinity" or His deity, or that He "abandoned a sovereign position." It has also been said, "When He left heaven and came to this earth, He gave up the voluntary use of His divine attributes." And another has written, "Jesus restricted the use of these divine attributes when he took on the form of man." Perhaps you have heard a speaker raise these questions: "While He was here on earth, was He omnipotent? ... God could not do many mighty works? That's what the Bible says. Was He omnipresent? No. He was restricted by time and space." It has also been asked, "How could Jesus be omniscient and not know the time of His return?" Another radio speaker has taught that God was downsized. "Think about how big the Word is. Think about how he downsized to become flesh—one cell..." Perhaps words such as these have warmed your heart at Christmas: "Those hands that formed all the worlds... would now have to be held... And the mouth that spoke, for by the word of the Lord were the heavens made, ...would now have to learn to speak Aramaic and Hebrew."

These are statements and questions about the nature of God as revealed in Holy Scripture and summarized in historic creeds of the Christian faith. They beg for answers to foundational questions of the faith. Would God be God if He did not know the future, or if He did not sovereignly rule the universe? Would Jesus be God if He did not know the future, or if He did not sovereignly rule the universe? When Jesus Christ was born in Bethlehem, did He continue, in His divine nature, to use His omnipotence, omniscience and omnipresence to sovereignly rule the universe?

Jesus clearly taught, and the rest of Holy Scripture confirms, that He is Son of God and Son of man (Matthew 16:13-17). In the Creed of Chalcedon the early fathers rightly affirmed that Christ "*must be acknowledged in two natures, without any commingling, or change, or division or separation.*"

The Creed of Athanasius offers an important analogy to help us understand Biblical statements about Christ's two natures: "As a rational soul and flesh are one man, so God and man are one Christ." Because I am a rational soul I can say, "I will never die." That statement is not true of my flesh, unless Christ returns before I die. On the other hand, because I am flesh I can also say, "I will not live forever." That statement is not true of my soul.

In the same manner, certain statements by or about Christ are true only if ascribed to the appropriate nature. For example, because Christ is God He could say "You are of this world, I am not of this world" (NAS John 8:23). This statement is not true of Christ's human nature. If we err in ascribing this statement to His human nature, we would conclude, as did the doceticists, that Christ was only a spirit. On the other hand, because Christ is man, He elsewhere says concerning His second coming: "But of that day and hour no one knows, not even the angels of heaven, nor the Son, but the Father alone" (NAS Matthew 24:36). This statement is not true of Christ's divine nature. If we ascribe this statement to His divine nature, we would conclude that as God, He did not know when He would return. He would not be omniscient, He would be less than God, and thus, not God at all, as the Arians argued.

KENOTIC THEOLOGY

Most kenoticists believe that Christ gave up His sovereign dominion when becoming incarnate. They follow the same logic as the Arians, but they are deceived into thinking their Christ is still God. These could be classified as neo-Arians. Other kenoticists believe that Christ continued being sovereign while on earth, but that His divine and human natures were not truly united into one Person. These could be classified as neo-Nestorian.

Most kenoticists thus either diminish the deity of Christ or they undermine the union of the two natures in one Person.

Much of what we hear and read has been gleaned from theologians who have disseminated their views in commentaries and doctrinal treatises. Rather than study the scriptures regarding the kenosis and two natures of Christ, many of these pastors, teachers, and radio and television personalities go to their commentaries or other books in their libraries to find answers that they do not test with Scripture.

In his excellent work on Philippians 2, Rodney Decker shows the following sources for many of the distorted views of the kenosis.
- *"Christ had a human soul, to which the Logos imparted his divinity, little by little until he became completely divine" (Dorner).*
- *Christ "laid aside his deity which was then restored at the ascension" (Gess and Beecher).*
- *He "abandoned certain prerogatives of the divine mode of existence in order to assume the human," e.g., omniscience (Gore).*
- *"He surrendered the external, physical attributes of omniscience, though retaining the attributes of love and truth" (A. M. Fairbairn). This was also held by Thomasius, Deilitzsch, and H. Crosby.*
- *Christ "lived a double life from two, non-communicating life centers. As God, he continued his Trinitarian and providential existence, and as man he was united with a human nature. He did not know consciously anything of his divine, Trinitarian existence" (Martensen).*
- *"He disguised his deity and attributes, not by giving them up, but by limiting them to a time-form appropriate to a human mode of existence ... His attributes could only be expressed in relation to the (human) time and space that his human form could experience" (Ebrard).*

- "He gave up the use of the attributes (cf. Carson, FD&FPJ, 35)."
- "He gave up the independent exercise of the divine attributes" (Strong, ST, 703).
- "He limited himself to the voluntary non-use of the attributes" (Walvoord).

Among Catholics the primary influence has come from Karl Rainer, one of the most influential theologians of the twentieth century. According to John O'Connel in the March/April 1997 issue of The Catholic Faith, Rainer speaks of Christ as gradually developing His self-consciousness: "This consciousness in Christ realized itself only gradually during his spiritual history, and this history does not consist only, or even first and foremost, in being occupied with this or that fact of external reality but consists rather in the never quite successful attaining of what and who one is oneself "... "So Christ in His human consciousness never became fully aware of His self-identity, nor was He fully cognizant that His Sacred Humanity was intimately united to the Logos."

IMPLICATIONS OF KENOTIC THEOLOGY

In trying to understand the mystery of the incarnation, kenoticists have fallen prey to the tendency to submit the authority of God's Word to human reason: "Understanding is believing" rather than "God said it, and I believe it." They do not properly acknowledge Christ's two natures during His 33 years on earth, and they ignore or subtly alter important Christological distinctions in God's Word. Dorner's view is at best a perversion of Biblical, orthodox Christology. The remaining views of the kenosis are senseless—what does the nonuse or non-exercise of omnipresence look like? And they are heretical.

1. ***They destroy the integrity of the atonement.*** *The redemption of all creation (Romans 8:18-22) and of everyone who would ever believe in Christ required not only a perfect human being,*

but also a sacrifice that was also infinite in every way. It required the "blood of God" (Acts 20:28). "It was the Father's good pleasure for all the fullness to dwell in Him, and through Him to reconcile all things to Himself, having made peace through the blood of His cross" (NAS Colossians 1:19-20). The fullness of the Father's divinity was in Christ during His ministry and passion, but most kenoticists substitute the word "partialness" for the word "fullness," or they diminish the unity of the Person of Christ in the kenosis. Limiting Christ's sovereign deity or separating His two natures would leave all of humanity, and all of creation hopelessly subject to God's curse and to His eternal wrath.

2. **They distort the Christian view of the incarnation.** *The Bible says, "The Word became flesh" (NAS John 1:14); kenoticists teach that God minus the use of His dominion attributes became flesh, or that the Word remained separate from the flesh. The Bible states, "God was in Christ reconciling the world to Himself" (NAS Second Corinthians 5:19); kenotic thinking holds that only God minus omnipotence, omniscience and omnipresence, was in Christ, or that God was not truly in Christ. The Bible affirms that Jesus is the only begotten Son of God (John 3:16). To be the Son of God is to have the same substance as God. Kenoticists teach a mutation: God birthed a Son Who either later became God minus boundlessness or Who was never really united to human flesh. "Great is the mystery of godliness: God was manifest in the flesh" (KJV First Timothy 3:16). According to kenotic thought the mystery of godliness lies not in the fact that "God was manifest in the flesh," but that God minus sovereignty was manifest in the flesh, yet was still mysteriously somehow God. Or as Martenson or Rainer would suggest, that God was not really manifest in the flesh, yet was still somehow mysteriously one Person. Such views tend "...to rupture the hypostatic union of Christ's divine and human natures."*

Sovereignty is an attribute of God. According to Don Fortner it means ruling "all things, everywhere, at all times absolutely."

If, by becoming man, Christ gave up the use of His divine attributes in any way, then He was not sovereign. If Jesus was not sovereign during His earthly ministry, then He was not God. If He was not God, the Word that was God (John 1:1) never became flesh—only part of the Word did. And the name "Immanuel," meaning "God with us" (NAS Matthew 1:23), is a lie, and God's Word is not true.

3. **They deny the immutability of God.** Most distorted views of the kenosis mutate the Immutable. In order for the God the Son to abandon His sovereignty in any way, He would have to change His character or being. This, God would never do. "I AM WHO I AM" (NAS Exodus 3:14). "But Thou art the same, And Thy years will not come to an end." (NAS Psalm 102:27). "Jesus Christ is the same yesterday and today, yes and forever." (NAS Hebrews 13:8). According to R.C. Sproul, "If God laid aside one of His attributes, the immutable undergoes a mutation, the infinite suddenly stops being infinite; it would be the end of the universe."

4. **They undermine the monotheistic distinctive of the Christian faith.** The only way to limit the use of attributes of one Person without limiting the attributes of all three members of the Godhead is to divide God into three divine Beings for each of the three Persons. Jesus could then suspend His omnipotence, omniscience, omnipresence, etc., while the Father and Holy Spirit would continue to exercise sovereign dominion over the universe. This view of the Trinity, however, is polytheistic, not Christian. The Christian faith is monotheistic. We believe there is only one God. "Hear O Israel! The Lord our God is one Lord" (Mark 12:29). The Creed of Athanasius affirms this truth: "The Father is God, the Son is God, and the Holy Spirit is God, but there are not three gods, but one God... The Father is omnipotent, the Son is omnipotent and the Holy Spirit is omnipotent, but there are not three omnipotent Beings, but one omnipotent Being ... We distinguish among the Persons, but we do not divide the Substance."

> *Kenotic theology has spawned two significant distortions of Scripture, that Christ, as God, emptied Himself of His glory, and that as God, Christ performed His miracles by the power of the Holy Spirit and did not use His own divine power to do the miracles. These two distortions of the kenosis must be examined in the light of infallible Scripture.*[3]

WHAT IS THE EMPTINESS OF THE *KENOSIS*?

A cogent answer to the heresies of the *Kenosis* can be discerned by studying the larger context of Philippians 2:7 in Philippians 2:6-8. The passage reads as follows:

> ⁶*In God's own form existed he,*
> *and shared with God equality,*
> *deemed nothing needed grasping.*
> ⁷*Instead, poured out in emptiness,*
> *a servant's form did he possess,*
> *a mortal man becoming.*
> *In human form he chose to be,*
> ⁸*and lived in all humility,*
> *death on a cross obeying.*

A careful exegetical analysis of the Greek text will demonstrate that the first line of Greek language poetry composed by the Apostle Paul in verse seven, which reads "…poured out in emptiness…" (Greek: ἐκένωσεν, *ekénōsen*) is defined by, modified by, and *explained* by the Messiah taking the form of a servant in his incarnation, and not by the temporary removal or setting aside of any of his attributes of deity. That servant's form is further defined in line number three of verse 7's poetry, in which the servant's form that he took is explained as God becoming a mortal man. Other aspects of his emptying of himself by taking the form of a servant include his human mortality, (verse 7d), his humble life circumstances (verse 8b), and his obedience to death on a Roman cross (verse 8c). Professor Wilson summarized the issue as follows:

---

3 Musick, Dan., Editor. *Kenosis: Christ "emptied Himself" (Philippians 2:7)* See http://kenosis.-info/index.shtml for more information

In former days, many good Christian men, who truly loved the Lord and relied humbly on His grace, believed in this doctrine; largely because they thought that the sayings of Jesus with regard to the Old Testament were not true in fact. Judging by the analogy of the Greek and Roman histories, they argued that the early history of the Old Testament consisted largely of myths and legends; and having given up their faith in its historic trustworthiness, and recognizing that Jesus believed in its trustworthiness, they preserved their faith in Him by taking refuge in kenosis. But today we know that the history of Israel, unlike that of Greece and Rome, is confirmed by a mass of evidence, which rules out all the old-time mythical theories as to its origin. Wherever the Old Testament records can be thoroughly tested, they have stood the test. As to writing, language, forms of literature, law, history and religion, it stands approved by the evidence of contemporaneous documents of unquestioned veracity and relativity. Its statements must be accepted on their face value unless it can be shown by evidence from outside that they are false.[4]

THE ORTHODOX VIEW OF THE INCARNATION

The orthodox, conservative view of the incarnation is that the divine attributes of Jesus were never set aside during the time of his mortality, though they were *veiled to human sight* for those 33-34 years, being manifest only on rare occasions as the circumstances warranted, and fully demonstrated in his post-resurrection appearances.

In his incarnation, Jesus never "emptied" himself of his divine attributes. He did, however, take on the attributes of a servant, veiling his deity to most people who met him. But he never made a mistake with respect to his understanding of the *Tanakh*. Accordingly, the only times he asked questions were when he was soliciting information or responses to his actions as *teachable moments* in which he could display his grace toward people or rebuke stubborn national

---
4   *Ibid*. p. 638.

leaders of Israel. He never attributed historical doubt, doctrinal error, myth, or hagiographic literary genres to the records of the Hebrew Scriptures…not even once. Overall, the confidence displayed by Jesus the Messiah in the essential *unbreakable nature* of the biblical text was absolutely unshakable.

The Brilliant *Simplicity* of the Hebrew Language

As we will demonstrate within this work, Jesus of Nazareth displayed an unwavering confidence in the historical reliability and internal integrity of the Hebrew Scriptures. He attributed the authorship of the Law (i.e., the first five books of the Old Testament, commonly called the *Torah*) to Moses, which would have been composed after the exodus of the ancient Israeli people from their years of slavery in Egypt (estimated by conservative scholars to around 1440 BC, or perhaps about 90 years earlier).

By the time Moses handed down the tablets of the Ten Commandments to Israel on Mount Sinai, the ancient Hebrews as a nation had enough accumulated knowledge of reading and writing that the transmission of a written set of history and laws to the nation (and the attendant transmission of the text of the *Torah* itself) could be accomplished with very high confidence. Copies of it would be read and used as a standard for everyday life and practice in national Israel.

The Hebrew language, when compared to the amazing complexity of other ancient languages that were in use during the mid-second millennium, BC, is brilliantly simple in its structure. The Hebrew alphabet itself consists of only 22 consonants, and no vowels. This simplicity of the Hebrew alphabet stands in stark contrast to the alphabets of other contemporaneous languages in use in the ancient world.

Comparing biblical Hebrew to other ancient alphabets

Consider, for example, the Hebrew alphabet in comparison to some of these other ancient languages. We've listed on the following page, two versions of the Hebrew alphabet dating

The Rabbi Who Believed the Bible

from ca. 8th century BC and ca. 6th century BC, respectively. Please note how both alphabets, while differing in outward appearance, nevertheless contain 22 identical letters. Contrast this simplicity with the Hittite alphabet, also posted on the previous page, which consists of about 375 separate characters. Other alphabets that are contemporaneous to ancient Hebrew include the Indus Valley Harappan language (about 417 symbols), the Luwian language of Anatolian (about 500 hieroglyphs), the Akkadian language (more than 1,500 Sumerian characters), the Egyptian language (more than 3,000 characters), and the Chinese language (about 10,000 pictograms).

✶	'alep	'	𐤋	lamed	l	א	'alep	'	ל	lamed	l
ꓱ	bet	b	𐤌	mem	m	ב	bet	b	מם	mem	m
ꓶ	gimel	g	𐤍	nun	n	ג	gimel	g	נן	nun	n
◁	dalet	d	𐤎	samek	s	ד	dalet	d	ס	samek	s
ꓱ	he	h	O	ayin	'	ה	he	h	ע	ayin	'
ꓬ	waw	w	ꓕ	pe	p	ו	waw	w	פף	pe	p
ꓘ	zayin	z	𐤑	tsade	ṣ	ז	zayin	z	צץ	tsade	ṣ
𐤇	het	ḥ	ꓑ	qop	q	ח	het	ḥ	ק	qop	q
⊗	tet	ṭ	ꓥ	reš	r	ט	tet	ṭ	ר	reš	r
ꓶ	yod	y	W	šin	š	י	yod	y	ש	šin	š
ꓬ	kap	k	X	taw	t	ךכ	kap	k	ת	taw	t

Figure 1: Proto-Hebrew Alphabet (ca. 8th century BC)

Figure 2: Hebrew Alphabet (ca. 6th century BC)

23

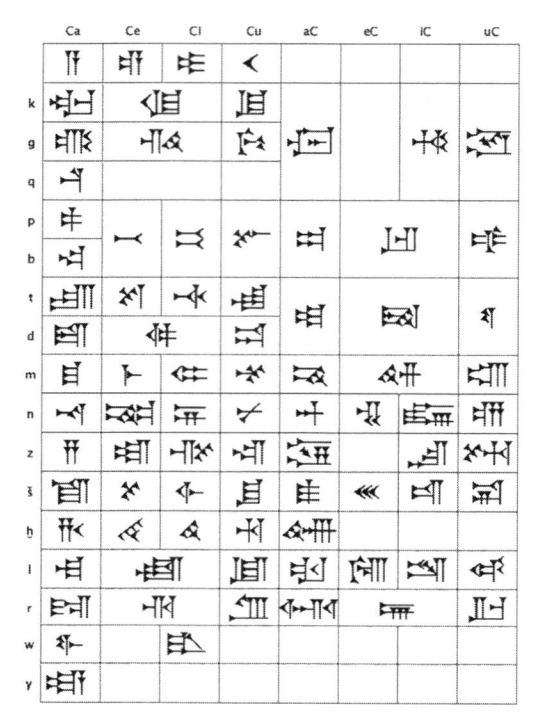

Figure 3: Hittite alphabet (ca. 1800 BC)

2 | WHY SHOULD YOU READ THIS BOOK?

Well now, maybe you don't need to. Maybe you've spent the last several decades of your life in more-or-less full time analysis of the 66 books that comprise the collection of ancient writings we call the Bible. Perhaps you've even done some of your readings in the original languages in which those books were written. But then again, it can take a lifetime to learn the subtle nuances involved in studying ancient *Koiné* Greek verbs, Hebrew *niphal* and other grammatical constructions and vocabulary, and more than a few Aramaic phrases thrown in as well. Bluntly speaking, becoming a competent Bible scholar is difficult work. For most of us, it takes a lifetime of study to begin even to start to articulate what the really difficult questions are that need to be asked and answered. On a personal note, it took me nearly fifteen years of study until I finally began to get the *beginnings* of an understanding regarding what the Apostle Paul meant when he talked about "veiling" of women in his first letter to the Corinthian congregation.

On the other hand, if you're anything remotely resembling what we might call the "average" Christian today, chances are your knowledge of the Bible is less than stellar. If you're a Christian, maybe you're one of those people who demand that the Ten Commandments should be posted in court room hallways, but you couldn't recite them in their biblical order if your life depended on your ability to do so.

Maybe you're not aware that there are two different wordings of the Ten Commandments in the Bible itself, and that they're not identical in wording![1] One of those wordings (I'll let you figure out which one by reading the footnote) is supposed by some to support a literal six-day creation of the Universe. The other wording doesn't make that claim *at all*, and it's clear from the biblical text that its author never intended it to do so! I'll leave the answer to that conundrum to your own study, with the counsel that this difference in wordings has been known by biblical scholars *for centuries*, and that there is a simple explanation for it that doesn't involve mysterious conspiracies or contradictions to the biblical text on any level.

THE EMERGING CHALLENGE OF THE EMERGENT CHURCH

One day not so long ago, Koinonia Institute founder Dr. Charles "Chuck" Missler and I were talking about a disturbing trend that has been infecting the evangelical culture of the United States of America. This disturbing trend concerns a church movement commonly called the "Emergent Church". Some observers call it the "Emerging Church". As best as I can tell by analyzing the component elements that comprise this movement, emergent churches share two basic common characteristics: *first*, their leaders avoid biblical doctrine, and *second*, their members provide only lip service at best to serious, systematic study of the biblical text. All of the other criticisms that

---

1   See Exodus 20 and Deuteronomy 5

I've observed of this movement—and there have been *hundreds* of these criticisms over the past few years—seem to trace their origin to these two basic flaws.

The Emergent Church movement has been described with remarkable clarity by the Internet encyclopedia *Wikipedia*, a public, open source press institution not generally known for its impartiality with respect to theological matters. *Wikipedia* opines:

> The **emerging church** *is a Christian movement of the late 20th and early 21st centuries that crosses a number of theological boundaries: participants are described as Protestant, post-Protestant, evangelical, post-evangelical, liberal, post-liberal, conservative, post-conservative, Anabaptist, Adventist, reformed, charismatic, neocharismatic, and post-charismatic. Emerging churches can be found throughout the globe, predominantly in North America, Western Europe, Australia, New Zealand, and Africa. Some attend local independent churches or house churches while others worship in traditional Christian denominations. Proponents believe the movement transcends such "modernist" labels of "conservative" and "liberal," calling the movement a "conversation" to emphasize its developing and decentralized nature, its vast range of standpoints, and its commitment to dialogue. Participants seek to live their faith in what they believe to be a "postmodern" society. What those involved in the conversation mostly agree on is their disillusionment with the organized and institutional church and their support for the deconstruction of modern Christian worship, modern evangelism, and the nature of modern Christian community.*[2]

CHARACTERISTICS OF THE EMERGENT CHURCH

An insightful analysis of the Emerging Church may be found in an interview conducted with Dr. John Piper that was published on his web site Desiring God (www.desiringgod.org) on the subject *What is the "Emerging Church"?* [3]

---

2 https://en.wikipedia.org/wiki/Emerging_church
3 http://www.desiringgod.org/interviews/what-is-the-emerging-church

Dr. Piper, a well-known and now-retired evangelical Christian pastor from the Reformed tradition, answered the question with this statement:

> *"Emerging" and "emergent" are sometimes distinguished.*
>
> *Emergent seems to be a reaction—among younger believers primarily, 20 and 30-somethings—to several things. In my judgment it's not a very healthy reaction, though I can understand why it might happen.*
>
> *On one hand it seems to be a reaction against the large, plastic, mega-church phenomenon where relationships are not paramount. The emphasis on bigness, success, slick marketing, and super-duper high-powered worship services all feels very plastic, commercial, and not real, poetic, gutsy and down-to-earth. So there is a reaction against that.*
>
> *On the other hand it's a reaction to formalized doctrinal statements. The emergent church tends to find creative ways of coming together, like sitting on sofas, using candles for lighting, painting the walls—strange and different things like that—because it's fresh and new and it gives release to different peoples' expressions, and so on. And if you try to push them on what they believe they don't like to tell you.*
>
> *If you Google the emergent church you'll find some emergent websites. You'll notice that they don't like statements of faith. They don't like them because they say that they alienate people. They push people apart instead of relationally nurturing people to come together.*
>
> *So that's the flavor. It's not defined. There is no list on "this is what it means to be emergent." It's just kind of a general reactionary movement.*
>
> *What concerns you most about the emergent church?*

The single greatest concern for me is their attitude towards doctrine. Stylistic things are neither here nor there. They come and go: whether you meet in a home or meet in a church, sit in a circle or sit in rows, paint on the walls or not—they're all just peripheral issues. They're the wineskins, not the wine.

The issue is their attitude towards truth. I'm deeply concerned about it, and I think that it will be the undoing of the emergent church as it has come to be. They don't believe that truth itself is an objective propositional thing that has a yes and a no. Nothing is ever either/or, good or bad, right or wrong, ugly or beautiful. It's all vague.

I've talked with some emergent types and tried to understand even their concept of truth, and you can't get your hand around it.

Here's a typical kind of response. One person made an accusation that the emergent church's view of doctrine is like trying to nail Jello to the wall. I mentioned that to one of them and his response to me was, "Why would you want to nail Jello to the wall?" That's clever, right? Yes it is, but it shows that that Jello is there. You just don't nail it to the wall. You eat Jello. You cut it in cubes, etc. But you don't nail it to the wall.

So all of this "nailing to the wall" of theses—doctrines that you would subscribe to—they're not at home with that kind of talk. They regard their position here as a virtue, I think, but I regard it as the undoing of their movement.

Now let me clarify one other thing. I said earlier that emergent and emerging aren't necessarily the same.

Emerging might be used by some people—like Mark Driscoll—to describe a proper reaction that is taking place against some of the negative things going on in the church, but a reaction that doesn't throw away the doctrines.

So Mark is a very vigilantly biblical, reformed person when it comes to what we ought to believe. And he would want to stress that a big piece of that emerging church is not just its reaction to certain unreal things in middle class Christianity but also a very intentional mission orientation. The word "missional" is kind of the "in" word today. And a church that is missional tends to be a church where everything is thought about in terms of making an impact on people around the church who are not Christians. You design everything to think that way. And I think that is a good thing.

So be careful, when you're talking emerging or emergent, to know which group you're talking about. The Mark Driscoll "emerging" type would put a very high premium on biblical faithfulness, truth, doctrine and propositions. But the emergent types would not put premium on that, but would explicitly say on their websites that they regard that kind of emphasis as harmful.[4]

Another insightful analysis of the Emerging Church may be found in Matt Slick's cogently written essay entitled *What is the Emerging Church?* [5] published on the web site maintained by *Christian Apologetics and Research Ministry*. Perhaps it is significant that Matt Slick founded CARM "to respond to the many false teachings of the cults on the Internet."[6] Perhaps it is not insignificant that Mr. Slick's personal doctrinal statement is theologically sound and above reproach.[7] An analysis of Mr. Slick's views on the Emerging Church make it clear that the man classifies this movement as heretical and aberrant. Here's a summary of what the man sees as the main characteristics of Emergent Theology:

Following are some of the common traits I have discovered by reading through Emerging Church material. But please understand that not all Emerging Churches adhere to all the points listed.

---

4 http://www.desiringgod.org/interviews/what-is-the-emerging-church
5 http://carm.org/what-emerging-church
6 http://carm.org/matt-slick
7 http://carm.org/what-i-believe-matt-slick

Why Should You Read this Book

1. *An awareness of and attempt to reach those in the changing postmodern culture.*
2. *An attempt to use technology, i.e., video, slide shows, internet.*
3. *A broader approach to worship using candles, icons, images, sounds, smells, etc.*
4. *An inclusive approach to various, sometimes contradictory belief systems.*
5. *An emphasis on experience and feelings over absolutes.*
6. *Concentration on relationship-building over proclamation of the gospel.*
7. *Shunning stale traditionalism in worship, church seating, music, etc.*
8. *A de-emphasis on absolutes and doctrinal creeds*
9. *A re-evaluation of the place of the Christian church in society.*
10. *A re-examination of the Bible and its teachings.*
11. *A re-evaluation of traditionally-held doctrines.*
12. *A re-evaluation of the place of Christianity in the world.*

Hopefully you can see some problems in the list. But, I have to say it again, not all Emerging Church adherents agree with all the points. Emerging Church pastors Mark Driscoll and Dan Kimball both acknowledge the necessity of preaching doctrinal truths which properly define Christianity while others like Brian McLaren are extremely lax when it comes to proclaiming the true biblical faith, so much so that he's been called a false teacher.[8]

WHAT GOOD CAN THERE BE IN HERESY?

Strictly defined, heresy is any deviation from the traditional, orthodox teachings of Christianity regarding the person, nature, work, or attributes of God. When applied to matters relating to the Church, the term generally refers to those teachings that attempt to redefine the role of the Church in relation to society. For example, the Scriptures make it clear that there will always be a tension of sorts

---
8 http://carm.org/what-emerging-church

between the things of the kingdom of this world and the kingdom of God. They will remain at war until the Messiah comes again to retake his creation by force.

It is helpful to remind Christians that the Messiah's eventual and final conquering of the kingdoms of this world will not come about by political reform, evangelistic efforts, or even by military conquest by mortal armies. The resurrected saints who accompany Jesus back to earth at his second coming are unarmed. While the Scriptures may indicate that the armies of the earth will gather together to attack God's armies (Revelation 19:19), the Bible indicates that they will never have an opportunity to begin their attack. Notice how the Apostle John describes the last battle called Armageddon:

> *[14] The armies of heaven, wearing fine linen, white and pure, follow him [i.e., Jesus the Messiah] on white horses. [15] A sharp sword comes out of his mouth to strike down the nations. He will rule them with an iron rod and tread the winepress of the fury of the wrath of God Almighty.*
>
> Revelation 19:14-15

This passage of Scripture makes it clear that when he comes again, God the Son will destroy all of his enemies in a single action, and with a single uttered statement. His saints will be unarmed because they will be immortal, incapable of even being injured, and because they'll be protected both by their own immortality and also by the presence of the Messiah himself.

When the Messiah is present in force, the enemy is routed. In a like manner, perhaps the presence of heresy in the Church comes pre-packaged, as it were, with its own set of unique benefits. Destructive as it is, the presence of heresy in the Church serves as a wake-up call to God's people, telling all of us that we need to re-order our priorities and re-examine our lives. In a sense, destructive movements such as the Emergent Church can serve as a form of "severe mercy," to borrow a phrase from C. S. Lewis, by which we learn to see our true present condition, compare it with the arena

Why Should You Read this Book

from which we have fallen, and turn to God for yet more grace so that we can become what we ought to be.

Thoughts on How to Start Fixing the Problem

In First Timothy 1:3-6, the Apostle Paul warns his young pastor protégé Timothy that he should:

> *³...instruct certain people to stop teaching false doctrine ⁴and occupying themselves with myths and endless genealogies. These things promote controversies rather than God's ongoing purpose, which involves faith. ⁵The goal of this instruction is love that flows from a pure heart, from a clear conscience, and from a sincere faith. ⁶Some people have left these qualities behind and have turned to fruitless discussion. ⁷They want to be teachers of the Law, yet they do not understand either what they are talking about or the things about which they speak so confidently.*
>
> 1 Timothy 1:3b-7

This counsel from the Apostle Paul is as relevant today as it was when it was first penned back in the mid-first century of our Christian era. In Second Timothy 3:1-6, the Apostle Paul continues his warnings to his Timothy by instructing him that:

> *¹...in the last days difficult times will come. ... ²People will be... ⁴lovers of pleasure rather than lovers of God. ⁵They will hold to an outward form of godliness but deny its power. Stay away from such people. ... ⁸Just as Jannes and Jambres opposed Moses, so these men oppose the truth. They are depraved in mind and their faith is a counterfeit. ⁹But they will not get very far because, as in the case of those two men, their stupidity will be plain to everyone.*
>
> Timothy 3:1b-6

In Second Peter 2:1-3, the Apostle Peter reminds the early church that:

...there were false prophets among the people, just as there also will be false teachers among you, who will secretly introduce destructive heresies and even deny the Master who bought them, bringing swift destruction on themselves. ²Many people will follow their immoral ways, and because of them the way of truth will be maligned. ³In their greed they will exploit you with deceptive words. The ancient verdict against them is still in force, and their destruction is not delayed.

2 Peter 2:1b-3

Jude, Jesus the Messiah's younger brother turned Apostle, warned the first century church about false religious leaders and teachers. Starting in verse three of his short book, he wrote that he:

Found it necessary to write to you and urge you to continue your vigorous defense of the faith that was passed down to the saints once and for all. ⁴For some people have slipped in among you unnoticed. … They turn the grace of our God into uncontrollable lust and deny our only Master and Lord, Jesus the Messiah. … ⁸In a similar way, these dreamers also defile their flesh, reject the Lord's authority, and slander his glorious beings. … ¹⁰Whatever these people do not understand, they slander. Like irrational animals, they are destroyed by the very things they know by instinct. ¹¹How terrible it will be for them! … ¹²These people are stains on your love feasts. They feast with you without any sense of awe. They are shepherds who care only for themselves. They are waterless clouds blown about by the winds. They are autumn trees that are fruitless, totally dead, and uprooted. ¹³They are wild waves of the sea, churning up the foam of their own shame. They are wandering stars for whom the deepest darkness has been reserved forever. … ¹⁶These people are complainers and faultfinders, following their own desires. They say arrogant things and flatter people in order to take advantage of them. … ¹⁷But you, dear friends, must remember the statements and predictions of the apostles of our Lord Jesus, the Messiah. ¹⁸They kept telling you, "In the last times there will be mockers, following their own ungodly desires." [19] *These are the people who cause divisions. They are worldly, devoid of the Spirit.*

Jude 3b-19

Jude's counsel regarding how we should respond to the presence of false teachers and leaders is cogent and simple. In verse 20 of the book of Jude, he writes:

[20] *But you, dear friends, must continue to build your most holy faith for your own benefit. Furthermore, continue to pray in the Holy Spirit.* [21] *Remain in God's love as you look for the mercy of our Lord Jesus the Messiah, which brings eternal life.* [22] *Show mercy to those who have doubts.* [23] *Save others by snatching them from the fire. To others, show mercy with fear, hating even the clothes stained by their sinful lives.*

Jude 20-23

Then Jude concludes his counsel with an important reminder about how God is eternally vigilant to watch out for the long-term interests of his Elect:

[24] *Now to the one who is able to keep you from falling and to make you stand joyful and faultless in his glorious presence,* [25] *to the only God, our Savior, through Jesus the Messiah, our Lord, be glory, majesty, power, and authority before all time and for all eternity! Amen.*

Jude 24-25

Jude reminds us that it is God himself who keeps his own from falling, causing them to stand before him faultless.

ON THE NEED FOR RENEWED EMPHASIS ON SYSTEMATIC BIBLICAL STUDY AND DOCTRINAL SOUNDNESS

The primary tool that Jesus the Messiah uses to equip his saints to perform their day-to-day duties as members of the Church is that of gifted, mature men who lead the Body of Christ. As the Apostle

Paul clearly explains in Ephesians 4:11-16, Jesus himself gave gifted men to the Church:

> *[11] ...some to be apostles, others to be prophets, others to be evangelists, and still others to be pastors and teachers, [12]to equip the saints, to do the work of ministry, and to build up the body of the Messiah [13]until all of us are united in the faith and in the full knowledge of God's Son, and until we attain mature adulthood and the full standard of development in the Messiah. [14]Then we will no longer be little children, tossed like waves and blown about by every wind of doctrine, by people's trickery, or by clever strategies that would lead us astray. [15]Instead, by speaking the truth in love, we will grow up completely and become one with the head, that is, one with the Messiah, [16]in whom the whole body is united and held together by every ligament with which it is supplied. As each individual part does its job, the body builds itself up in love.*
>
> Ephesians 4:1b1-16

Let me make things clear: this passage *does not* say that gifted men equip the saints for the work of the ministry. The giver of the gifted men is the one who equips the saints, and that is Jesus the Messiah himself. As valuable as they are, pastors, teachers, evangelists, and even the early apostles and prophets are not the equippers of the saints for their works of ministry. Jesus the Lord of his church is the one who does the equipping.

The Messiah's primary tool for making this all happen is the instructional ministry and day-to-day discipleship function of godly leaders who turn young, relatively immature believers into a "whole body" that is "united and held together by every ligament with which it is supplied" (Ephesians 4:16). The resultant outcome of this process will be Christian maturity, which includes doctrinal solidarity and steadfastness.

Now if Jesus the Messiah uses gifted men to go about perfecting the saints, and if those gifted men are to do that perfecting through the ministry of the Word of God, it stands to reason that those gifted men should be comfortable in their understanding of the historical accuracy and reliability of the Scriptures if they're going to be teaching that Word of God to the members of their local congregations.

This book has been written in order to present, in a systematic way, what Jesus the Messiah believed about the Scriptures that existed during the time of his mortality, in the first century of the Christian era. By demonstrating what he believed about the Bible of his day, we can be equipped with the tools we need upon which to build the foundation of our own teaching ministries.

We will begin our analysis of the view of Jesus regarding the reliability of the Scriptures by presenting a very brief overview of the four gospel narratives that make up the first four books of the New Testament. These four books contain everything that Jesus himself had to say about the Hebrew Scriptures of his day.

BACKGROUND TO THE NEW TESTAMENT RECORDS

THE GOSPEL OF MATTHEW

The ***Gospel of Matthew***, Matthew's record of the life of Jesus, is widely perceived as having been written to a largely Jewish audience, since it focuses on what Jesus had to say, presenting him as the rightful Messiah entitled to sit on David's throne.

Early Christian tradition identified the four Gospels with icons based on the four faces of angelic creatures described in the books of Ezekiel and Revelation (cf. Ezekiel 1:10; 10:14; Revelation 4:7ff; 21:13ff) and also reflecting the encampment of ancient Israel in the wilderness. Matthew's Gospel has been symbolized as a lion, representing the camp of Judah standing east of the Tabernacle that serves as an expression of the character of the Messiah's royalty by presenting Jesus as King of kings and Lord of lords.

The book is traditionally attributed to Matthew, a descendent of Levi who also served for a time as a tax collector for local Roman authorities. In that capacity, Matthew would have been skilled in the art of *tachygraphy*, an ancient Greco-Roman system of shorthand that could have enabled him to record the public discourses of Jesus in substantially a word-for-word format.

Many conservative scholars date this work to sometime after the destruction of the Jerusalem Temple in 70 AD, even though evidence exists that this work—along with the rest of the New Testament—was actually completed antecedent to that date. One school of textual criticism suggests that Matthew was the first writer to have composed his Gospel, originally recoding its contents in Hebrew or Aramaic, with copies of it translated or transcribed at a later time into Greek for dissemination to the larger Christian community.

The Messianic Theme of this work is *The Gospel for Jews—What did the Messiah Say?*

The Gospel of Mark

The **Gospel of Mark**, John Mark's record of the life of Jesus, is widely perceived as having been written to a largely Roman audience. Accordingly, this work focuses on what Jesus did as it presents him as a forceful man of action in control of the events surrounding him as he served those in need while demonstrating the great power and ability of Jesus as the Messiah, the Son of God.

Many see this work as being written to provide courage and confidence to believers who were being persecuted in the mid-60's AD. Mark records fewer parables than does Matthew and Luke, but describes more miracles in which the hand of Jesus is frequently mentioned to emphasize a sense of his personal service. Portions of the final addendum are disputed as to authenticity by some scholars due to conflicting evidence relating to the textual transmission history of parts of the record of post-resurrection events leading up to the ascension of Jesus to heaven.

Mark's Gospel has been symbolized as an ox, representing the camp of Ephraim standing west of the Tabernacle and serving as an expression of the character of the Messiah's labor and service by presenting Jesus as the servant of God and the servant of men.

Some scholars hold that this work was the first written Gospel rather than the *Gospel of Matthew*. Traditionally attributed to

Why Should You Read this Book

John Mark, a companion of Peter and Paul in several missionary activities, it is generally agreed that the *Gospel of Mark* was written in Rome, first intended for use by Roman citizens living there. Pertinent evidence for this theory includes frequent quotation of Aramaic words, followed by a translation of them, along with explanations of Jewish customs clearly intended primarily for non-Jewish readers.

Conservative scholars who hold to a very early date for the writing of this Gospel attribute this work to the late 60's or early 70's AD, most likely before the destruction of the Jerusalem Temple in 70 AD. Some note that allusions to persecution contained in the work (cf. 8:34-38; 10:38-40) seem to be too general to have been written down after the commencement of persecution under Nero in ca. 60 AD. Therefore it is surmised that a more likely post-persecution date for the writing of this work would have resulted in a more intense literary focus consistent with such persecution, had this book been composed at a date later than before 64 AD.

The Messianic Theme of this work is *The Gospel for Romans—What did the Messiah Do?*

THE GOSPEL OF LUKE

The ***Gospel of Luke***, Luke's record of the life of Jesus is widely perceived as having been written to a largely Greek audience, or at least to gentiles in general. Accordingly, this work focuses on who Jesus knew as it presents him in close interaction with men, women, and even a few children.

Authorship is traditionally attributed to the Greek physician (or Hellenistic Jew) Luke, who appears to have used a number of existing oral and/or written accounts to compose and compile his work, this book is actually part one of a two part compendium of the life of Jesus, the second part of which is the Book of Acts. Some conservative scholars suggest that Luke and Acts were composed under sponsorship of a sympathetic Roman authority named Theophilos (cf. Luke 1:1-4 and Acts 1:1) as part of the Apostle Paul's written testimony that would have been assembled in preparation for his trial in Rome before Caesar. A record of events surrounding Paul's trip to Rome is recorded in the second half of Acts.

Luke's Gospel has been symbolized as a man, representing the camp of Reuben standing south of the Tabernacle and serving as an expression of the character of the Messiah's brotherly sympathy with humanity by presenting Jesus as the fully human, loving friend, companion, associate, and leader.

The earliest possible date for the completion of Luke's Gospel must be the conclusion of events recorded in Acts 28, which records the Apostle Paul's arrest and two years of his captivity in Rome in the very early 60's AD. The second half of Luke's narrative history contains no concluding statement recording Paul's execution in Rome, which history records as having happened ca. 64 AD. Many conservative scholars surmise that Luke and Acts were completed shortly after the two year period noted in Acts 28:30 while Paul was still living. Otherwise, a notation would have been added regarding Paul's death in Rome to the end of the book of Acts.

The Messianic Theme is *The Gospel for Gentiles—Who Knew the Messiah?*

THE GOSPEL OF JOHN

The **Gospel of John**, John's record of the life of Jesus is widely perceived as having been written to a largely Christian audience. Accordingly, this work focuses on the divine nature of Jesus, presenting him as the pre-existent, eternal Word of God who pitched his tent (as the literal Greek of John 1:14 records the event) for a time among the people whom he came to save. This work focuses on a number of "I AM" claims made by Jesus regarding his nature that link the identity, essential character, and nature of Jesus directly and unmistakably to the Name of God recorded in Exodus 3:14.

John's Gospel has been symbolized as an eagle, representing the camp of Dan standing north of the Tabernacle and serving as an expression of the character of the Messiah's soaring majesty by presenting him as the Word, God Himself in full, majestic, eternal, and all-powerful Deity and now permanently incarnate as a human being.

Early church tradition attributed this work to John, arguably one of the closest friends that Jesus maintained while in ministry. Highly developed and intricate claims portraying Jesus as both Messiah and as God incarnate are cited in John's narrative of what Jesus—and not merely John as the writer of this book—had to say about his nature and person, since the "I AM" statements are recorded as actual quotations from Jesus himself, not merely theological statements or conclusions about his nature. The early church father Irenaeus wrote that the Apostle John published this Gospel "during his residence at Ephesus in Asia" (*Against Heresies* 3.1.1).

Conservative scholars suggest that this work was completed well before the destruction of Jerusalem's Temple in 70 AD, since no mention is made about this momentous event within it. Speculation by non-conservative critics that this Gospel was composed as late as ca. 170 AD were refuted by discovery of the *Roberts Fragment* $\mathcal{P}^{52}$, which contains parts of John 8:31–38, demonstrating that John's Gospel had gained enough history and wide-spread acceptance to have been circulated extensively by the early years of the second century AD, which in turns suggests that the *Gospel of John* had been complete for many decades before the beginning years of the second century AD.

The Messianic Theme is *The Gospel for Believers—Who is the Messiah?*

3 | JESUS AND THE HEBREW SCRIPTURES

That Jesus of Nazareth demonstrated high confidence in the authenticity, reliability, and accuracy of the Hebrew Scriptures can be seen in his citations of this collection of 24 separate books that comprise what we Christians call the "Old Testament" and what the Jews call the *Tanakh* and in the New Testament gospels of Matthew, Mark, Luke, and John. In the ancient Jewish canonical order, what the Christian community considers to be the 39 books of the Old Testament were looked at as 24 separate books. The twelve minor prophets were considered one book, and 1 and 2 Chronicles and Ezra were concatenated as one book, 1 and 2 Kings were concatenated as one book, and 1 and 2 Samuel were considered a single book as well. Taken together, the word *Tanakh* was coined by the Jews as an acronym taken from the three Hebrew words that described, first, the Law of Moses (*Torah*), second, the Prophetic Writings (*Neviim*), and third, the Historic Writings (*Chetubim*).

We begin our analysis by inviting the reader to consider, for example, the following general statements from Jesus the Messiah himself about the historical accuracy, doctrinal reliability, and general trustworthiness of the Hebrew Scriptures.

CLAIM #1: JESUS CLAIMED THAT MOSES SPECIFICALLY MENTIONED HIM, EVEN THOUGH THE *TORAH* HAD BEEN WRITTEN ABOUT 1,500 YEARS BEFORE JESUS HAD BEEN BORN.

Arguably the most astonishing claim that Jesus made about his relationship to and view of the Hebrew Scriptures has been recorded for us by the Apostle John in the fifth chapter of his Gospel. The extended context of his remarks was a doctrinal fight in which he became involved following his appearance at the Bethesda Pool in Jerusalem, which John tells us was located near the Sheep Gate entrance to the city. That location is in what today is the Muslim Quarter of the Old City portion of modern Jerusalem. John

Figure 4: Model of Pool of Bethesda at the Model of Ancient Jerusalem, Israel Museum.

mentions in his Gospel that it was surrounded by five colonnades, which could accommodate the presence of what John 5:4 tells us was "a large number of sick people" who "were laying—blind, lame, or paralyzed".

For many years, higher critics doubted the veracity of John's record of the healing that Jesus performed at the Bethesda Pool on the sophomoric grounds that they believed John's claim about the five colonnades was a "hagiographic interpolation"—in other words, that John *made up the story about the colonnades* without actually having been there. They claimed that the reference to the five colonnades was *added* by a later author as a sly reference to the five books of Moses. Apparently, it never occurred to these higher critics that *John himself* wrote the original account, that he visited the pool himself, and that there really were five colonnades.

Also, since the text of the account in John 5:5 *specifically* notes that "One particular man was there who had been ill for 38 years," one would think that a man who knew enough about the incident to record the detail that the individual in question had been ill for exactly 38 years would also know how many sets of colonnades surrounded the pool! More accurately, these higher critics denied that the gospel account had been written by John himself, since there was no evidence that there were five colonnades surrounding the pool, or that there ever had been.

Figure 5: Ruins of Byzantine era chapel near the site of the Pool of Bethesda

But then in the nineteenth century, archaeologists discovered the remains of the pool. It *precisely* fitted the description of the Bethesda Pool, right down to the five colonnades. There was one colonnade on each of the four sides of a rectangular structure, and a fifth one that dissected the pool across the middle of the structure.

You can see what the pool looked like in the model of the Bethesda Pool located in the model of ancient Jerusalem that was been constructed on the site of the modern Israeli Museum in Jerusalem. There's a photo of the model of the Bethesda Pool on the previous page. At any rate, as a direct result of the archaeological discoveries, the theories of the higher critics that the pool carried only a metaphorical, rather than a historical, reality were finally laid to rest.

The context of Jesus the Messiah's comment that the ancient Hebrew Scriptures contained accounts written by Moses in which the greatest authority in ancient Israel wrote about Jesus is a theological dispute regarding what Jesus did one Sabbath day when Jesus was visiting Jerusalem to attend one of the Jewish national festivals. At that festival, Jesus decided to heal the man who had been ill for 38 years. As John relates the story in John 5:8-12:

> *⁸Jesus told him, "Stand up, pick up your mat, and walk!"*
> *⁹The man immediately became well, and he picked up his mat and started walking. Now that day was a Sabbath.*
> *¹⁰So the Jewish leaders told the man who had been healed, "It is the Sabbath, and it is not lawful for you to carry your mat."*
> *¹¹But he answered them, "The man who made me well told me, 'Pick up your mat and walk.'"*
> *¹²They asked him, "Who is the man who told you, 'Pick it up and walk'?"*
>
> John 5:8-12

Notice, if you would please, how the theological argument was not initially caused by Jesus' healing of the ill man. It was because the previously ill, but now healed, man was carrying the mat on which he had been laying on the Sabbath day! John 5:16 records how and why the fight began: "So the Jewish leaders began persecuting Jesus, because he kept doing such things on the Sabbath."

The succinct, blunt reply of Jesus to the Jewish leaders only made things worse! John 5:17-18 records the following remarkable statement:

> *¹⁷But Jesus answered them, "My Father has been working until now, and I, too, am working." ¹⁸So the Jewish leaders were trying all the harder to kill him, because he was not only breaking the Sabbath but was also calling God his own Father, thereby making himself equal to God.*
>
> John 5:17-18

Notice, if you would, that there were *two* complaints against the rabbi from Nazareth. *First*, they objected to Jesus "working" on the Sabbath day; and *second*, they didn't appreciate him calling God his Father, because by doing so, he was "thereby making himself equal to God".

In making his reply to the Jewish leaders, Jesus answered *both* objections in a single answer. He did this by linking the authority to work on the Sabbath to his *eternal existence* as part of his divine nature. In simple terms, his claim to have authority to work on the Sabbath day springs directly from his nature as sharing the same divine character qualities as God the Father. That's because in Jewish thought, to be "a son of" someone means that the individual shares the same characteristic of the person named. So for Jesus to call himself "the Son of God the Father," what Jesus meant in rabbinic thought was that the old proverb "like father, like son" applied quite literally to himself: Jesus was claiming to make himself equal in character to God himself.

CLAIM #2: JESUS LINKED HIS CLAIM THAT HE WOULD JUDGE THE DEAD AT THE DAY OF RESURRECTION TO HIM HAVING BEEN WRITTEN ABOUT BY MOSES IN THE *TORAH*.

Notice how the argument in which Jesus was engaged with the Jewish leaders reaches its crescendo in John 5:24-29, in which he lays the foundation for what will be his astonishing claim that Moses himself mentioned him way back 1,500 years earlier when the man composed the *Torah*:

> [24] *Truly, I tell all of you emphatically, whoever hears what I say and believes in the one who sent me has eternal life and will not be judged, but has passed from death to life.* [25] *Truly, I tell all of you emphatically, the time approaches, and is now here, when the dead will hear the voice of the Son of God, and those who hear it will live.* [26] *Just as the Father has life in himself, so also he has granted the Son to have life in himself,* [27] *and he has given him authority to judge, because he is the Son of Man.* [28] *Don't be amazed at this, because the time is*

approaching when everyone in their graves will hear the Son of Man's voice [29] *and will come out—those who have done what is good to the resurrection that leads to life, and those who have practiced what is evil to the resurrection that ends in condemnation.*

John 5:24-29

Now what strikes me as remarkable about this astonishing statement isn't merely that Jesus is claiming to be the one who will judge everyone who has ever lived for each of their actions at the Resurrection Day.

That's remarkable enough in its own right, but if you read through this section of John's narrative again very carefully, you'll see that all of his remarks are a setup for what happens next: Jesus links the origin of the Law of God written by Moses to himself! In John 5:39-40 and John 5:45-47, Jesus complained to the Jewish leaders that:

[39] *You examine the Scriptures carefully because you suppose that in them you have eternal life. Yet they testify about me.* [40] *But you are not willing to come to me to have life. …* [45] *Do not suppose that I will be the one to accuse you before the Father. Your accuser is Moses, on whom you have set your hope,* [46] *because if you believed Moses, you would believe me, since he wrote about me.* [47] *But if you do not believe what he wrote, how will you believe my words?"*

John 5:39-40, 45-47

CLAIM #3: JESUS CLAIMED THAT THE HEBREW SCRIPTURES IN GENERAL SPOKE OF HIM, EVEN THOUGH THE LAST BOOK OF THE *TANAKH* HAD BEEN WRITTEN ABOUT 430 YEARS BEFORE HE HAD BEEN BORN.

Notice how, at the end of the mortal ministry of Jesus, John Mark records in his Gospel a seemingly off-the-cuff remark about the man's relationship to the entire corpus of divinely revealed writings called the Hebrew Scriptures. His apparently off-hand remark is recorded in Mark 14:17-21, specifically at verse 21:

[17] When evening came, Jesus arrived with the Twelve. [18] While they were at the table eating, Jesus said, "I tell all of you with certainty, one of you is going to betray me, one who is eating with me."

[19] They began to be very sad and asked him, one after the other, "Surely I am not the one, am I?"

[20] He told them, "It's one of you Twelve, the one who is dipping his bread into the bowl with me. [21] For the Son of Man is going away, just as it has been written about him, but how terrible it will be for that man by whom the Son of Man is betrayed! It would have been better for him if he had never been born."

Mark 14:17-21

By making the claim that his upcoming execution had been written about in the Hebrew Scriptures, Jesus the Messiah is claiming that his "going away" noted in verse 21 was described by these ancient documents. The last of the books (the book of Malachi) written by the ancient prophets was completed during the mid-400's BC.

CLAIM #4: JESUS ENDORSED THE ABSOLUTE RELIABILITY AND ENDURING NATURE OF THE HEBREW SCRIPTURES SO EMPHATICALLY THAT HE CLAIMED NOT A SINGLE LETTER OR PORTION OF A LETTER WOULD FAIL.

The fifth through the seventh chapters of the Gospel of Matthew record a verbatim transcript of Jesus the Messiah's first public manifesto regarding what life in the Kingdom from Heaven is all about. Skilled as he was in the ancient speed writing skill of *tachygraphy*, Matthew recorded what we call *"The Kings Speech"* word-for-word. After beginning his Sermon on the Mount, Jesus engaged in what for lack of a better term we'll call a "pre-emptive strike" against criticism by the contemporary Jewish leaders of Jesus' view of the integrity of the Scriptures.

So radical was his *conservative view of the biblical record* that he would be attacked time and time again for his presumed tendency to depart from Scripture. As a point of fact, Jesus wasn't departing from Scriptural truth. Instead, he claimed to be upholding that truth. What Jesus was attacking was the *oral tradition* handed down for generations by the Jewish leaders, not the *written records* of the biblical text itself. Matthew 5:17-19 sets forth Jesus the Messiah's corrective exhortation:

> [17] *"Do not think that I came to destroy the Law or the Prophets. I didn't come to destroy them, but to fulfill them,* [18] *because I tell all of you with certainty that until heaven and earth disappear, not one letter or one stroke of a letter will disappear from the Law until everything has been accomplished.* [19] *So whoever sets aside one of the least of these commandments and teaches others to do the same will be called least in the kingdom from heaven. But whoever does them and teaches them will be called great in the kingdom from heaven.*
>
> Matthew 5:17-19

At this point, let's make a brief comment about Jesus the Messiah's use of the term "the Law and the Prophets" as referring to the entirety of the then-existing written revelation of the Word of God. Strictly speaking, the complete Jewish term for what we Christians call the "Old Testament" consisted of three parts, not two. As we noted earlier, the Old Testament was divided into the *Torah* (consisting of the books of Genesis through Deuteronomy), the *Neviim* (the major and minor prophetic books), and the *Chetubim* (the historical writings).

But in his Sermon on the Mount, Jesus mentions only the first two divisions of the Hebrew Scriptures (the Law and the Prophets) without mentioning the historical book section that the Jews called the *Chetubim*. His omission is deliberate, but it's not because he believed that the *Writings* from Psalms to Second Chronicles had a lesser sense of reliability than the Law and the Prophets. As a point of fact, we'll see in later chapters, below, that one of the most common references to the Hebrew Scriptures mentioned by Jesus was to the Psalms, specifically, to Psalm 110. And the Psalms were part of the *Chetubim*. Jesus was using a form of oral shorthand, so to speak, by referring to the entire *Tanakh* by its first two divisions only. His regular reference to and quoting of the Psalms demonstrates that he held the same high view of the third section of the Hebrew Scriptures that he did to the first two sections. Now with respect to Jesus' view of the Hebrew Scriptures, he makes specific mention to the *verbal, plenary* reliability of every word, letter, and stroke of a letter of the entire Hebrew and Aramaic corpus of the text. Note, if you would, please, this striking statement in Matthew 5:18:

> *"…because I tell all of you with certainty that until heaven and earth disappear, not one letter or one stroke of a letter will disappear from the Law until everything has been accomplished."*
>
> Matthew 5:18

The smallest letter in the Hebrew and Aramaic alphabets in which the Hebrew Scriptures were composed is the Hebrew letter *yod*. It looks like this: ׳

When Jesus referred to "one stroke of a letter" in Matthew 5:18, he was talking about the small, differential stroke appended to certain forms of the individual letters by which a reader could distinguish between what would otherwise be identical in shape but different in meaning. Consider, for example, these five different Hebrew letters:

ב ר ד ה ח

Read left to right, they represent the Hebrew/Aramaic letters "B," "R," "D", "H," and "Ch," respectively.

- You'll notice that the letter "B" consists of two strokes: a lower horizontal stroke and an upper horizontal stroke that curves down to the right and intersects the lower horizontal stroke.

- The letter "R" lacks the lower horizontal stroke that occurs in the letter "B".
- The only distinguishing difference between the letter "R" and the letter "D" is the extremely small extension of the upper horizontal stroke on the "D":

ר ד ☞ Extender

- The letter "H" is formed by adding a small vertical stroke to the letter "D":

ד   Extender ☞ ה

- The only distinguishing difference between the letter "Ch" and the letter "H" is that the small vertical stroke added to the letter "D" extends all the way to the top horizontal line of the letter "Ch," but not to the top horizontal line of the letter "H":

Extender ☞ ח   Extender ☞ ה

It was to these strokes that Jesus was referring when he said that not even a stroke of a letter would pass away from the Law and the Prophets before the Word of God would be fulfilled. Jesus wasn't the only one who held this view. The *Talmud* itself said the same thing:

- *Should anyone, in Deuteronomy 6:4, change (d) to (r), he would ruin the world, because instead of reading "Listen, Israel! The Lord is our God, the Lord alone," the verse would read "Listen, Israel! The Lord our God is a false Lord."*
- *Should anyone, in Exodus 34:14, change (r) to (d), he would ruin the world, because instead of reading "…you are not to bow down in worship to any other*

Jesus and the Hebrew Scriptures

- *god,", the verse would read "…you are not to worship the one true God."*

- *Should anyone, in Leviticus 22:32, change (ch) to (h), he would ruin the world, because instead of reading, "You are not to defile my sacred name," the verse would read "Neither are to praise my sacred name."*

- *Should anyone, in Psalm 150:6, change (h) to (ch), he would ruin the world because instead of reading, "Let everyone who breathes praise the Lord!" the verse would read "Let everyone who breathes profane the Lord."*

- *Should anyone, in Jeremiah 5:12, change (b) to (k), he would ruin the world, because instead of reading, "They have lied about the Lord," the verse would read "They have lied like the Lord."*

- *Should anyone, in First Samuel 2:2, change (k) to (b), he would ruin the world, because instead of reading, "Indeed, there is no one holy like the Lord," the verse would read "Indeed, there is no holiness in the Lord."*[1]

By claiming that not a single letter or stroke of a letter of the Hebrew Scriptures would ever fail, Jesus the Messiah was claiming that the Bible of his day was reliable in its record of the history that it records, that it was trustworthy in the teachings about God that it contains, and that it was accurate in all aspects of its predictive history that we call prophetic literature.

That the *Talmud concurs* with the assessment by Jesus the Messiah as to the reliability of the Hebrew Scriptures is, I suspect, an unwitting *endorsement* of the man's view of the Bible. That's because the *Talmud* was being compiled during the lifetime of Jesus, and was not formally completed until about five hundred years after his earthly ministry was concluded. I know of no instances in which, if the historical record of Scripture were thoroughly tested in comparison with outside evidence contemporaneous to the claimed

---

1 The *Talmud* at *Vayikra Rabba* (s.19). Cited by Katherine Bushnell in her classic work, *God's Word to Women*, p. 14. Source: https://godswordtowomen.files.wordpress.com/2010/10/gods_-word_to_women1.pdf.

date of the biblical events, that the *prima facie* accounts of the Bible should not be taken as correct where it cannot yet be tested.

Perhaps you're thinking that all of the above may be very well and good, but the analysis of the letters and strokes of a letter of those five letters was undertaken on the *modern* Hebrew alphabet. What about the actual Hebrew alphabet characters in use during Jesus' life time? Well now, the table below lists a selection of letters from the Early, Middle, and Late Hebrew alphabets:[2]

\multicolumn{7}{c}{Ancient Semitic/Hebrew}
Early	Middle	Late	Name	Picture	Meaning
⌂	⌐	ב	Bet	Tent floorplan	Family, House, "In"
ឧ	ዋ	ר	Resh	Head of a man	First, Top, Beginning
▽	△	ד	Dal	Door	Move, Hang, Entrance
⚶	ⅎ	π	Hey	Man with arms raised	Look, Reveal, Breath
目	日	Π	Hhet	Tent wall	Outside, Divide, Half

The very same pattern of letters and strokes of a letter that applies to the modern Hebrew alphabet also applies to Early, Middle, and Late Hebrew. This striking similarity of appearance is particularly evident in Middle Hebrew, where:

- *The "Ch" and the "H" letter forms differ only by a single added descending stroke to the left side of the letter "Ch" or a slightly longer upper top level horizontal stroke for the letter "H"; and,*

日	Π	Hhet
ⅎ	π	Hey

- *In the presence of a descender on the "B" that isn't present in the "D"; and,*

---

2   Compiled by Jeff A. Benner. Cited from http://www.ancient-hebrew.org/alphabet_chart.html.

ב	ב	Bet
ד	ד	Dal

- *The difference between the "B" and "R" is only evident in the curvature of the descender for the letter "B".*

ב	ב	Bet
ר	ר	Resh

To sum up, no mere scholarly assumption, theory, claim, or *opinion* carries enough internal credibility sufficient to warrant maintaining doubt regarding the truth of documents that are twenty or thirty *centuries* old. Speculation, theory, and "learned opinion" ***are not*** evidence sufficient to impeach the integrity of Jesus the Messiah's faith in the Scriptures. As Professor Robert Dick Wilson observed:

> *as far as any one today knows, every reference that He made to the Old Testament is true… Today we know that the history of Israel, unlike that of Greece and Rome, is confirmed by a mass of evidence, which rules out all the old-time mythical theories as to its origin. Wherever the Old Testament records can be thoroughly tested, they have stood the test. As to writing, language, forms of literature, law, history and religion, it stands approved by the evidence of contemporaneous documents of unquestioned veracity and relativity. Its statements must be accepted on their face value unless it can be shown by evidence from outside that they are false.*[3]

ON THE BIBLICAL TEXT OF JESUS' DAY

Unlike the situation faced by those who study the manuscript transmission history of the Greek New Testament, students of biblical Hebrew don't have to be concerned much with sorting out which manuscripts of the Old Testament are more reliable or trustworthy

---

3 Robert Dick Wilson. *Jesus and the Old Testament. Princeton* Theological Review Vol. 24 No. 4 (1926), p. 638

than others. That's because with respect to biblical Hebrew, unlike the vast catalog of literally *thousands* of Greek manuscripts of the New Testament that we have to study, *only two* different manuscripts of the Hebrew Old Testament exist to be studied. They are the *Leningrad Codex* and the *Aleppo Codex*, named after the cities of Leningrad, Russia and Aleppo, Syria, where they were stored originally.

The *Aleppo Codex* is now stored in Israel. The *Leningrad Codex* resides in the National Library of Russia. Both manuscripts are about 1,000 years old, but the *Aleppo Codex* is slightly older than the *Leningrad Codex*, dating from the 10th century AD. It was endorsed with respect to its accuracy by Maimonides, the great Jewish scholar of the Middle Ages. However, it lacks most of the *Torah* and other parts. Furthermore, shortly after World War II (i.e., between 1947 and 1958), 193 of its 487 original pages disappeared from the manuscript and are probably in the hands of private collectors.

Figure 6: Page from the Aleppo Codex

In contrast to the *Aleppo Codex*, the *Leningrad Codex* is quite complete. It's the oldest complete codex of the Old Testament that has survived until the 21st century. Accordingly, the *Leningrad Codex* is the primary source document for recovery of details that are presently missing from the *Aleppo Codex*. Now with respect to both of these codices, V. S. Herrell has observed:

> *The Hebrew text ... is clearly not the original Hebrew, nor even the Hebrew that was in use in the 1st century AD. The Hebrew*

of the 1st century AD was closely akin to the Greek Septuagint that we have today; this is clear because, although the Hebrew was little used, when it was used in ancient writing it was clearly in agreement with the Greek Septuagint rather than the Masoretic Text. For example, although Philo and Josephus both used the Greek Septuagint, it is believed by most scholars that they frequently had access to a Hebrew Bible and even consulted it on a few occasions. It is through evidence like this that we see that the then current Hebrew disagreed with the Hebrew Masoretic Text of today. In the 1st century, the Christians and all other Greek speaking Israelites, including 1,000,000 of them who lived in Alexandria, Egypt, used the Greek Septuagint. Jesus and His Apostles wrote in Greek and quoted the Greek Septuagint. Of this there can be no doubt. This is a fact that can be confirmed in any encyclopedia or scholarly book on the subject. As we have already pointed out, we know this because the quotations of the Greek New Testament are exactly aligned with the Greek Septuagint, but in sharp opposition to the Hebrew Masoretic Text. There is, however, no reason to believe that they were in disagreement with the Hebrew that was current in the 1st century AD.[4]

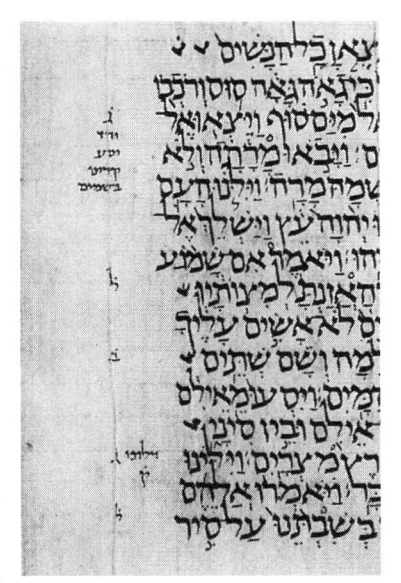

Figure 7: Exodus 15:2-16:3 from Lenin-grad Codex

No substantial manuscript problems exist that call into question the essential accuracy of the text of the Hebrew Scriptures of Jesus' generation. With respect to our modern English language translations of the text of the Bible that Jesus studied, virtually all of them are reliable. While a few notable differences of opinion exist

---

4 V. S. Herrell. *The Masoretic Text of the Old Testament.* Cited from http://www.bible-believers.org.-au/masorete.htm.

as to the modern day translation of some Hebrew words,[5] they are reliable in their translation of the history of Israel, the poetic books, and the prophecies of the Old Testament.

To sum up, when you add the testimony of the New Testament to the mix, sacred history and the doctrines of redemption are so well rendered that anyone who reads them may learn by such reading how they may become wise unto salvation through faith in Jesus the Messiah. In those occasions when he refers to the Law, Jesus recognizes the verbal accuracy and the authority of the Biblical texts bearing upon the Sabbath and divorce; and, then, as the Lord of both Sabbath and of man, he makes known a higher and better Law.

---

5   Such as, for example, whether the Hebrew word *almah* used in Isaiah 7:14 means "young woman" or "virgin". In our work *Ten Test Questions for the World's Finest Woman: A Protestant Theologian looks at the life of Mary, the Mother of Jesus,* we addressed that subject, demonstrating that the Septuagint's rendering of *alma* as *parthenos*, or "virgin", was the correct choice by the pre-Christian translators of the Hebrew Scriptures into Greek.

4 | JESUS AND MOSES

That Jesus of Nazareth demonstrated high confidence in the authenticity, reliability, and accuracy of the Hebrew Scriptures can be seen in his references to Moses throughout the days of his public ministry. We invite the reader to consider, for example, the following direct quotes from the New Testament record:

CLAIM #5: **JESUS CONSIDERED THE LAWS CONTAINED IN THE *TORAH* TO HAVE BEEN AUTHORED BY MOSES.**

Immediately upon completing his delivery of the Sermon on the Mount, the Apostle Matthew recorded the following incident in Matthew 8:1-4:

> [1] *When Jesus came down from the hillside, large crowds followed him.* [2] *Suddenly, a leper came up to him, fell down before him, and said, "Sir, if you want to, you can make me clean."*
> [3] *So Jesus reached out his hand, touched him, and said, "I do want to. Be clean!" And instantly his leprosy was made clean.*

59

> *⁴Then Jesus told him, "See to it that you don't speak to anyone. Instead, go and show yourself to the priest, and then offer the sacrifice that Moses commanded as proof to the authorities."*
>
> Matthew 8:1-4

The offerings to which Jesus refers are recorded in Leviticus 14:1-32. Notice how the text of this passage begins with an affirmation that it was dictated by God Himself directly to Moses, who then set them down in permanent written form for use by the believing community of ancient Israel.

Also, if you read through the extended section from Leviticus that we've reproduced for your perusal, below, you'll see why Jesus did not specifically tell the cleansed man which offering to present when he appeared before the priests in the Temple. Specifically, the Mosaic law provided a *range of offerings*, all of which were based on the ability of the offeror to pay, based on his economic stance in the community of Israel. It would be up to the offeror to examine his own circumstances and choose which type of offering to present in the Temple at his appearance before the Lord in the Temple.

Furthermore, the directive by Jesus to the man not to speak to anyone until he had presented himself to the Temple authorities was 100% consistent with the *Torah's* command that he would not be considered legally cleansed (even with the Messiah's supernatural cleansing!) until he had completed the Law's required offerings. You can read this requirement in Leviticus 14:1-32:

> *¹The LORD told Moses, ²"This is the law concerning those who have infectious skin diseases, after they have been cleansed: ³The priest is to go outside the camp and examine the infectious skin disease to confirm that the person has been healed. ⁴If he has been healed, then the priest is to command that two live and clean birds, some cedar wood, some crimson thread, and hyssop be brought for the one cleansed.*
> *⁵Then the priest is to command that one bird be slaughtered on an earthen vessel over flowing water. ⁶He is to take the live bird, the cedar wood, the crimson thread, and the hyssop,*

and dip them together in the blood of the bird that had been slaughtered over the flowing water. ⁷ He is to sprinkle the blood seven times on the person with the infectious skin disease and then pronounce him clean. Then he is to release the live bird into the open fields. ⁸ The person who is clean is to wash his clothes, shave all his hair, and bathe in water, after which he is to be declared clean. Then he can be brought back to the camp, but he is to remain outside his tent for seven days. ⁹ On the seventh day, he is to shave the hair on his head, chin, back, and eyebrows. After he has shaved all his hair, washed his clothes, and bathed himself with water, then he will be clean."

¹⁰ "On the eighth day, he is to take two lambs without defect, a one year old ewe lamb without defect, one third of a measure of fine flour mixed with olive oil for a meal offering, and one log of oil. ¹¹ The priest who will pronounce him clean is to present the person to be cleansed and these offerings in the LORD's presence at the entrance to the Tent of Meeting.

¹² The priest is to take one of the lambs and present it as a guilt offering, along with one log of olive oil, which he is to wave as a raised offering in the LORD's presence. ¹³ Then he is to slaughter the lamb in the place where he slaughtered the sin and burnt offerings—that is, at a place in the sanctuary. Just as the sin offering is for the priest, so also is the guilt offering. It's a most holy thing.

¹⁴ "Then the priest is to take some of the blood from the guilt offering and place it on the right earlobe of the person to be cleansed, on his right thumb, and on his right great toe.
¹⁵ Then the priest is to take some of the log of olive oil and pour it into his own left hand. ¹⁶ The priest is to dip his right finger in the olive oil that is in his left palm and sprinkle some of the olive oil with his finger seven times in the LORD's presence.
¹⁷ "As to the remainder of the olive oil in his palm, he is to place some on the right earlobe of the person to be cleansed, on his right thumb, on his right great toe, and on the blood of

the guilt offering. ¹⁸ Then he is to place the rest of the oil in his palm on the head of the person to be cleansed, thus making atonement for him in the LORD's presence. ¹⁹ This is how the priest is to present the sin offering to make atonement for the person being cleansed of his impurity. After this, he is to slaughter the whole burnt offering. ²⁰ The priest is to offer both the whole burnt and the grain offerings on the altar. After the priest makes atonement for him, he will be clean."

²¹ "If the offeror is poor and cannot afford the regular offering, then he is to take one lamb for a guilt offering that will be presented in the form of a wave offering to atone for him, one tenth of a measure of fine flour mixed with olive oil for a grain offering, one log of olive oil, ²² and two turtledoves or two young pigeons, whichever he can afford. One is for a sin offering and the other is for a whole burnt offering.

²³ "On the eighth day, he is to bring them for cleansing to the priest in the LORD's presence at the entrance to the Tent of Meeting. ²⁴ The priest is to take the lamb for a guilt offering and the olive oil and wave them as a raised offering in the LORD's presence. ²⁵ Then he is to take the lamb for the guilt offering and place some blood from the guilt offering on the right earlobe of the person to be cleansed, on his right thumb, and on his right great toe. ²⁶ Then the priest is to pour olive oil into his left palm ²⁷ and use his right finger to sprinkle oil from his left palm seven times in the LORD's presence. ²⁸ The priest is to place oil from his palm on the right earlobe of the person being cleansed, on his right thumb, on his right great toe, and where the blood for the guilt offering is poured.

²⁹ "As to the remainder of the oil in his palm, the priest is to use it to anoint the head of the person to be cleansed, in order to make atonement for him in the LORD's presence.

³⁰ Then he is to offer one of the turtledoves or the young pigeons, whichever he can afford. ³¹ Based on what he can afford, one is for a sin offering and the other is for a whole

burnt offering. Along with the grain offering, the priest is to make atonement for the person to be cleansed in the LORD's presence. ³²This is the regulation concerning one who has an infectious skin disease but who cannot afford his cleansing."
Leviticus 14:1-32

Perhaps in closing our discussion of this subject, we might do well to point out one other factor regarding the regulations set forth in the *Torah* regarding cleansing from leprosy. That observation is this: back in the days of Moses and the early Israeli nation, leprosy *was a permanent disease*. Once it was contracted, it was incurable.

That certain disease that we call today "leprosy" bears only a surface resemblance to biblical era leprosy. Biblical era leprosy was far more virulent than its modern equivalent, most notably in the area of *communicable nature*. The ancient form of the disease was so dangerous that its victims required complete isolation from other members of the community. While modern leper colonies continue this social tradition to some extent, today's disease is very difficult to contract by direct physical contact. Given the virulent nature of the disease, and the extreme likelihood that its sufferers would have carried the disease *for life*, we wonder if the ultimate purpose of the regulations for cleansing were put in place *in anticipation* of the day that would come when the Messiah would arrive with the power and authority to cleanse lepers with a touch or a word of healing.

I do not mean to appear crass here, but have you ever stopped to consider that whenever you read in the New Testament that Jesus healed a leper with a touch, he was violating the non-contact provisions of the regulations for dealing with leprosy set forth in the *Torah*? He did this for the same reason that as Lord of the Sabbath, he could override its provisions for the sake of the good of humanity. So also, as Lord of healing, whenever Jesus touched a leper, instead of Jesus being made unclean, the leper was healed, because he came to serve humanity and fulfill the Law.

CLAIM #6: **JESUS CONSIDERED CIRCUMCISION TO HAVE BEEN HANDED DOWN FROM THE DAYS OF THE PATRIARCHS THROUGH THE AUTHORITY OF MOSES.**

In one of his many dialogs with the Jewish leaders of his day, Jesus claimed that the regulation that circumcision be performed on the eighth day of life was given through the authority of Moses, who passed the requirement on to national Israel from the time of Abraham. John 7:19-22 records the claim by Jesus:

> [22] *"Moses gave you circumcision—not that it is from Moses, but from the Patriarchs—and so you circumcise a man on the Sabbath."*
>
> John 7:22

By this statement, Jesus affirmed the historical viability not only of Moses, but also of Abraham, Isaac, and Jacob, as well.

JESUS ON THE *TORAH*: THE SINGULAR UNITY OF THE TEXT

Many generations ago, a group of German-based higher critics began to promulgate a theory that the *Torah* was composed and compiled about the time of the exile to Babylon, or shortly thereafter, and not in the mid-15th century BC, as the conservative scholarly community (and Jesus himself!) contends. They made their determination by *assuming* that the development of the *Tanakh* was evolutionary in method. By making this erroneous assumption, these textual critics rejected the unity of the authorship of the *Torah*, thus standing in irreconcilable opposition to the view of Jesus regarding the five books of Moses. That's because Jesus considered the entire *Torah* to be the product of a single author, whom he identified as the man who led the nascent nation of Israel out of Egypt into Canaan.

In contrast to Jesus' view of the essential unity of the *Torah*, the German higher critics believed they could determine who wrote the *Torah* by segmenting the text into differing authors based on how they used the various names of God in their writings. The late Dr. Gleason Archer, *Professor of Old Testament and Semitic Languages* at Trinity Evangelical Divinity School, summarized the documentary hypothesis of textual criticism by which the authors of the *Torah* were described by letters of the alphabet:

- *J—written about 850 B.C. by an unknown writer in the Southern Kingdom of Judah. He was especially interested in personal biography, characterized by vivid delineation of character. He often portrayed or referred to God in anthropomorphic terms (i.e., as if He possessed the body, parts, and passions of a human being). He also had a prophet-like interest in ethical and theological reflection, but little interest in sacrifice or ritual.*

- *E—written about 750 B.C. by an unknown writer in the Northern Kingdom of Israel. He was more objective than J in his narrative style and was less consciously tinged with ethical and theological reflection. He tended rather to dwell upon concrete particulars (or the origins of names or customs of particular importance to Israelite culture). In Genesis, E shows an interest in ritual and worship, and he represents God as communicating through dreams and visions (rather than through direct anthropomorphic contact, after the fashion of J). In Exodus through Numbers, E exalts Moses as a unique miracle worker, with whom God could communicate in anthropomorphic guise.*

- *About 650 B.C. an unknown redactor combined J and E into a single document: J-E.*

- *D—composed possibly under the direction of the high priest Hilkiah, as an official program for the party of reform sponsored by King Josiah in the revival of 621 B.C. Its object was to compel all the subjects of the kingdom of Judah to abandon their local sanctuaries on the "high places" and bring all their sacrifices and religious contributions to the temple in Jerusalem. This document was strongly under the influence of the prophetic movement, particularly of Jeremiah. Members*

> of this same Deuteronomic school later reworked the historical accounts recorded in Joshua, Judges, Samuel, and Kings.
>
> - P—composed in various stages, all the way from Ezekiel, with his Holiness Code (Lev. 17–26) ca. 570 B.C. (known as H to Ezra, "the ready scribe in the law of Moses" under whose guidance the latest priestly sections were added to the Torah. P is concerned with a systematic account of the origins and institutions of the Israelite theocracy. It shows a particular interest in origins, in genealogical lists, and details of sacrifice and ritual.[1]

Each of these separate writers had their work compiled and/or redacted by yet another unnamed person into the document we now know as the *Torah*. The usual suspect for the man who did the editing is someone such as Ezra, who lived after the exile to Babylon was completed, but there appears to be no universal consensus among higher critics as to the "true" identity of this mythical editor.

There is no textual transmission evidence of any kind that supports this documentary theory regarding the origin of the *Torah*. Surviving copies of the Septuagint (the Greek translation of the Hebrew text that was completed during the 2nd century, BC) are substantially in agreement with the Hebrew editions. Virtually *no one* dared to suggest that the *Torah* was written by anyone other than Moses himself [2] …until, that is, the German rationalist higher critics assumed that Moses could not have composed it and therefore the work had to be the product of a committee of some kind that assembled all of the historical myths (which included the Levitical regulations!) into a single document about 800 years after Israel had been using them to conduct their ministries in the Tabernacle and the Temple.

---

1   Gleason Archer Jr., *A Survey of Old Testament Introduction*, 3rd. ed. (Chicago: Moody Press, 1994), 97–98.
2   As far back as 1670, the Spanish pantheistic Benedict Spinoza had expressed the view in his *Tractatus Theologico-Politicus* that the *Pentateuch* was not written by Moses, because he is referred to in the third person rather than by the first, and because he could not have recorded his own death, as is done in Deuteronomy 34. Spinoza proposed Ezra as the final composer of the *Torah*. But Spinoza's theory was largely ignored until the rise of the German higher critics.

CLAIM #7: **JESUS HAD LITTLE RESPECT FOR THE *TRADITIONS* HANDED DOWN ABOUT HOW TO OBEY THE *TORAH*, BUT HE HAD HIGH RESPECT FOR THE AUTHORITY OF THE *TORAH* ITSELF.**

The Apostle Matthew recorded the following details regarding a theological fight that Jesus had with the Pharisees and *Torah* experts who were active during Jesus' public ministry. The incident is recorded in Matthew 15:1-6:

> [1] *Then some Pharisees and scribes came from Jerusalem to Jesus and asked,* [2] *"Why do your disciples disregard the tradition of the elders? They don't wash their hands when they eat."* [3] *But he answered them, "Why do you also disregard the commandment of God because of your tradition?* [4] *Because God said, 'You are to honor your father and your mother,' and, 'Whoever curses father or mother must certainly be put to death.'* [5] *But you say, 'Whoever tells his father or his mother, "Whatever support you might have received from me has been given to God,"* [6] *does not have to honor his father.' Because of your tradition, then, you have disregarded the authority of God's word.*
>
> Matthew 15:1-6

We invite the reader to notice that this incident records the *high contrast* that Jesus makes between the authority of the Law of Moses and the traditions of the elders of first century Israel. Jesus clearly held the view that the traditions put in place over the centuries following Moses' giving the Law to Israel had the effect of disregarding the authority of the *Torah*.

CLAIM #8: **JESUS BELIEVED THAT THE AUTHORITY OF THE *TORAH* ORIGINATED FROM THE EARLIEST DAYS OF HUMANITY, NOT MERELY FROM MOUNT SINAI.**

Claim #9: Jesus believed that the book of Genesis was written by Moses.

Matthew 19:1-8 records a theological debate between Jesus and a group of Pharisees that took place in the territory of Judea late in his ministry. The debate began with what on the surface appeared to be an innocent question about what the *Torah* had to say about the grounds for divorce. But things quickly morphed into an insightful rebuttal by Jesus in the form of some point-counterpoint questions that were targeted back at the Pharisees. As Matthew records the incident:

> [1] *When Jesus had finished saying these things, he left Galilee and went to the territory of Judea on the other side of the Jordan.* [2] *Large crowds followed him, and he healed them there.*
> [3] *Some Pharisees came to him in order to test him. They asked, "Is it lawful for a man to divorce his wife for any reason?"* [4] *He answered them, "Haven't you read that the one who made them at the beginning 'made them male and female'* [5] *and said, 'That is why a man will leave his father and mother and be united with his wife, and the two will become one flesh'?* [6] *So they are no longer two, but one flesh. Therefore, what God has joined together, man must never separate."*
>
> Matthew 19:1-6

Jesus bases his answer to the Pharisees on the authority of the *Torah*. Specifically, he cites Genesis 1:27 and Genesis 2:24 as the foundation of his argument to rebut the Pharisees. He concludes his initial stance by *assuming the literalness* of a proper interpretation of the origin of marriage.

In doing so, Jesus rejects as untenable all theories of the origin and evolution of the marriage institution as a cultural norm that rose gradually as a means to preserve humanity throughout future generations. Instead, he states that marriage is an institution so serious in its form and function that to separate the marital union by divorce is akin to cutting apart a human body. Furthermore, as Dr. Robert Dick Wilson observed:

> *This is objected to on the ground that it affirms monogamy to have been the original family bond. This has been challenged by the evolutionists who regard the monogamous relation as the result of a long process of development. But can anyone maintain that this has been conclusively proved to be the case? If man is really a fallen creature, as the Bible affirms, he may have departed rapidly and far from this primitive ideal. If man is not a fallen being, not merely does our whole theology need to be radically reconstructed, but the need of redemption is annulled and God's revelation of free and abundant grace through Jesus Christ, the Son of God, becomes an absurd delusion.*[3]

At any rate, the serious answer by Jesus to the Pharisees prompted them to attempt to trap him in a contradiction. In Matthew 19:7-8, they quizzed him:

> *⁷They asked him, "Why, then, did Moses order us 'to give a certificate of divorce and divorce her'?"*
> *⁸He told them, "It was because of your hardness of heart that Moses allowed you to divorce your wives. But from the beginning it was not this way."*
>
> Matthew 19:7-8

This incident is also recorded by the apostle John Mark in Mark 10:2-3, where he said:

> *²Some Pharisees came to test him. They asked, "Is it lawful for a man to divorce his wife?"*
> *³"What did Moses command you?" he responded.*
> *⁴They said, "Moses allowed a man to write a certificate of divorce and to divorce her."*
>
> Mark 10:2-4

---

3 Robert Dick Wilson. *Jesus and the Old Testament.* Princeton Theological Review Vol. 24 No. 4 (1926), p. 630.

By giving this answer, Jesus recognized as *historical* fact that there was a beginning to humanity, and by extension, he confirmed the historical veracity of the creation of Adam and Eve.

Claim #10: Jesus believed that Moses also authored the books of Leviticus, Exodus, and Deuteronomy.

Mark 7: 8-13 provides us with yet another instance of theological debate between Jesus the Messiah and the Pharisees of his day. The occasion was an inquiry from those Pharisees about why the followers of Jesus did not follow the traditions of the Jews relating to washing before meals. Jesus' reply was to accuse the Jews, telling them:

> *⁸"You abandon the commandment of God and hold to human tradition." ⁹Then he told them, "You have such a fine way of rejecting the commandment of God in order to keep your own tradition! ¹⁰Because Moses said, 'Honor your father and your mother,' and 'Whoever curses his father or mother must certainly be put to death.'*
>
> Mark 7: 8-10

His accusation against the Pharisees is bolstered by Jesus citing two *separate* of the *Torah*. In verse ten, he quotes from both Exodus 20:12 and Deuteronomy 5:16 when he tells them that Moses said "Honor your father and your mother." Then he quotes from both Leviticus 20:9 and Exodus 21:17, thus confirming his trust in the authorship by Moses of Leviticus, Exodus, and Deuteronomy.

> *¹¹But you say, 'If anyone tells his father or mother, "Whatever support you might have received from me is Corban,"' (that is, an offering to God) ¹²'you no longer let him do anything for his father or mother.' ¹³You are destroying the word of God through your tradition that you have handed down. And you do many other things like that."*
>
> Mark 7:11-13

Claim #11: Jesus believed that the Ten Commandments were authoritative and binding upon national Israel.

That Jesus endorsed the validity of the Ten Commandments is stressed so seriously by New Testament writers that all three of the Synoptic Gospels record an incident when Jesus was quizzed about how an individual could obtain eternal life. Here are the records set forth by the Apostles Matthew, Mark, and Luke, respectively:

16 Just then a man came up to Jesus. "Teacher," he asked, "what good deed should I do to have eternal life?"
17 Jesus asked him, "Why ask me about what is good? There is only one who is good. If you want to get into that life, you must keep the commandments."
18 The young man asked him, "Which ones?"
Jesus said, "'You must not murder, you must not commit adultery, you must not steal, you must not give false testimony, 19 honor your father and mother,' and, 'you must love your neighbor as yourself.'"

Matthew 19:16-19

17 As Jesus was setting out again, a man ran up to him, knelt down in front of him, and asked him, "Good Teacher, what must I do to inherit eternal life?"
18 "Why do you call me good?" Jesus asked him. "Nobody is good except for one—God. 19 You know the commandments: 'Never murder.' 'Never commit adultery.' 'Never steal.' 'Never give false testimony.' 'Never cheat.' 'Honor your father and mother.'"

Mark 10:17-19

18 Then an official asked Jesus, "Good Teacher, what must I do to inherit eternal life?"
19 "Why do you call me good?" Jesus asked him. "Nobody is good except for one—God. 20 You know the commandments: 'Never commit adultery. Never murder. Never steal. Never give false testimony. Honor your father and mother.'"

Luke 18:17-20

Please note, if you would, that:
- *Even though Jesus **omitted** from his listing of the Ten Commandments the requirement to keep the Sabbath; and,*
- *Even though Matthew's edition of the incident shows Jesus **adding** the command to love your neighbor as yourself to the list (see Matthew 19:19); and,*
- *Even though Mark's edition of this account has Jesus **adding** a prohibition of cheating in business (see Mark 10:19) to the listing,*

Nevertheless it is clear from even a casual reading of the above verses that the authoritative nature of the Ten Commandments forms the basis of Jesus' answer to his inquirer.

Claim #12: Jesus linked his claim to have been the only person to have gone to heaven with the historical reality of the incident of the serpent in the wilderness.

The Apostle John records a claim by Jesus that he was eternally existent in heaven and that he had come to visit the earth. In doing so, he linked the validity of his claim to an historical incident in the life of Moses recorded in the *Torah*. John 3:13-15 tells us:

> [13] *"No one has gone up to heaven except the one who came down from heaven, the Son of Man who is in heaven.* [14] *Just as Moses lifted up the serpent in the wilderness, so must the Son of Man be lifted up,* [15] *so that everyone who believes in him would have eternal life."*
>
> John 3:13-15

The incident to which Jesus is referring can be found in Numbers 21:4-9, where Moses recorded an incident of rebellion against God in which the Israelis incited the anger of the Lord following a military victory against Hormah. The passage tells us that the Israelis…

> [4] *…traveled from Mount Hor along the caravan route by way of the Sea of Reeds and went around the land of Edom.*

But when the people got impatient because it was a long route, ⁴the people complained against the LORD *and Moses. "Why did you bring us out of Egypt to die in the wilderness?" they asked. "There's no food and water, and we're tired of this worthless bread."*
⁶In response, the LORD *sent poisonous serpents among the people to bite them. As a result, many people of Israel died. ⁷Then the people approached Moses and admitted, "We've sinned by speaking against the* LORD *and you. Pray to the* LORD*, that he'll remove the serpents from us." So Moses prayed in behalf of the people.*
⁸Then the LORD *instructed Moses, "Make a poisonous serpent out of brass and fasten it to a pole. Anyone who has been bitten and who looks at it will live." ⁹So Moses made a bronze serpent and fastened it to a pole. If a person who had been bitten by a poisonous serpent looked to the serpent, he lived.*

Numbers 21:4b-9

A number of specific observations spring from examining how Jesus used the incident of the serpent in the wilderness in his dialog with the Pharisees:

- *First, Jesus assumes that Moses himself recorded the incident in the Torah; and,*

- *Second, the historical reality of the incident is assumed to be accurate as it is described by Moses, because Jesus bases the reality of his crucifixion on the reality of the incident in the wilderness.*

- *Third, Jesus compares the activity of the Israelis in the wilderness who wished to be healed from the snake attacks (merely looking at the image of the serpent) with the activity of faith in himself.*

CLAIM #13: JESUS ASSUMED THAT THE CLAIM OF ANCIENT ISRAEL THAT MOSES DELIVERED THE LAW TO THE NATION HAD HISTORICAL VALIDITY.

In John 7:14-24 the Apostle records yet another debate with the Jewish leaders of his day regarding how the Messiah kept the Sabbath. As part of his debate, Jesus asked the Jews the following rhetorical question and supplied his own built-in rebuke to them, all in the same short answer:

> [19] *"Moses gave you the Law, didn't he? Yet none of you is keeping the Law. Why are you trying to kill me?"...*
>
> John 7:19

CLAIM #14: JESUS ASSUMED THAT THE *TORAH* CONTINUED IN FULL IMMUTABLE FORCE AND EFFECT THROUGH THE COMPLETION OF THE LIFE MINISTRY OF JOHN THE BAPTIZER.

Luke 16:16-17 records Jesus repeating his claim about the immutability of the Law and the Prophets (which term is, as we noted earlier, is an abbreviated term that means the entirety of the *Torah*). But he does note that the *applicability* of the *Torah* will have reached its culmination in the ministry of John the Baptizer. After him, there will be no more prophetic writings, and Jesus by his sacrifice will fulfill the atonement requirements of the Law:

> [16] *"The Law and the Prophets were fulfilled with John. Since then, the good news about the kingdom of God is being proclaimed, and everybody enters it enthusiastically.* [17] *However, it is easier for heaven and earth to disappear than for one stroke of a letter in the Law to be dropped.*
>
> Luke 16:16-17

The really puzzling part of this quotation by Jesus is his comments about the Law and the Prophets enduring through John the Baptizer. How can Jesus say the Law is eternal, that the earth will pass away before a single letter of it fails, yet in *the very same sentence* he claims that it has been fulfilled in John's day? I believe that the answer to this conundrum lies in making three distinguishing divisions of God's Law as set forth in the *Torah*. The divisions rather conveniently can be listed as an acrostic that spells out the word "LAW". The three divisions of the law distinguish between:

L = *Life in God's Society*
A = *Atonement Requirements*
W = *Witness of God's Eternal Character*

The overwhelming stress on keeping the Law of God as expressed in the New Testament has nothing to do with the Law as an expression of the first two distinguishing characteristics.

Life in God' Society is that portion of the Law of God that pertained to the theocratic structure of Israel. This part of the law mandated that a railing be constructed around roofs so nobody would fall off of them. It also **mandated** that housetops be flat so people could live on the roofs! It was not possible to enforce this aspect of the Law outside of national Israel and it is not binding to the Christian today. If it were, I'd be asking you why, for example, (1) you don't have a flat roof on your home that people can use to visit together, and (2) why you don't have a parapet constructed around that flat roof! And what about the Law's requirement that people not mix different types of clothing together? Put in that light, I think the abrogation of the requirement to practice this part of the Law today is obvious.

Atonement Requirements are that portion of the Law of God that pertained to maintaining both national and personal relationship and fellowship with God through the sacrificial systems of the Old Testament. These were fulfilled in the death and atonement of Jesus. They are not so much as abrogated by his death as they are fulfilled by them. Animal sacrifices are not mandated today, but will be instituted in the Millennial Temple described by Ezekiel's description of that building set forth in the last 10 chapters or so of Ezekiel's book. But these sacrifices do not appear to be atonement oriented. They're more likely thanksgiving offerings.

The Witness of God's Eternal Character is binding on the Christian today. All aspects of the Ten Commandments except those that pertain to Life in God's Society (keeping the Sabbath as the fourth commandment is one of these) are included as part of this aspect of God's Law. The Apostle Paul points out that it was the Tenth Commandment that particularly grieved him, since it prohibits coveting.

It is debatable whether execution for adultery falls under the Witness of God's Eternal Character (enduring for all times and cultures) or Life in God's Society (abrogated by the destruction of Israel's national sovereignty under Rome). The first century Jewish community had abrogated the death penalty for adultery, since the Romans had taken that right away from them. Instead, the offenders would be excommunicated from the community of the faithful. Given that the only case where Jesus was challenged to rule on the death penalty (the woman caught in adultery described in the eighth chapter of John), he merely *outed her publicly* because all of the eyewitnesses refused to testify, I'm inclined to suggest that the death penalty should not apply to moral failures. I note that the penalty that the Apostle Paul mandated for the Corinthian fornicator was not that he be executed for violating the seventh commandment..

By not making distinctions between these parts of God's Law described above, it is possible to create confusion in the minds of Christians who don't know any better, and this can lead to a charge of making Christians fulfill the Law in order to be acceptable to God. An early church council, described rather thoroughly in the book of Acts, addresses this concern, and concludes that certain aspects of the Law are binding on Christians, including abstaining from eating blood and from fornication.

Claim #15: Jesus claimed that throughout the entirety of the Hebrew Scriptures, its writers mentioned him.

Perhaps one of the most remarkable of Jesus' claims regarding the Hebrew Scriptures is delivered by him during the 40 day period that followed his resurrection. The Apostle Luke records an incident

Jesus and Moses

in Luke 23:14-27 involving two of Jesus' followers. It took place on the road to Emmaus during the week following his crucifixion:

> *¹⁴They were talking with each other about all these things that had taken place. ¹⁵While they were discussing and analyzing what had happened, Jesus himself approached and began to walk with them, ¹⁶but their eyes were prevented from recognizing him.*
>
> *¹⁷He asked them, "What are you discussing with each other as you're walking along?" They stood still and looked gloomy.*
>
> *¹⁸The one whose name was Cleopas answered him, "Are you the only visitor to Jerusalem who doesn't know what happened there in the past few days?"*
>
> *¹⁹He asked them, "What things?"*
>
> *They answered him, "The events involving Jesus of Nazareth, who was a prophet, mighty in what he said and did before God and all the people, ²⁰and how our high priests and leaders handed him over to be condemned to death and had him crucified. ²¹But we kept hoping that he would be the one to redeem Israel. What is more, this is now the third day since these things occurred. ²²Even some of our women have startled us by what they told us. They were at the tomb early this morning ²³and didn't find his body there, so they came back and told us that they had seen a vision of angels, who were saying that he was alive. ²⁴Then some of those who were with us went to the tomb and found it just as the women had said. However, they didn't see him."*
>
> *²⁵Then Jesus told them, "O, how foolish you are! How slow you are to believe everything the prophets said! ²⁶The Messiah had to suffer these things and then enter his glory, didn't he?" ²⁷Then, beginning with Moses and all the Prophets, he explained to them all the passages of Scripture about himself.*
>
> Luke 23:14-27

At the conclusion of this impromptu executive briefing by Jesus the Messiah for the benefit of his two followers, the two men returned to Jerusalem in search of the surviving eleven disciples. After they were located, the two explained what had happened. Then, rather unexpectedly, Jesus appeared to the disciples. In Luke 23:44-47, Luke tells us what Jesus said to them:

> [44]… *"These are the words that I spoke to you while I was still with you—that everything written about me in the Law of Moses, the Prophets, and the Psalms had to be fulfilled."* [45]*Then he opened their minds so that they might understand the Scriptures.* [46]*He told them, "This is how it is written: the Messiah was to suffer and rise from the dead on the third day,* [47]*and then repentance and forgiveness of sins is to be proclaimed in his name to all the nations, beginning at Jerusalem.*
>
> Luke 23:44b-47

Biblical scholars have wished that a transcript of what Jesus said on these two occasions had been left for posterity. I suggest that one practical effect of Jesus not letting a record of the content of his briefing be left for us to read is that the deliberate omission of a transcript of the briefing has required diligent readers to search the Scriptures in order to assemble their own listing of passages in the *Tanakh* that refer to Jesus. Here's a partial listing of passages that Jesus may well have mentioned in his briefing:

1. THE COMING OF SHILOH

Genesis 49:10 records a prophetic statement uttered by Jacob regarding a descendant of Judah. The passage is translated by the *Holy Bible: International Standard Version* reads as follows:

> [10]*The scepter will never depart from Judah,*
> *nor a ruler's staff from between his feet,*
> *until the One comes, who owns them both,*
> *and to him will belong the allegiance of nations.*

Some of the older English translations (such as the Authorized "King James" Version) render the third line of this as "until Shiloh

Jesus and Moses

comes." This prophecy has traditionally been interpreted to be an unmistakable claim that it will be from Judah's house that Messiah shall descend.

The *Targum of Onkelos* (see sample page in the image below), produced by non-Christians ca. 35-120 AD as an Aramaic language edition of the *Torah*, translates this passage by rendering "ruler"

Figure 8: Targum of Onkelos.
Hebrew text (right) and Aramaic Onkelos (left) in Hebrew Bible dating from ca. 1299. Source: Bodleian Library. Image credit: https://upload.wikimedia.org/wikipedia/commons/1/1c/Kennicott_Bible_fol_21r.jpg

as "scribe," the phrase "the One comes, who owns them both" as "the Messiah, whose is the kingdom," and "to him will belong the allegiance of nations" as "and him shall the peoples [of the world] obey. The *Targum of Jonathan*, also produced by non-Christian Jews ca. first century, AD, does not appear to me to have been rendered in poetic format from the Hebrew to the Aramaic. It reads:

> *Kings and sultans shall not cease from those of the house of Judah nor scribes from the thousands of the law from his descendants until the time when the king Messiah shall come, the least of his sons, and on account of him shall the peoples pass away.*

The Samaritan Targum reads:

> *The scepter shall not cease from Judah nor a leader from between his ranks until that Shiloh come, and to him shall the peoples be assembled.*

The Greek Septuagint translation of the *Tanakh*, produced ca. mid-second century, BC, renders this verse:

> *A ruler shall not depart from Judah nor a leader from his loins until the things that are instore for him shall come; and he is the expectation of the nations.*

The Latin Vulgate reads:

> *The scepter shall not be taken away from Judah nor a leader from his loins until he who is to be sent shall come; and he shall be the expectation of the nations.*

The Arabic translation of Saadya Gaon (ca. 10th century, AD) reads:

> *The scepter shall not pass away from Judah nor a lawgiver from his command until that he to whom it belongs shall come and unto him shall the tribes be gathered.*

Even the most skeptical of readers of the Christian New Testament cannot help but notice that each of these ancient renderings (all of which were produced for the *Jewish* community except for the Latin Vulgate) interpret this verse as referring to the Messiah.

There is no textual transmission or manuscript evidence *of any kind* that even *begins to suggest* that these words were not originally spoken by Jacob himself, that they were not written down in permanent form by Moses for transmission to future generations, or that they do not refer to Jesus.

As a point of *historical certainty*, so confident were the rabbinic authorities of the late first century BC and early first century AD that when Roman hegemony was finally extended over national Israel during the reign of Herod, certain Jewish religious authorities were heard to lament, "Woe to us! For the scepter has departed from Israel, and Messiah has not come!" It is unfortunate for them that they did not know at the time that over in Bethlehem, a descendant of Israel's ancient King David (through his son Nathan, as the Gospel of Luke records) had been born.

Figure 9: Three pages from Samaritan Pentateuch.
Source: https://upload.wikimedia.org/wikipedia/commons/thumb/b/b7/Samaritan_Pentateuch_%28detail%29.jpg/800px-Samaritan_Pentateuch_%28detail%29.jpg

2. The Star from Jacob

Numbers 24:17-19 contains a prophetic statement spoken by the false (!) prophet Balaam regarding the future of Israel's greater Son:

> *17... A star streams forth from Jacob;*
> *a scepter arises from Israel.*
> *He will crush Moab's forehead,*
> *along with all of Seth's descendants.*
> *18 Edom will be a conquered nation*
> *and Seir will be Israel's defeated foe,*
> *while Israel performs valiantly.*
> *19 He will rule over Jacob,*
> *annihilating those who survive in the city.*
>
> Numbers 24:17b-19

The Jewish Targums of Onkelos and Jonathan renderings of "star" as "king" and "scepter" as "Messiah" have *never* been questioned by Jewish scholars and textual interpreters until the coming of the higher critics.

3. The Seed of the Woman

One of the earliest records of humanity recorded by Moses in the book of Genesis documents a conversation between God and the creature called *The Shining One*. Genesis 3:15 is called the *Protoevangelium* because this verse contains the very first prediction of how God will repair the damages caused by the Fall of Adam and Eve in the Garden of Eden. The verse reads:

> *15 "I'll place hostility between you and the woman,*
> *between your offspring and her offspring.*
> *He'll strike you on the head,*
> *and you'll strike him on the heel."*
>
> Genesis 3:15

This verse has been interpreted to mean that the Messiah would destroy the power of the Devil. It is on the shoulders of skeptics to demonstrate that this is **not** the correct meaning of the verse, given that the prophecy has been *historically and universally accepted* as being a reference to the Messiah.

4. THE PROPHET LIKE MOSES

At one point during the early ministry of John the Baptizer, a group of men were sent by the Pharisees to quiz the man about his identity. At the time of the interview, Jesus had not yet revealed himself to national Israel. In John 1:19-25, the Apostle John recites how the conversation went:

> *[19] This was John's testimony when the Jewish leaders sent priests and descendants of Levi to him from Jerusalem to ask him, "Who are you?"*
> *[20] He spoke openly and, remaining true to himself, admitted, "I am not the Messiah."*
> *[21] So they asked him, "Well then, are you Elijah?"*
> *John said, "I am not."*
> *"Are you the Prophet?"*
> *He answered, "No."*
> *[22] "Who are you?" they asked him. "We must give an answer to those who sent us. What do you say about yourself?"*
> *[23] He replied, "I am*
> *'...a voice crying out in the wilderness,*
> *"Prepare the Lord's highway,"'*
> *as the prophet Isaiah said."*
> *[24] Now those men had been sent from the Pharisees.*
> *[25] They asked him, "Why, then, are you baptizing if you are not the Messiah, or Elijah, or the Prophet?"*
>
> John 1:19-25

Notice, if you would please, how the Pharisees specifically ask John the Baptizer if he were "the Prophet" in verses 21 and 25. John emphatically refuses to be identified with this individual. You'll find the same reference to "the Prophet" clearly noted in one of the miraculous feeding instances that Jesus performed during his public ministry. John 6:13-15 tells us that after feeding thousands of men (not counting women and children):

> [13]...*they collected and filled twelve baskets full of pieces of the five barley loaves left over by those who had eaten.*
> [14] *When the people saw the sign that he had done, they kept saying, "Truly this is the Prophet who was to come into the world!"* [15] *Then Jesus, realizing that they were about to come and take him by force to make him king, withdrew again to the hillside by himself.*
>
> John 6:13-15

The term "the Prophet" finds its origin in Deuteronomy 18:18-19, where Moses records a conversation between God and him that took place one day regarding the future prophets who would arise in years to come. Moses records God as having told him:

> [18] *I will raise up a prophet like you from among their relatives, and I will place my words in his mouth so that he may expound everything that I have commanded to them.* [19] *But if someone will not listen to those words that the prophet speaks in my name, I will hold him accountable.*
>
> Deuteronomy 18:18-19

Throughout the history of Israel from the time of Moses until the final entry into Roman captivity of national Israel and the destruction of Herod's Temple in 70 AD, *absolutely no one* has arisen that even begins to demonstrate any of the public recognition (either in favor of or against) that would characterize "the Prophet". Who's to say that the Prophet isn't a not-so-oblique reference to the Messiah?

Claim #16: Jesus certified that the feeding of national Israel in the wilderness with manna actually occurred.

Nobody knows what the manna was made of that fed national Israel for about 40 years during the wilderness wanderings described in the *Torah*. We don't know by what agency it was supplied to the ancient Israelis. All we know is that the text of the Hebrew Scriptures attributes its origin to the daily, supernatural supply by God to meet the nutritional needs of his people. As a point of *linguistic fact*, the Hebrew word for "manna" is merely a question that is literally translated as "What is it?" The substance *has no formal name in the Hebrew language!* The text of the *Torah* tells us that:

- *It was delivered during the night to the area surrounding the encampment of national Israel in the wilderness; and,*
- *The supply continued unabated for decades; and,*
- *It was delivered only in quantities sufficient for a single day, except on the morning before the Sabbath, at which time a quantity sufficient to alleviate collection on the seventh day of the week was provided; and,*
- *Its substance would only last for a few hours. If any were kept overnight, it would spoil rapidly and be inedible the next morning (except for the quantity gathered in anticipation of the Sabbath day).*

Jesus commented on the manna in a discussion with some Jewish leaders, as recorded by John 6:30-32 and by John 6:49:

> *[30] So they asked him, "What sign are you going to do so that we may see it and believe in you? What actions are you performing? [31] Our ancestors ate the manna in the wilderness, just as it is written, 'He gave them bread from heaven to eat.'" [32] Jesus told them, "Truly, I tell all of you emphatically, it was not Moses who gave you the bread from heaven, but it is my Father who gives you the true bread from heaven. ... [49] Your ancestors ate the manna in the wilderness and died."*
>
> John 6:30-32, 49

In regards to the manna in the wilderness, Robert Dick Wilson comments:

> *But just what God did there in the wilderness, we do not know, nor how He did it. Nor do we know how Jesus fed the five thousand. Neither do we know how He made the universe and the mountains and the cattle on a thousand hills. He is the greatest of all physicists, electricians and mechanics, the maker of chemists and chemicals, the fashioner of our bodies and spirits*

and the one who cares for them. When He wills to go beyond the ordinary processes and laws of the nature, which He has created, we pause in adoration and wonder and exclaim: "What has God wrought?" We read Job and Isaiah and cry out: "What is man that thou are mindful of him?" [4]

Claim #17: Jesus believed and stated publicly that the Scripture cannot be disregarded or broken.

John 10:34-36 contains a quote by Jesus the Messiah that comes directly from Psalm 82:6. After quoting the Psalm, note that Jesus calls attention to a question that he wants his inquirers to answer. But Jesus' question has a built-in assumption, the truth value of which he takes quite literally for granted: the Scripture cannot be disregarded. The literal Greek reads, "It is not possible to break the Scripture." For those of our readers who understand Koiné Greek, the verse reads: καὶ οὐ δύναται λυθῆναι ἡ γραφή *(kaì ou dúnatai luthēnai hē graphē)*:

> *³⁴Jesus replied to them, "Is it not written in your Law, 'I said, "You are gods"'? ³⁵If he called those to whom a message from God came 'gods' (and the Scripture cannot be disregarded), ³⁶how can you say to the one whom the Father has consecrated and sent into the world, 'You're blaspheming,' because I said, 'I'm the Son of God'?"*

John 10:34-36

The Greek verb used by Jesus in this parenthetical phrase, **λυθῆναι** *(luthēnai)*, means "to undo" what is tied up or constrained. It has been used to refer to the breakage of a seal on a legal document (such as a will), "to loosen, set free, or untie" an animal, a restraining chain, or a prisoner from a jail, or "to remove" a wrapping, such as the grave-clothes that bound Lazarus in John 11:44.[5] Jesus claimed in a rather matter-of-fact way that the Scripture cannot be overturned in such a manner.

---

4   Robert Dick Wilson. *Jesus and the Old Testament*. Princeton Theological Review Vol. 24 No. 4 (1926), p. 649-650.
5   William Arndt, Frederick W. Danker, and Walter Bauer, *A Greek-English Lexicon of the New Testament and Other Early Christian Literature* (Chicago: University of Chicago Press, 2000), 606.

CLAIM #18: JESUS BELIEVED AND STATED PUBLICLY THAT THE AUTHORITY OF MOSES SHOULD BE RESPECTED AND OBEYED.

Even though Jesus of Nazareth remained at odds with the Jewish religious authorities throughout his entire public ministry, he was *never* at odds with respect to the authority of the Hebrew Scriptures, the authority of Moses himself, or with respect to the authority of the descendants of Moses who occupied Moses' seat of authority.

The high contrast that is evident in regards to the high value of the Hebrew Scriptures always stood out in contrast with the hypocrisy of the Jewish leaders. One of the more startling examples of this dichotomy stands out with crystal clarity when one examines Matthew 23:1-7:

> *[1] Then Jesus told the crowds and his disciples, [2] "The scribes and the Pharisees administer the authority of Moses, [3] So do whatever they tell you and follow it, but stop doing what they do, because they don't do what they say. [4] They tie up burdens that are heavy and unbearable and lay them on people's shoulders, but they refuse to lift a finger to remove them. [5] "They do everything to be seen by people. They increase the size of their phylacteries and lengthen the tassels of their garments. [6] They love to have the places of honor at festivals, the best seats in the synagogues, [7] to be greeted in the marketplaces, and to be called 'Rabbi' by people.*
>
> Matthew 23:1-7

CLAIM #19: JESUS BELIEVED AND STATED PUBLICLY THAT THE SUFFERING AND BETRAYAL THAT HE WOULD UNDERGO WAS PREDICTED IN THE HEBREW SCRIPTURES BY THE PROPHETS.

Luke records a statement by Jesus to his followers by which he declares that the salient events relating to his upcoming crucifixion were predicted by the Hebrew Scriptures. Luke 18:31-33 records what he said:

> *[31] Jesus took the Twelve aside and told them, "Pay attention! We're going up to Jerusalem. Everything written by the*

prophets about the Son of Man will be fulfilled, [32] because he'll be handed over to the unbelievers, and will be mocked, insulted, and spit on. [33] After they have whipped him, they'll kill him, but on the third day he'll rise again."

Luke 18:31-33

Now with respect to this surprising claim that *everything* written by the prophets whose writings contributed to the Hebrew Scriptures would reach their fulfillment over the next few days, it may surprise our readers to learn just how many prophecies contained in the Old Testament are considered by biblical scholars to have been completed in the life of Jesus. Listed below are 355 of them:[6]

HEBREW SCRIPTURE PROPHECIES FULFILLED BY JESUS THE MESSIAH

Scripture	Prophecy	Fulfillment
1. Genesis 3:15	Seed of a woman (virgin birth)	Galatians 4:4-5; Matthew 1:18
2. Genesis 3:15	He will bruise Satan's head	Hebrews 2:14; 1 John 3:8
3. Genesis 3:15	Christ's heel would be bruised with nails on the cross	Matthew 27:35; Luke 24:39-40
4. Genesis 5:24	The bodily ascension to heaven illustrated	Mark 16:19; Revelation 12:5
5. Genesis 9:26-27	The God of Shem will be the Son of Shem	Luke 3:23-36
6. Genesis 12:3	Seed of Abraham will bless all nations	Galatians 3:8; Acts 3:25, 26
7. Genesis 12:7	The Promise made to Abraham's Seed	Galatians 3:16
8. Genesis 14:18	A priest after the order of Melchizedek	Hebrews 6:20
9. Genesis 14:18	King of Peace and Righteousness	Hebrews 7:2
10. Genesis 14:18	The Last Supper foreshadowed	Matthew 26:26-29
11. Genesis 17:19	Seed of Isaac (Genesis 21:12)	Romans 9:7
12. Genesis 22:8	The Lamb of God promised	John 1:29

---

6   Cited from http://www.accordingtothescriptures.org/prophecy/353prophecies.html

Jesus and Moses

Scripture	Prophecy	Fulfillment
13. Genesis 22:18	As Isaac's seed, will bless all nations	Galatians 3:16
14. Genesis 26:2-5	The Seed of Isaac promised as the Redeemer	Hebrews 11:18
15. Genesis 28:12	The Bridge to heaven	John 1:51
16. Genesis 28:14	The Seed of Jacob	Luke 3:34
17. Genesis 49:10	The time of His coming	Luke 2:1-7; Galatians 4:4
18. Genesis 49:10	The Seed of Judah	Luke 3:33
19. Genesis 49:10	Called Shiloh or One Sent	John 17:3
20. Genesis 49:10	Messiah to come before Judah lost identity	John 11:47-52
21. Genesis 49:10	Unto Him shall the obedience of the people be	John 10:16
22. Exodus 3:13-15	The Great "I AM"	John 4:26; 8:58
23. Exodus 12:3-6	The Lamb presented to Israel 4 days before Passover	Mark 11:7-11
24. Exodus 12:5	A Lamb without blemish	Hebrews 9:14; 1 Peter 1:19
25. Exodus 12:13	The blood of the Lamb saves from wrath	Romans 5:8
26. Exodus 12:21-27	Christ is our Passover	1 Corinthians 5:7
27. Exodus 12:46	Not a bone of the Lamb to be broken	John 19:31-36
28. Exodus 15:2	His exaltation predicted as Yeshua	Acts 7:55-56
29. Exodus 15:11	His Character-Holiness	Luke 1:35; Acts 4:27
30. Exodus 17:6	The Spiritual Rock of Israel	1 Corinthians 10:4
31. Exodus 33:19	His Character-Merciful	Luke 1:72
32. Leviticus 1:2-9	His sacrifice a sweet smelling savor unto God	Ephesians 5:2
33. Leviticus 14:11	The leper cleansed-Sign to priesthood	Luke 5:12-14; Acts 6:7
34. Leviticus 16:15-17	Prefigures Christ's once-for-all death	Hebrews 9:7-14
35. Leviticus 16:27	Suffering outside the Camp	Matthew 27:33; Hebrews 13:11, 12
36. Leviticus 17:11	The Blood-the life of the flesh	Matthew 26:28; Mark 10:45

Since He Wrote about Me

Scripture	Prophecy	Fulfillment
37. Leviticus 17:11	It is the blood that makes atonement	Romans 3:23-24; 1 John 1:7
38. Leviticus 23:36-37	The Drink-offering: "If any man thirst"	John 7:37
39. Numbers 9:12	Not a bone of Him broken	John 19:31-36
40. Numbers 21:9	The serpent on a pole-Christ lifted up	John 3:14-18; 12:32
41. Numbers 24:17	Time: "I shall see him, but not now."	John 1:14; Galatians 4:4
42. Deuteronomy 18:15	"This is of a truth that prophet."	John 6:14
43. Deuteronomy 18:15-16	"Had ye believed Moses, ye would believe me."	John 5:45-47
44. Deuteronomy 18:18	Sent by the Father to speak His word	John 8:28-29
45. Deuteronomy 18:19	Whoever will not hear must bear his sin	Acts 3:22-23
46. Deuteronomy 21:23	Cursed is he that hangs on a tree	Galatians 3:10-13
47. Joshua 5:14-15	The Captain of our salvation	Hebrews 2:10
48. Ruth 4:4-10	Christ, our kinsman, has redeemed us	Ephesians 1:3-7
49. 1 Sam. 2:35	A Faithful Priest	Hebrews 2:17; 3:1-3, 6; 7:24-25
50. 1 Samuel 2:10	Shall be an anointed King to the Lord	Matthew 28:18; John 12:15
51. 2 Samuel 7:12	David's Seed	Matthew 1:1
52. 2 Samuel 7:13	His Kingdom is everlasting	2 Peter 1:11
53. 2 Samuel 7:14a	The Son of God	Luke 1:32; Romans 1:3-4
54. 2 Samuel 7:16	David's house established forever	Luke 3:31; Revelation 22:16
55. 2 Kings 2:11	The bodily ascension to heaven illustrated	Luke 24:51
56. 1 Chronicles 17:11	David's Seed	Matthew 1:1; 9:27
57. 1 Chronicles 17:12-13	To reign on David's throne forever	Luke 1:32-33
58. 1 Chronicles 17:13	"I will be His Father, He...my Son."	Hebrews 1:5
59. Job 9:32-33	Mediator between man and God	1 Timothy 2:5

Scripture	Prophecy	Fulfillment
60. Job 19:23-27	The Resurrection predicted	John 5:24-29
61. Psalm 2:1-3	The enmity of kings foreordained	Acts 4:25-28
62. Psalm 2:2	To own the title, Anointed (Christ)	John 1:41; Acts 2:36
63. Psalm 2:6	His Character-Holiness	John 8:46; Revelation 3:7
64. Psalm 2:6	To own the title King	Matthew 2:2
65. Psalm 2:7	Declared the Beloved Son	Matthew 3:17; Romans 1:4
66. Psalm 2:7, 8	The Crucifixion and Resurrection intimated	Acts 13:29-33
67. Psalm 2:8, 9	Rule the nations with a rod of iron	Revelation 2:27; 12:5; 19:15
68. Psalm 2:12	Life comes through faith in Him	John 20:31
69. Psalm 8:2	The mouths of babes perfect His praise	Matthew 21:16
70. Psalm 8:5, 6	His humiliation and exaltation	Hebrews 2:5-9
71. Psalm 9:7-10	Judge the world in righteousness	Acts 17:31
72. Psalm 16:10	Was not to see corruption	Acts 2:31; 13:35
73. Psalm 16:9-11	Was to arise from the dead	John 20:9
74. Psalm 17:15	The resurrection predicted	Luke 24:6
75. Psalm 18:2-3	The horn of salvation	Luke 1:69-71
76. Psalm 22:1	Forsaken because of sins of others	2 Corinthians 5:21
77. Psalm 22:1	"My God, my God, why hast thou forsaken me?"	Matthew 27:46
78. Psalm 22:2	Darkness upon Calvary for three hours	Matthew 27:45
79. Psalm 22:7	They shoot out the lip and shake the head	Matthew 27:39-44
80. Psalm 22:8	"He trusted in God, let Him deliver Him"	Matthew 27:43
81. Psalm 22:9-10	Born the Savior	Luke 2:7
82. Psalm 22:12-13	They seek His death	John 19:6
83. Psalm 22:14	His blood poured out when they pierced His side	John 19:34

Since He Wrote about Me

Scripture	Prophecy	Fulfillment
84. Psalm 22:14-15	Suffered agony on Calvary	Mark 15:34-37
85. Psalm 22:15	He thirsted	John 19:28
86. Psalm 22:16	They pierced His hands and His feet	John 19:34, 37; 20:27
87. Psalm 22:17-18	Stripped Him before the stares of men	Luke 23:34-35
88. Psalm 22:18	They parted His garments	John 19:23-24
89. Psalm 22:20-21	He committed Himself to God	Luke 23:46
90. Psalm 22:20-21	Satanic power bruising the Redeemer's heel	Hebrews 2:14
91. Psalm 22:22	His Resurrection declared	John 20:17
92. Psalm 22:27-28	He shall be the governor of the nations	Colossians 1:16
93. Psalm 22:31	"It is finished"	John 19:30; Hebrews 10:10, 12, 14, 18
94. Psalm 23:1	"I am the Good Shepherd"	John 10:11; 1 Peter 2:25
95. Psalm 24:3	His exaltation predicted	Acts 1:11; Philippians 2:9
96. Psalm 30:3	His resurrection predicted	Acts 2:32
97. Psalm 31:5	"Into thy hands I commit my spirit"	Luke 23:46
98. Psalm 31:11	His acquaintances fled from Him	Mark 14:50
99. Psalm 31:13	They took counsel to put Him to death	Matthew 27:1; John 11:53
100. Psalm 31:14-15	"He trusted in God, let Him deliver him"	Matthew 27:43
101. Psalm 34:20	Not a bone of Him broken	John 19:31-36
102. Psalm 35:11	False witnesses rose up against Him	Matthew 26:59
103. Psalm 35:19	He was hated without a cause	John 15:25
104. Psalm 38:11	His friends stood afar off	Luke 23:49
105. Psalm 38:12	Enemies try to entangle Him by craft	Mark 14:1; Mt. 22:15
106. Psalm 38:12-13	Silent before His accusers	Matthew 27:12-14
107. Psalm 38:20	He went about doing good	Acts 10:38

Jesus and Moses

Scripture	Prophecy	Fulfillment
108. Psalm 40:2-5	The joy of His resurrection predicted	John 20:20
109. Psalm 40:6-8	His delight-the will of the Father	John 4:34; Hebrews 10:5-10
110. Psalm 40:9	He was to preach the Righteousness in Israel	Matthew 4:17
111. Psalm 40:14	Confronted by adversaries in the Garden	John 18:4-6
112. Psalm 41:9	Betrayed by a familiar friend	John 13:18
113. Psalm 45:2	Words of Grace come from His lips	John 1:17; Luke 4:22
114. Psalm 45:6	To own the title, God or Elohim	Hebrews 1:8
115. Psalm 45:7	A special anointing by the Holy Spirit	Matthew 3:16; Hebrews 1:9
116. Psalm 45:7-8	Called the Christ (Messiah or Anointed)	Luke 2:11
117. Psalm 45:17	His name remembered forever	Ephesians 1:20-21; Hebrews 1:8
118. Psalm 55:12-14	Betrayed by a friend, not an enemy	John 13:18
119. Psalm 55:15	Unrepentant death of the Betrayer	Matthew 27:3-5; Acts 1:16-19
120. Psalm 68:18	To give gifts to men	Ephesians 4:7-16
121. Psalm 68:18	Ascended into Heaven	Luke 24:51
122. Psalm 69:4	Hated without a cause	John 15:25
123. Psalm 69:8	A stranger to own brethren	John 1:11; 7:5
124. Psalm 69:9	Zealous for the Lord's House	John 2:17
125. Psalm 69:14-20	Messiah's anguish of soul before crucifixion	Matthew 26:36-45
126. Psalm 69:20	"My soul is exceeding sorrowful."	Matthew 26:38
127. Psalm 69:21	Given vinegar in thirst	Matthew 27:34
128. Psalm 69:26	The Savior given and smitten by God	John 17:4; 18:11
129. Psalm 72:10-11	Great persons were to visit Him	Matthew 2:1-11
130. Psalm 72:16	The corn of wheat to fall into the Ground	John 12:24-25

Since He Wrote about Me

Scripture	Prophecy	Fulfillment
131. Psalm 72:17	Belief on His name will produce offspring	John 1:12, 13
132. Psalm 72:17	All nations shall be blessed by Him	Galatians 3:8
133. Psalm 72:17	All nations shall call Him blessed	John 12:13; Revelation 5:8-12
134. Psalm 78:1-2	He would teach in parables	Matthew 13:34-35
135. Psalm 78:2b	To speak the Wisdom of God with authority	Matthew 7:29
136. Psalm 80:17	The Man of God's right hand	Mark 14:61-62
137. Psalm 88	The Suffering and Reproach of Calvary	Matthew 27:26-50
138. Psalm 88:8	They stood afar off and watched	Luke 23:49
139. Psalm 89:27	Firstborn	Colossians 1:15, 18
140. Psalm 89:27	Emmanuel to be higher than earthly kings	Luke 1:32-33
141. Psalm 89:35-37	David's Seed, throne, kingdom endure forever	Luke 1:32-33
142. Psalm 89:36-37	His character-Faithfulness	Revelation 1:5; 19:11
143. Psalm 90:2	He is from everlasting (Micah 5:2)	John 1:1
144. Psalm 91:11-12	Identified as Messianic; used to tempt Christ	Luke 4:10-11
145. Psalm 97:9	His exaltation predicted	Acts 1:11; Ephesians 1:20
146. Psalm 100:5	His character-Goodness	Matthew 19:16-17
147. Psalm 102:1-11	The Suffering and Reproach of Calvary	John 19:16-30
148. Psalm 102:25-27	Messiah is the Preexistent Son	Hebrews 1:10-12
149. Psalm 109:25	Ridiculed	Matthew 27:39
150. Psalm 110:1	Son of David	Matthew 22:42-43
151. Psalm 110:1	To ascend to the right-hand of the Father	Mark 16:19
152. Psalm 110:1	David's son called Lord	Matthew 22:44-45
153. Psalm 110:4	A priest after Melchizedek's order	Hebrews 6:20
154. Psalm 112:4	His character-Compassionate, Gracious, et al	Matthew 9:36

Scripture	Prophecy	Fulfillment
155. Psalm 118:17-18	Messiah's Resurrection assured	Luke 24:5-7; 1 Corinthians 15:20
156. Psalm 118:22-23	The rejected stone is Head of the corner	Matthew 21:42-43
157. Psalm 118:26a	The Blessed One presented to Israel	Matthew 21:9
158. Psalm 118:26b	To come while Temple standing	Matthew 21:12-15
159. Psalm 132:11	The Seed of David (the fruit of His Body)	Luke 1:32; Act 2:30
160. Psalm 129:3	He was scourged	Matthew 27:26
161. Psalm 138:1-6	The supremacy of David's Seed amazes kings	Matthew 2:2-6
162. Psalm 147:3, 6	The earthly ministry of Christ described	Luke 4:18
163. Prov. 1:23	He will send the Spirit of God	John 16:7
164. Prov. 8:23	Foreordained from everlasting	Revelation 13:8; 1 Peter 1:19-20
165. Song. 5:16	The altogether lovely One	John 1:17
166. Isaiah 2:3	He shall teach all nations	John 4:25
167. Isaiah 2:4	He shall judge among the nations	John 5:22
168. Isaiah 6:1	When Isaiah saw His glory	John 12:40-41
169. Isaiah 6:8	The One Sent by God	John 12:38-45
170. Isaiah 6:9-10	Parables fall on deaf ears	Matthew 13:13-15
171. Isaiah 6:9-12	Blinded to Christ and deaf to His words	Acts 28:23-29
172. Isaiah 7:14	To be born of a virgin	Luke 1:35
173. Isaiah 7:14	To be Emmanuel-God with us	Matthew 1:18-23; 1 Timothy 3:16
174. Isaiah 8:8	Called Emmanuel	Matthew 28:20
175. Isaiah 8:14	A stone of stumbling, a Rock of offense	1 Peter 2:8
176. Isaiah 9:1-2	His ministry to begin in Galilee	Matthew 4:12-17
177. Isaiah 9:6	A child born-Humanity	Luke 1:31
178. Isaiah 9:6	A Son given-Deity	Luke 1:32; John 1:14; 1 Timothy 3:16

Scripture	Prophecy	Fulfillment
179. Isaiah 9:6	Declared to be the Son of God with power	Romans 1:3-4
180. Isaiah 9:6	The Wonderful One, Peleh	Luke 4:22
181. Isaiah 9:6	The Counsellor, Yaatz	Matthew 13:54
182. Isaiah 9:6	The Mighty God, El Gibor	1 Corinthians 1:24; Titus 2:3
183. Isaiah 9:6	The Everlasting Father, Avi Adth	John 8:58; 10:30
184. Isaiah 9:6	The Prince of Peace, Sar Shalom	John 16:33
185. Isaiah 9:7	To establish an everlasting kingdom	Luke 1:32-33
186. Isaiah 9:7	His Character-Just	John 5:30
187. Isaiah 9:7	No end to his Government, Throne, and Peace	Luke 1:32-33
188. Isaiah 11:1	Called a Nazarene-the Branch, Netzer	Matthew 2:23
189. Isaiah 11:1	A rod out of Jesse-Son of Jesse	Luke 3:23, 32
190. Isaiah 11:2	Anointed One by the Spirit	Matthew 3:16-17; Acts 10:38
191. Isaiah 11:2	His Character-Wisdom, Knowledge, et al	Colossians 2:3
192. Isaiah 11:3	He would know their thoughts	Luke 6:8; John 2:25
193. Isaiah 11:4	Judge in righteousness	Acts 17:31
194. Isaiah 11:4	Judges with the sword of His mouth	Revelation 2:16; 19:11, 15
195. Isaiah 11:5	Character: Righteous & Faithful	Revelation 19:11
196. Isaiah 11:10	The Gentiles seek Him	John 12:18-21
197. Isaiah 12:2	Called Jesus-Yeshua	Matthew 1:21
198. Isaiah 22:22	The One given all authority to govern	Revelation 3:7
199. Isaiah 25:8	The Resurrection predicted	1 Corinthians 15:54
200. Isaiah 26:19	His power of Resurrection predicted	Matthew 27:50-54
201. Isaiah 28:16	The Messiah is the precious corner stone	Acts 4:11-12

Jesus and Moses

Scripture	Prophecy	Fulfillment
202. Isaiah 28:16	The Sure Foundation	1 Corinthians 3:11; Matthew 16:18
203. Isaiah 29:13	He indicated hypocritical obedience to His Word	Matthew 15:7-9
204. Isaiah 29:14	The wise are confounded by the Word	1 Corinthians 1:18-31
205. Isaiah 32:2	A Refuge-A man shall be a hiding place	Matthew 23:37
206. Isaiah 35:4	He will come and save you	Matthew 1:21
207. Isaiah 35:5-6	To have a ministry of miracles	Matthew 11:2-6
208. Isaiah 40:3-4	Preceded by forerunner	John 1:23
209. Isaiah 40:9	"Behold your God."	John 1:36; 19:14
210. Isaiah 40:10	He will come to reward	Revelation 22:12
211. Isaiah 40:11	A shepherd-compassionate life-giver	John 10:10-18
212. Isaiah 42:1-4	The Servant-as a faithful, patient redeemer	Matthew 12:18-21
213. Isaiah 42:2	Meek and lowly	Matthew 11:28-30
214. Isaiah 42:3	He brings hope for the hopeless	John 4
215. Isaiah 42:4	The nations shall wait on His teachings	John 12:20-26
216. Isaiah 42:6	The Light (salvation) of the Gentiles	Luke 2:32
217. Isaiah 42:1, 6	His is a worldwide compassion	Matthew 28:19-20
218. Isaiah 42:7	Blind eyes opened.	John 9:25-38
219. Isaiah 43:11	He is the only Savior.	Acts 4:12
220. Isaiah 44:3	He will send the Spirit of God	John 16:7, 13
221. Isaiah 45:21-25	He is Lord and Savior	Philippians 3:20; Titus 2:13
222. Isaiah 45:23	He will be the Judge	John 5:22; Romans 14:11
223. Isaiah 46:9-10	Declares things not yet done	John 13:19
224. Isaiah 48:12	The First and the Last	John 1:30; Revelation 1:8, 17
225. Isaiah 48:16-17	He came as a Teacher	John 3:2

Since He Wrote about Me

Scripture	Prophecy	Fulfillment
226. Isaiah 49:1	Called from the womb - His humanity	Matthew 1:18
227. Isaiah 49:5	A Servant from the womb.	Luke 1:31; Philippians 2:7
228. Isaiah 49:6	He will restore Israel	Acts 3:19-21; 15:16-17
229. Isaiah 49:6	He is Salvation for Israel	Luke 2:29-32
230. Isaiah 49:6	He is the Light of the Gentiles	John 8:12; Acts 13:47
231. Isaiah 49:6	He is Salvation unto the ends of the earth	Acts 15:7-18
232. Isaiah 49:7	He is despised of the Nation	John 1:11; 8:48-49; 19:14-15
233. Isaiah 50:3	Heaven is clothed in black at His humiliation	Luke 23:44-45
234. Isaiah 50:4	He is a learned counselor for the weary	Matthew 7:29; 11:28-29
235. Isaiah 50:5	The Servant bound willingly to obedience	Matthew 26:39
236. Isaiah 50:6a	"I gave my back to the smiters."	Matthew 27:26
237. Isaiah 50:6b	He was smitten on the cheeks	Matthew 26:67
238. Isaiah 50:6c	He was spat upon	Matthew 27:30
239. Isaiah 52:7	Published good tidings upon mountains	Matthew 5:12; 15:29; 28:16
240. Isaiah 52:13	The Servant exalted	Acts 1:8-11; Ephesians 1:19-22; Philippians 2:5-9
241. Isaiah 52:14	The Servant shockingly abused	Luke 18:31-34; Matthew 26:67, 68
242. Isaiah 52:15	Nations startled by message of the Servant	Luke 18:31-34; Matthew 26:67-68
243. Isaiah 52:15	His blood shed sprinkles nations	Hebrews 9:13-14; Revelation 1:5
244. Isaiah 53:1	His people would not believe Him	John 12:37-38
245. Isaiah 53:2	Appearance of an ordinary man	Philippians 2:6-8
246. Isaiah 53:3a	Despised	Luke 4:28-29
247. Isaiah 53:3b	Rejected	Matthew 27:21-23

Scripture	Prophecy	Fulfillment
248. Isaiah 53:3c	Great sorrow and grief	Matthew 26:37-38; Luke 19:41; Hebrews 4:15
249. Isaiah 53:3d	Men hide from being associated with Him	Mark 14:50-52
250. Isaiah 53:4a	He would have a healing ministry	Matthew 8:16-17
251. Isaiah 53:4b	Thought to be cursed by God	Matthew 26:66; 27:41-43
252. Isaiah 53:5a	Bears penalty for mankind's iniquities	2 Corinthians 5:21; Hebrews 2:9
253. Isaiah 53:5b	His sacrifice provides peace between man and God	Colossians 1:20
254. Isaiah 53:5c	His sacrifice would heal man of sin	1 Peter 2:24
255. Isaiah 53:6a	He would be the sin-bearer for all mankind	1 John 2:2; 4:10
256. Isaiah 53:6b	God's will that He bear sin for all mankind	Galatians 1:4
257. Isaiah 53:7a	Oppressed and afflicted	Matthew 27:27-31
258. Isaiah 53:7b	Silent before his accusers	Matthew 27:12-14
259. Isaiah 53:7c	Sacrificial lamb	John 1:29; 1 Peter 1:18-19
260. Isaiah 53:8a	Confined and persecuted	Matthew 26:47; 27:31
261. Isaiah 53:8b	He would be judged	John 18:13-22
262. Isaiah 53:8c	Killed	Matthew 27:35
263. Isaiah 53:8d	Dies for the sins of the world	1 John 2:2
264. Isaiah 53:9a	Buried in a rich man's grave	Matthew 27:57
265. Isaiah 53:9b	Innocent and had done no violence	Luke 23:41; John 18:38
266. Isaiah 53:9c	No deceit in his mouth	1 Peter 2:22
267. Isaiah 53:10a	God's will that He die for mankind	John 18:11
268. Isaiah 53:10b	An offering for sin	Matthew 20:28; Galatians 3:13
269. Isaiah 53:10c	Resurrected and live forever	Romans 6:9
270. Isaiah 53:10d	He would prosper	John 17:1-5
271. Isaiah 53:11a	God fully satisfied with His suffering	John 12:27

Scripture	Prophecy	Fulfillment
272. Isaiah 53:11b	God's servant would justify man	Romans 5:8-9; 18-19
273. Isaiah 53:11c	The sin-bearer for all mankind	Hebrews 9:28
274. Isaiah 53:12a	Exalted by God because of his sacrifice	Matthew 28:18
275. Isaiah 53:12b	He would give up his life to save mankind	Luke 23:46
276. Isaiah 53:12c	Numbered with the transgressors	Mark 15:27-28
277. Isaiah 53:12d	Sin-bearer for all mankind	1 Peter 2:24
278. Isaiah 53:12e	Intercede to God in behalf of mankind	Luke 23:34; Romans 8:34
279. Isaiah 55:3	Resurrected by God	Acts 13:34
280. Isaiah 55:4a	A witness	John 18:37
281. Isaiah 55:4b	He is a leader and commander	Hebrews 2:10
282. Isaiah 55:5	God would glorify Him	Acts 3:13
283. Isaiah 59:16a	Intercessor between man and God	Matthew 10:32
284. Isaiah 59:16b	He would come to provide salvation	John 6:40
285. Isaiah 59:20	He would come to Zion as their Redeemer	Luke 2:38
286. Isaiah 60:1-3	He would shew light to the Gentiles	Acts 26:23
287. Isaiah 61:1a	The Spirit of God upon him	Matthew 3:16-17
288. Isaiah 61:1b	The Messiah would preach the good news	Luke 4:16-21
289. Isaiah 61:1c	Provide freedom from the bondage of sin	John 8:31-36
290. Isaiah 61:1-2a	Proclaim a period of grace	Galatians 4:4-5
291. Jeremiah 11:21	Conspiracy to kill Jesus	John 7:1; Matthew 21:28
292. Jeremiah 23:5-6	Descendant of David	Luke 3:23-31
293. Jeremiah 23:5-6	The Messiah would be both God and Man	John 13:13; 1 Timothy 3:16
294. Jeremiah 31:22	Born of a virgin	Matthew 1:18-20
295. Jeremiah 31:31	The Messiah would be the new covenant	Matthew 26:28

Jesus and Moses

Scripture	Prophecy	Fulfillment
296. Jeremiah 33:14-15	Descendant of David	Luke 3:23-31
297. Ezekiel 34:23-24	Descendant of David	Matthew 1:1
298. Ezekiel 37:24-25	Descendant of David	Luke 1:31-33
299. Daniel 2:44-45	The Stone that shall break the kingdoms	Matthew 21:44
300. Daniel 7:13-14a	He would ascend into heaven	Acts 1:9-11
301. Daniel 7:13-14b	Highly exalted	Ephesians 1:20-22
302. Daniel 7:13-14c	His dominion would be everlasting	Luke 1:31-33
303. Daniel 9:24a	To make an end to sins	Galatians 1:3-5
304. Daniel 9:24a	To make reconciliation for iniquity	Romans 5:10; 2 Corinthians 5:18-21
305. Daniel 9:24b	He would be holy	Luke 1:35
306. Daniel 9:25	His announcement	John 12:12-13
307. Daniel 9:26a	Cut off	Matthew 16:21; 21:38-39
308. Daniel 9:26b	Die for the sins of the world	Hebrews 2:9
309. Daniel 9:26c	Killed before the destruction of the temple	Matthew 27:50-51
310. Daniel 10:5-6	Messiah in a glorified state	Revelation 1:13-16
311. Hosea 11:1	He would be called out of Egypt	Matthew 2:15
312. Hosea 13:14	He would defeat death	1 Corinthians 15:55-57
313. Joel 2:32	Offer salvation to all mankind	Romans 10:9-13
314. Jonah 1:17	Death and resurrection of Christ	Matthew 12:40; 16:4
315. Micah 5:2a	Born in Bethlehem	Matthew 2:1-6
316. Micah 5:2b	Ruler in Israel	Luke 1:33
317. Micah 5:2c	From everlasting	John 8:58
318. Haggai 2:6-9	He would visit the second Temple	Luke 2:27-32
319. Haggai 2:23	Descendant of Zerubbabel	Luke 2:27-32
320. Zechariah 3:8	God's servant	John 17:4
321. Zechariah 6:12-13	Priest and King	Hebrews 8:1
322. Zechariah 9:9a	Greeted with rejoicing in Jerusalem	Matthew 21:8-10

Scripture	Prophecy	Fulfillment
323. Zechariah 9:9b	Beheld as King	John 12:12-13
324. Zechariah 9:9c	The Messiah would be just	John 5:30
325. Zechariah 9:9d	The Messiah would bring salvation	Luke 19:10
326. Zechariah 9:9e	The Messiah would be humble	Matthew 11:29
327. Zechariah 9:9f	Presented to Jerusalem riding on a donkey	Matthew 21:6-9
328. Zechariah 10:4	The cornerstone	Ephesians 2:20
329. Zechariah 11:4-6a	At His coming, Israel to have unfit leaders	Matthew 23:1-4
330. Zechariah 11:4-6b	Rejection causes God to remove His protection	Luke 19:41-44
331. Zechariah 11:4-6c	Rejected in favor of another king	John 19:13-15
332. Zechariah 11:7	Ministry to "poor," the believing remnant	Matthew 9:35-36
333. Zechariah 11:8a	Unbelief forces Messiah to reject them	Matthew 23:33
334. Zechariah 11:8b	Despised	Matthew 27:20
335. Zechariah 11:9	Stops ministering to those who rejected Him	Matthew 13:10-11
336. Zechariah 11:10-11a	Rejection causes God to remove protection	Luke 19:41-44
337. Zechariah 11:10-11b	The Messiah would be God	John 14:7
338. Zechariah 11:12-13a	Betrayed for thirty pieces of silver	Matthew 26:14-15
339. Zechariah 11:12-13b	Rejected	Matthew 26:14-15
340. Zechariah 11:12-13c	Thirty pieces of silver cast in the house of the Lord	Matthew 27:3-5
341. Zechariah 11:12-13d	The Messiah would be God	John 12:45
342. Zechariah 12:10a	The Messiah's body would be pierced	John 19:34-37
343. Zechariah 12:10b	The Messiah would be both God and man	John 10:30
344. Zechariah 12:10c	The Messiah would be rejected	John 1:11
345. Zechariah 13:7a	God's will He die for mankind	John 18:11
346. Zechariah 13:7b	A violent death	Mark 14:27

Scripture	Prophecy	Fulfillment
347. Zechariah 13:7c	Both God and man	John 14:9
348. Zechariah 13:7d	Israel scattered as a result of rejecting Him	Matthew 26:31-56
349. Zechariah 14:4	He would return to the Mt. of Olives	Acts 1:11-12
350. Malachi 3:1a	Messenger to prepare the way for Messiah	Mark 1:1-8
351. Malachi 3:1b	Sudden appearance at the temple	Mark 11:15-16
352. Malachi 3:1c	Messenger of the new covenant	Luke 4:43
353. Malachi 3:6	The God who changes not	Hebrews 13:8
354. Malachi 4:5	Forerunner in spirit of Elijah	Matthew 3:1-3; 11:10-14; 17:11-13
355. Malachi 4:6	Forerunner would turn many to righteousness	Luke 1:16-17

CLAIM #20: JESUS HELD THE BOOKS OF LEVITICUS AND DEUTERONOMY IN SUCH HIGH ESTEEM THAT HE LINKED THE ENTIRETY OF THE LAW AND THE PROPHETS TO THEIR INTEGRITY.

While Jesus clearly recognized the validity and authority of the Ten Commandments, he also unmistakably linked the authority of the books of Deuteronomy and Leviticus to the theological integrity of the Hebrew Scriptures. In Matthew 22:35-40 (and reiterated in Mark 12:28-34), Jesus indicated that the integrity of the Law and the Prophets rested on two commandments that were never included in the original set:

> [35] One of them, an expert in the Law, tested him by asking,
> [36] "Teacher, which is the greatest commandment in the Law?"
> [37] Jesus told him, "'You must love the Lord your God with all your heart, with all your soul, and with all your mind.' [38] This is the greatest and most important commandment.
> [39] The second is exactly like it: 'You must love your neighbor as yourself.' [40] All the Law and the Prophets depend on these two commandments."
>
> Matthew 22:35-40

> [28] Then one of the scribes came near and heard the Sadducees arguing with one another. He saw how well Jesus answered them, so he asked him, "Which commandment is the most important of them all?"
> [29] Jesus answered, "The most important is, 'Hear, O Israel, the Lord our God is one Lord, [30] and you must love the Lord your God with all your heart, with all your soul, with all your mind, and with all your strength.' [31] The second is this: 'You must love your neighbor as yourself.' No other commandment is greater than these."
> [32] Then the scribe told him, "Well said, Teacher! You have told the truth that 'God is one, and there is no other besides him.' [33] To love him with all your heart, with all your understanding, and with all your strength, and to love your neighbor as yourself is more important than all the burnt offerings and sacrifices."
> [34] When Jesus saw how wisely the man answered, he told him, "You are not far from the kingdom of God." After that, no one dared to ask him another question.
>
> Mark 12:28-34

Notice how these two commandments are recorded in the books of Deuteronomy and Leviticus:

> [4] "Listen, Israel! The LORD is our God, the LORD alone. [5] You are to love the LORD your God with all your heart, all your soul, and all your strength.
>
> Deuteronomy 6:4-5

> You are not to seek vengeance or hold a grudge against the descendants of your people. Instead, love your neighbor as yourself. I am the LORD.
>
> Leviticus 19:18

CLAIM #21: JESUS HELD CONVERSATIONS FROM TIME TO TIME WITH SATAN, WHICH DEMONSTRATED THAT HE BELIEVED THIS CREATURE EXISTED AND HAD INFLUENCE IN THE WORLD.

Jesus and Moses

CLAIM #22: JESUS HELD THE BOOK OF DEUTERONOMY IN SUCH HIGH ESTEEM THAT HE USED IT TO REBUT THE TEMPTATIONS OF SATAN DURING HIS TIME IN THE WILDERNESS.

Jesus endured several occasions of temptation by Satan during his pre-ministry time of spiritual testing in the wilderness. It comes as a surprise to many to learn that it was from the book of Deuteronomy in the Hebrew Scriptures that Jesus quoted his answers to Satan's accusations. Notice how he cites the book of Deuteronomy in rebuttal to all three temptations:

> [3] *The Devil told him, "Since you are the Son of God, tell this stone to become a loaf of bread."*
> [4] *Jesus answered him, "It is written,*
> *'One must not live on bread alone,*
> *but on every word of God.'"*
>
> Luke 4:3-4 (citing Deuteronomy 8:3)

The larger context of Jesus' answer from Deuteronomy comes from Deuteronomy 8:1-20:

> [1] *"Be careful to observe every command that I'm instructing you today, in order that you may live, increase, and enter and take possession of the land that the Lord promised by an oath to your ancestors.* [2] *Remember how the LORD your God led you all the way these 40 years in the desert, to humble and test you in order to make known what was in your heart, whether or not you would keep his commands.* [3] *He humbled you, causing you to be hungry, yet he fed you with manna that neither you nor your ancestors had known, in order to teach you that human beings are not to live by food alone—instead human beings are to live by every word that proceeds from the mouth of the LORD.*
> [4] *"The clothes you wore did not wear out, nor did your feet blister during these 40 years.* [5] *Be convinced in your heart that as a father disciplines his son, so the LORD your God disciplines you.* [6] *Observe the commands of the LORD your God by walking in his ways and by fearing him,* [7] *because*

the Lord your God is bringing you to a good land—a land with rivers and deep springs flowing to the valleys and hills. ⁸It's a land filled with wheat, barley, vines, fig trees, and pomegranates. It's a land filled with olive oil and honey— ⁹a land without scarcity. You'll eat food in it and lack nothing. It's a land where its rocks are iron and you can dig copper from its mountains."

¹⁰"When you have eaten and are satisfied, bless the Lord your God for the good land that he has given you. ¹¹Be careful! Otherwise, you will forget the Lord your God by failing to keep his commands, ordinances, and statutes that I'm commanding you this day. ¹²Otherwise, when you eat and are satisfied, when you have built beautiful houses and lived in them, ¹³when your cattle and oxen multiply, when your silver and gold increase, ¹⁴then you will become arrogant. You'll neglect the Lord your God, ¹⁵who brought you out of the land of Egypt, from the house of slavery, and who led you through the vast and dangerous desert, that parched land without water, with its poisonous snakes and scorpions. He brought water out of solid rock for you, ¹⁶and fed you in the desert with manna that neither you nor your ancestors had known, to humble and test you so that things go well with you later. ¹⁷You may say to yourselves, 'I have become wealthy by my own strength and by my own ability.' ¹⁸But remember the Lord your God, because he is the one who gives you the ability to produce wealth, in order to confirm his covenant that he promised by an oath to your ancestors, as is the case today. ¹⁹If you neglect the Lord your God, follow other gods, and serve and worship them, I testify to you today that you will certainly be destroyed. ²⁰Just like the nations whom the Lord destroyed before you, so will you be destroyed, because you did not listen to the voice of the Lord your God.

Deuteronomy 8:1-20

Several biblical scholars have speculated over the centuries that the threats contained in verses 19-20 of this chapter from Deuteronomy were prophetic references to what happened when Jerusalem was finally destroyed in 70 AD under Roman General Titus. We'll have more to say on this subject starting on page 121.

> *⁵The Devil also took him to a high place and showed him all the kingdoms of the world in an instant. ⁶He told Jesus, "I will give you all this authority, along with their glory, because it has been given to me, and I give it to anyone I please. ⁷So if you will worship me, all this will be yours." ⁸But Jesus answered him, "It is written, 'You must worship the Lord your God and serve only him.'"*
>
> Luke 4:5-8 (citing Deuteronomy 6:13)

This dialog between Jesus and Satan demonstrates the high regard Jesus had for Deuteronomy 6:10-15, since it is from that passage that Jesus drew his first response to the Temptation in the wilderness. The original passage reads:

> *¹⁰When the LORD your God brings you to the land that he promised to your ancestors Abraham, Isaac, and Jacob, he will give you large and beautiful cities that you didn't build, ¹¹houses filled with every good thing that you didn't supply, wells that you didn't dig, and vineyards and olive groves that you didn't plant. When you eat and are satisfied, ¹²be careful not to forget the LORD your God, who brought you out of the land of Egypt and slavery. ¹³Fear the LORD your God, serve him, and make your oaths in his name. ¹⁴Do not follow other gods, from the gods of the peoples around you. ¹⁵For the LORD your God who is among you is a jealous God. He will turn his anger against you and destroy you from the surface of the land.*
>
> Deuteronomy 6:10-15

The answer of Jesus to Satan from this portion of Deuteronomy includes in its larger context the motivational warning that disobeying it would incite the disciplinary wrath of God.

> *⁹The Devil also took him into Jerusalem and had him stand on the highest point of the Temple. He told Jesus, "Since you are the Son of God, throw yourself down from here, ¹⁰because it is written,*
> *'God will put his angels in charge of you*
> *to watch over you carefully.*
> *¹¹With their hands they will hold you up,*
> *so that you will never hit your foot against a rock.'"*
> *¹²Jesus answered him, "It has been said, 'You must not tempt the Lord your God.'"*
>
> Luke 4:9-12 (citing Deuteronomy 6:16)

Jesus cites the very next verses in Deuteronomy 6:16-19 to answer Satan's third challenge in the wilderness. The original passage from Deuteronomy reads:

> *¹⁶"Don't test the L*ORD *your God like you did in Massah. ¹⁷Be sure to observe the commands of the L*ORD *your God, his testimonies and his decrees that he gave you. ¹⁸Do what is good and right in the L*ORD*'s sight so it may go well with you. Then you'll enter and possess the good land that the L*ORD *your God promised to your ancestors, ¹⁹expelling all your enemies before you, as the L*ORD *said."*
>
> Deuteronomy 6:16-19

CLAIM #23: JESUS HELD DEUTERONOMY IN SUCH HIGH ESTEEM THAT HE CITED IT AS THE BASIS FOR CHURCH DISCIPLINE.

In one of his discourses on Church relations, Jesus addressed the issue of discipline for disobedient believers in Matthew 18:15-16:

> *¹⁵"If your brother sins against you, go and confront him while the two of you are alone. If he listens to you, you have won back your brother. ¹⁶But if he doesn't listen, take one or two*

others with you so that 'every word may be confirmed by the testimony of two or three witnesses.'"

Matthew 18:15-16

The citation from the Hebrew Scriptures cited in Matthew 18:16 is from Deuteronomy 19:15, the larger context of which reads in Deuteronomy 19:15-21:

> [15] *"The testimony of one person alone is not to suffice to convict anyone of any iniquity, sin, or guilt. But the matter will stand on the testimony of two or three witnesses.* [16] *When a malicious witness takes the stand against a man and accuses him,* [17] *then both must stand with their dispute in the* LORD's *presence, the priests, and the judges at that time.* [18] *The judges will investigate thoroughly. If the false witness lies in testifying against his relative,* [19] *do to him just as he intended to do to his relative. By doing this you will purge evil from your midst.* [20] *When others hear of this, they will be afraid and will not do such an evil deed again in your midst.* [21] *Your eyes must not show pity—life for life, eye for eye, tooth for tooth, hand for hand, and foot for foot."*

Deuteronomy 19:15-21

JESUS ON ADMINISTRATION OF JUSTICE

Jurisprudence is *the philosophy of the administration of law*. It is an admirable goal to attempt to conform a nation's laws to biblical truth. But the outworking of those standards runs squarely into this challenge: the entire presuppositional structure of western jurisprudence stands in conflict with the biblical standard of the administration of law. Until we come to understand this fundamental conflict, and adjust our application of jurisprudence to a nation's judicial standards, those standards will, of necessity, result in continual dichotomy.

For example, the modern model of jurisprudence dictates that criminal trials are *adversarial* in form and function. There is a prosecuting attorney who represents the interests of the national, state, regional, or municipal government. The prosecutor's function is to bring an indictment against the accused. The accused is provided a defense attorney, either at the accused's own expense or at the expense of the state. The judge in the proceeding acts as the referee between the adversarial parties. The jury acts as the adjudicators of the evidence in order to determine either innocence or guilt beyond reasonable doubt. Witnesses to the crime are called by the prosecutor, using subpoena powers to compel testimony even if the witness is reluctant to testify.

Everything described above with respect to the modern model is *antithetical* to the jurisprudence in force in the Jewish community of the Bible. In Jerusalem at the time of Jesus the Messiah, (i.e., ca. the early to mid-30's A.D.), there was no prosecuting attorney. The *witnesses* or the aggrieved victim were the prosecutors. If they declined to press charges, there would be no trial, whether for a criminal or a civil matter. There was no jury. The judge represented the interests of the *defendant*.

In cases where capital punishment was called for as the penalty for a criminal conviction, the witnesses were responsible for initiating the carrying out of the death penalty, which in the biblical economy required the guilty party to be taken to a high place, thrown from there to the ground (thus stunning the convicted criminal), and then large boulders were to be cast at the individual, killing the criminal.

The first stones were to be cast by the *witnesses*. The penalty for perjury in any trial was that the party whose testimony's validity was impeached was to suffer the same penalty that fit the crime on trial. You can read the specific statute about this in Deuteronomy 19:19, above. In the case of a capital offense, the penalty for perjury was death by stoning. The first stone would be cast by the person who had been falsely accused.

What made the biblical system of jurisprudence so fair and just was that it provided much room for grace and leniency. The penalty for theft was not prison time. It was four-fold restitution from the criminal. The penalty for rape was execution, but only if the victim testified as the prosecuting witness against the attacker. If the witness decided to forgive the attacker, no case could be brought against the attacker. If the criminal was repentant, the judge had broad discretionary authority to dismiss the charges.

Under the biblical system of jurisprudence, the penalty for moral offences against God, against his people, and against his Word remained high, thus reflecting the moral outrage of God at rebellion and lawlessness.

But in actual practice, the Bible records only a couple of instances when the harsh penalties for disobedience to God's law were enforced to the limits of ancient jurisprudence. In the book of Exodus, a man was stoned to death for violating the Sabbath. In this instance, the act of disrespect was considered to be a "sin with a high hand," i.e., disobedience carried out in direct rebellion against God's right to insist that people live life according to his standards. David, despite committing the sins of murder and adultery, was never prosecuted nor executed because he repented for his behavior when confronted by the prophet Nathan.

In the New Testament, the only time Jesus himself was confronted with a demand that the biblical standard of jurisprudence be brought to bear with respect to a criminal matter, it was to enforce a biblical penalty for the commission of an act of *porneia*, that is, for an incident of sexual immorality, where the woman had been caught in the very act. It is to this famous story that we now must turn in order to extract some principles by which a suggested set of guidelines for administering justice with respect to Law can be crafted.

GUIDELINES FROM JESUS ADJUDICATING A CAPITAL CRIMINAL CASE

When you add up the sum of all things relating to the Christian worldview of life, it really doesn't matter whether your background is traditional Catholicism, the Protestant Community, Orthodox Church, or something else: **_everybody_** agrees that the standards set by Jesus of Nazareth are the *sine qua non* (that is the essential element, indispensable component, or necessary factor) relating to what defines godly, wise, and just behavior.

Frankly speaking, *nobody* will ever be rebuked by God the Father because he or she behaved *too much* like Jesus. Bearing this principle in mind, the Apostle John records an incident in John 8:2-11 where a woman caught in the very act of adultery is brought before Jesus:

> *²At daybreak he appeared again in the Temple, and all the people came to him. So he sat down and began to teach them. ³But the scribes and the Pharisees brought a woman who had been caught in adultery. After setting her before them, ⁴they told him, .3"Teacher, this woman has been caught in the very act of adultery. ⁵Now in the Law, Moses commanded us to stone such women to death. What do you say?" ⁶They said this to test him, so that they might have a charge against him. But Jesus bent down and began to write on the ground with his finger.*
> *⁷When they persisted in questioning him, he straightened up and told them, "Let the person among you who is without sin be the first to throw a stone at her." ⁸Then he bent down again and continued writing on the ground. ⁹When they heard this, they went away one by one, beginning with the oldest, and he was left alone with the woman standing there. ¹⁰Then Jesus stood up and asked her, "Dear lady, where are your accusers? Hasn't anyone condemned you?"*
> *¹¹"No one, sir," she replied.*
> *Then Jesus said, "I don't condemn you, either. Go home, and from now on don't sin anymore."*
>
> John 8:2-11

We can dismiss from consideration the transparent motives of the Pharisees in bringing this case to Jesus to begin with. They weren't interested in having justice done. Their objective was to place Jesus squarely on the horns of an impossible dilemma.

If Jesus were to act as trial judge and call for her death by stoning, he would run afoul of Roman authorities, who had removed from Jewish leaders the authority to execute criminals. In the case of the woman caught in adultery, the Pharisees intended to bring a charge of sedition against Jesus if he agreed to act as judge in the case that had been brought before him. If Jesus were to refuse to prosecute, the Pharisees could bring a charge of failing to enforce the Law of Moses in his role as acting judge of the criminal proceeding. In short, it was a case of "damned if you do, damned if you don't".

But Jesus called their bluff, so to speak, and took the case. He fulfilled the requirements of the law perfectly, by reminding the witnesses that as judge of the trial, he would be cross-examining the witnesses. The witnesses whose testimony could not be refuted, that is, whose testimony was "without sin," as the rabbis used the term in the first century A.D., would be required to cast the first stone.

Of course, the very same law that called for the death of the woman caught in adultery *applied equally well to the woman's partner*, whom the Pharisees rather conveniently neglected to arrest. Jesus knew that the penalty for committing perjury in a capital case was that the false witness *was required to be stoned*, along with any witness whose testimony could be demonstrated to be incomplete or otherwise inconsistent with truth—by the accused woman in the case of the woman noted in John 8. Accordingly, by accepting the invitation to act as judge in the case, Jesus was putting the witnesses on notice that their lives were on the line and subject to forfeit if he were able to prove on cross-examination that perjury had been committed.

And so the witnesses walked away from the trial. The case against the woman collapsed due to lack of witnesses, not because she was innocent of the charges, but because nobody would testify against her. So Jesus let her go with a warning, even though she was guilty as charged. The resultant outcome was that all requirements of God's justice were met, and a repentant woman was extended saving grace.

5 | JESUS AND BIBLE HISTORY

That Jesus of Nazareth demonstrated high confidence in the authenticity, reliability, and accuracy of the Hebrew Scriptures can be seen in his absolute declarations that various historical figures cited in the *Tanakh* actually lived and that various events—including the supernatural events—actually occurred.

In essence, Jesus the Messiah *denied* that the supernatural events recorded in Scripture were *hagiographic* in intent; that is, he denied that they were spiritual embellishments by anonymous ancient authors intended to enhance the credibility of sacred history. To put things in simple terms, if time travel were possible, Jesus of Nazareth held the view that it would be possible to go back into biblical history and personally meet Adam, Eve, Abel, Noah, Abraham, King David, King Solomon, Elijah the Prophet, the Queen of Sheba, Jonah, Isaiah, Daniel, Zechariah, Hosea, and Malachi.

It would also be possible to have witnessed the creation of Adam (and of Eve from Adam's body), to have seen Abel killed by his brother Cain, to have observed Noah's flood, to have met Abraham as the man dined with the three divine visitors just before the destruction of the cities of the plain, or to have watched the region of Sodom and Gomorrah while those cities were being destroyed by fire. A time traveler could have met Jonah on the beach on the west coast near ancient Nineveh, where he was deposited on shore following his experience with the sea creature.

Claim #24: Jesus' publicly stated belief that Adam and Eve existed formed the basis of his high view of marriage.

Matthew 19:3-6 demonstrates from the dialogues in which Jesus engaged with the Pharisees that Jesus took it for granted that Adam and Eve existed:

> ³*Some Pharisees came to him in order to test him. They asked, "Is it lawful for a man to divorce his wife for any reason?"* ⁴*He answered them, "Haven't you read that the one who made them at the beginning 'made them male and female'* ⁵*and said, 'That is why a man will leave his father and mother and be united with his wife, and the two will become one flesh'?* ⁶*So they are no longer two, but one flesh. Therefore, what God has joined together, man must never separate."*
>
> Matthew 19:3-6

Before we proceed any further in our discussion of Jesus' view on creation, perhaps we should take a moment to discuss Jesus obvious reluctance to refer to himself with first person pronouns when talking about his claimed divine attributes. He also rarely utilized active verbs when talking about his claims to be able to exercise divine authority. For example, notice Jesus' comments about himself in Mark 2:10:

> *"I want you to know that the Son of Man has authority on earth to forgive sins…"*
>
> Mark 2:10

Jesus does not say, "I want you to know that I have authority on earth to forgive sins…" To do so would create the appearance of arrogance. So he avoids creating an impression of presumption by referring to himself in the third person singular. In other places in the New Testament, the reader also will observe that when referring to his actions as God, Jesus will utilize passive verbs instead of employing the active voice. For example, consider this statement made by Jesus in Matthew 10:26-28 during an address he made to his followers about why it's important never to be afraid of those who persecute them:

> [26] *"So never be afraid of them, because there is nothing hidden that will not be revealed, and nothing secret that will not be made known.* [27] *What I tell you in darkness you must speak in the daylight, and what is whispered in your ear you must shout from the housetops.* [28] *Stop being afraid of those who kill the body but can't kill the soul. Instead, be afraid of the one who can destroy both body and soul in hell."*
>
> Matthew 10:26-28

In these four short sentences, Jesus is telling his followers that:
- *First, nothing can be hidden forever, because he will uncover all things hidden, a power that only God possesses.*
- *Second, nobody can keep secrets from him, because he will reveal them, a power of omniscience that can be wielded only by God.*
- *Third, instead of fearing other people, the followers of Jesus should fear him, because he can destroy human beings in hell, a prerogative that only God possesses.*

JESUS' USE OF THE PASSIVE VOICE TO DESCRIBE HIS DEITY

An observant reader of the New Testament Gospels will also note that in the records of his public dialogs, Jesus refers to his possession of divine attributes in an almost casual, off-handed way, displaying a matter-of-factness that, frankly speaking, is incongruous with respect to the man's obvious humility, his heart as a servant of humanity, and with respect to the astounding claims that are being made by these verbs in the passive voice, third person singular.

Jesus is saying: "I can destroy the ungodly in hell," and, "I will reveal all hidden and secret evil activities undertaken by the ungodly." And he makes these statements obliquely, with *humility*, almost as if he's sharing a secret that only a select few people are privileged to hear. We do not wish to appear indelicate here, but nowadays people who speak that way about themselves have a tendency to be placed in rubber rooms by court-ordered psychologists on the grounds of mental instability. An incident recorded in Luke 7:48-50 provides a significant insight concerning the dynamics that were at work in Jesus' comments about his authority to forgive. The context of the incident recorded by Luke concerns a conversation Jesus had with a woman during an evening meal:

> [48] *Then Jesus told her, "Your sins are forgiven!"*
> [49] *Those who were at the table with them began to say among themselves, "Who is this man who even forgives sins?"*
> [50] *But Jesus told the woman, "Your faith has saved you. Go in peace."*
>
> Luke 7:48-50

Those sitting at the table watching the interaction between Jesus and the woman whose actions had drawn their attention during the dinner concluded that there was something unusual about the person of Jesus himself.

In simple terms, what Jesus said to the woman would, in other circumstances, be considered the highest arrogance at least, and downright blasphemous at worse. His comments were out of school, out of place, and far out of the protocol of a dinner discussion. And yet there is a casualness, a presuppositional set of assumptions that pervades the character of Jesus as he talks casually to the woman. That casualness is the self-confidence displayed as he tells the woman, "Go in peace." He tells her something that only God can truly know (that her sins had been forgiven), even though the extension of forgiveness is something that only God can accomplish.

And therein lies the consternation expressed by the dinner guests. They knew that one of only three possible conclusions could be drawn from what Jesus was saying to the woman: either Jesus was committing blasphemy, or he was claiming to know a fact that only God could know, or that he was claiming to be God himself.[1]

All of the above discussion regarding Jesus' tendency to veil any references to his divine abilities behind his employment of *passive verbs* applies directly to Matthew 19:4, because the "one who made them" at the beginning was Jesus of Nazareth himself, acting at the very beginning of creation to create Adam and Eve. The Apostle John addresses this truth about Jesus of Nazareth in John 1:3, where he writes:

> *³Through him all things were made, and apart from him nothing was made that has been made.*
>
> John 1:3

The wide-reaching extent of this claim is absolutely breathtaking: John informs his readers that everything that exists came about through the creative activity of Jesus of Nazareth during his pre-incarnate state. Stars, planets, galaxies, asteroids, meteors, interstellar dust clouds, angels, and all life on earth, including Adam and Eve, came from his creative hand.

On another occasion recorded in Mark 10:5-9, Jesus explained that Moses delivered the *Torah's* divorce regulations to Israel because God anticipated that the stubborn, hard-hearted disobedience of national Israel would lead to a failure to maintain God's high standards relating to marriage.

> *⁵But Jesus told them, "It was because of your hardness of heart that he wrote this command for you. ⁶But from the beginning of creation, 'God made them male and female.' ⁷That's why 'a man will leave his father and mother and be united with his wife, ⁸and the two will become one flesh.' So they're no longer two, but one flesh. ⁹Therefore, what God has joined together, man must never separate."*
>
> Mark 10:5-9

---

1   For a more detailed discussion of the remarkable claims of Jesus regarding his claims to being God incarnate, see our previous work *I, Jesus: an Autobiography*, written by this author with Dr. Chuck Missler.

Claim #25: Jesus' publicly stated belief that Abel and Zechariah existed formed the basis of his rebuke and warning that judgment was coming to national Israel.

Luke 11:48-51 demonstrates from Jesus' rebuke to the Pharisees that Jesus took it for granted that Able existed and that Zechariah was a historical figure:

⁴⁸So you are witnesses and approve of the deeds of your ancestors, because they killed those for whom you are building monuments. ⁴⁹That is why the Wisdom of God said, 'I will send them prophets and apostles. They will kill some of them and persecute others,' ⁵⁰so those living today will be charged with the blood of all the prophets that was shed since the foundation of the world, ⁵¹from the blood of Abel to the blood of Zechariah, who died between the altar and the sanctuary. Yes, I tell you, it will be charged against this generation!

Luke 11:48-51

Claim #26: Jesus' publicly stated belief that Able and Zechariah existed formed the basis of his warning about how Israel would soon be destroyed as a nation, an event that occurred in 70 AD.

During the final week of Jesus' mortal life and public ministry, he provided a massive, extended rebuke to the religious leaders of Israel. You'll find the entire discourse recorded in the 23rd chapter of Matthew's Gospel. In that discourse, Jesus took it for granted that Able and Zechariah were historical figures, and that their shed blood would be requited by the destruction of national Israel, and event that occurred during the lifetimes of many of the very people who heard his rebuke. The reference to Abel and Zechariah is found in Luke 11:49-51:

⁴⁹That is why the Wisdom of God said, 'I will send them prophets and apostles. They will kill some of them and persecute others,' ⁵⁰so those living today will be charged with the blood of all the prophets that was shed since the foundation of the world, ⁵¹from the blood of Abel to the blood of Zechariah, who died between the altar and the sanctuary. Yes, I tell you, it will be charged against this generation!

Luke 11:49-51

Abel's death at the hand of his brother Cain is described in Genesis 4:8. The assassination of Zechariah is described in Second Chronicles 24:20-21:

*²⁰Then Jehoiada the priest's son Zechariah was clothed by the Spirit of God, and he stood above the people and told them, "This is what God has to say: 'Why are you breaking the LORD's commandments. You'll never be successful! Because you have abandoned the Lord, he has abandoned you.'"
²¹But the people conspired against him, and at the direct orders of the king they stoned him to death in the courtyard of the LORD's Temple. ²²This is how King Joash failed to remember the kindness that Zechariah's father Jehoiada had shown him: he killed his son. As he lay dying, Zechariah cried out, "May the LORD watch this and avenge."*

2 Chronicles 24:20-22

The destruction that Jesus mentioned in Luke 11:51 was fulfilled by the invasion of Jerusalem by Roman General Titus in 70 AD.

THE DESTRUCTION OF JERUSALEM

Luke's Gospel alone records a portion of a private, executive level counsel from Jesus the Messiah about what lay ahead for the city of Jerusalem leading up to the coming destruction of the Temple and related events. Consistent with Luke's pattern to emphasize the relational aspects of the events surrounding the life of Jesus, Luke's comments on the destruction of Jerusalem will focus on how the divine pattern of judgment sees its outworking and effect on the citizens of Jerusalem. As one observer notes:

Figure 10: Wilhelm von Kaulbach's The Siege and Destruction of Jerusalem, 1846. Displayed currently at Neue Pinakothek Museum, Munich, Germany. Photo credit: © Ad Meskens / Wikimedia Commons.

What Luke does is easier to understand when we grasp how divine history was read by the Jews, as well as by the prophets. The belief was that God's judgment followed certain patterns. How he judged in one era resembled how he would judge in another. Because God's character was unchanging and because he controlled history, such patterns could be noted. Thus deliverance in any era was compared to the exodus. One event mirrored another. Exilic judgments, whether Assyrian or Babylonian, were described in similar terms. This "mirror" or "pattern" interpretation of history has been called a typological-prophetic reading of the text, with the "type" reflecting a basic pattern in God's activity. This way of reading history sees events as linked and mirroring one another. Sometimes the events are described

Figure 11: The Siege and Destruction of Jerusalem, by David Roberts (1850).

in such a way that we modern readers would not readily notice that distinct events are being discussed. Sometimes a text offers clarifying reflection after more events detailing God's program have been revealed. Jesus' eschatological discourse links together two such events, the destruction of Jerusalem in AD 70 and the events of the end signaling his return to earth. Because the events are patterned after one

Figure 12: Detail of von Kaulbach's work showing suicide of the Jerusalem Temple's High Priest. Photo credit: © Ad Meskens / Wikimedia Commons.

another and mirror one another, some of Jesus' language applies to both. Mark and Matthew highlight the mirror's long-term image, while Luke emphasizes the short-term event. Either focus is a correct portrayal of Jesus' teaching. Failure to appreciate the typological background to this speech, however, has led to an overemphasis of one image against the other within the Synoptics. Some readers insist that the portrait of one writer must exactly match that of another. Instead, complementary emphases are possible. But appreciation of typology allows each author to speak for himself and allows the accounts of all the Synoptic writers to be viewed not in contradictory or one-sided terms but as complementary. The speech makes several points.

- *First, Luke clearly shows how the destruction of AD 70 is distinct from but related to the end. The two events should not be confused, but Jerusalem's destruction, when it comes, will guarantee as well as picture the end, since one event mirrors the other. Both are a part of God's plan as events move toward the end.*

- *Second, Jesus' prophetic character is highlighted by this section. God is speaking through Jesus about unfolding events in the plan. Such prophetic gifts were highly respected in the ancient world (Philo Life of Moses 2.9.50-51).*

- *Third, the Jewish nation's fate was clearly tied to its reaction to Jesus. The reader is not to question that the events Jesus describes will result from the nation's failure to respond to him (19:41-44). In fact, if one were to ask why Jerusalem was being judged, Luke has given many reasons. It is filled with hypocrisy (11:37-54), has oppressed the poor (18:7; 20:47), has rejected Messiah (13:33-34; 20:13-18), has missed the day of visitation (19:44), has rejected the gospel (Acts 13:46-48; 18:5-6; 28:25-28) and has slain God's Son (Lk 9:22; 18:31-33; 19:47; 20:14-19; 22:1-2, 52; 23:1-25; Stein 1992:521).*

- *Fourth, the passage offers reassurance to disciples that God will enable them to face persecution and deliver them from it, whether by giving them words to say in their own defense or by saving them after martyrdom.*

- *Fifth, the call is to remain steadfast because God is in control.*

So the speech offers information and exhortations. It provides a general outline but not a detailed, dated calendar of future events. Such a general portrait without detailed dates is a common form for biblical apocalyptic material. We must be careful not to get more specific than Scripture does about the events of the future. Even though the portrait Jesus gives is general, he is saying, in effect, "Rest assured, God's plan is being fulfilled." [2]

Luke 21:20

20"So when you see Jerusalem surrounded by armies, then understand that its devastation is approaching.

Luke's employment of the slightly disjunctive Greek phrase Ὅταν δὲ ἴδητε, *Hótan dè ídete*, (literally, "Now when you observe...") suggests that by the Messiah using the second person plural verb, his followers to whom the Messiah is speaking will one day serve as personal eyewitnesses of what is to come. This use of the Greek present tense sets what Jesus will be saying about the future invasion of Jerusalem apart from his answering response to the question asked by the disciples regarding the end of the age, since the end of the age will not take place until the Gospel is proclaimed throughout all nations of the earth. To sum up, the end of the age will not take place for centuries, but the destruction of Jerusalem will be accomplished within a generation; i.e., in less than about 40 years, and some of the people listening to him at that moment would live to see that destruction. The siege of Jerusalem in 70 AD was the decisive event of the First Jewish–Roman War. The Roman army, led by the future Emperor Titus, with Tiberius Julius Alexander as his second-in-command, besieged and conquered the city of Jerusalem,[3] which had been occupied by its Jewish defenders in 66 AD. The siege ended with the sacking of the city and the destruction of its Temple on the ninth day of the Jewish month of Av, which also "happened" to be the anniversary of the destruction of Solomon's Temple by

---

2   Cited from https://www.biblegateway.com/resources/commentaries/IVP-NT/Luke/Jerusalems-Destruction-End.
3   http://en.wikipedia.org/wiki/Siege_of_Jerusalem_%28AD_70%29.

Nebuchadnezzar. (The destruction of both the first and second temples is still mourned annually as the Jewish fast *Tisha B'Av*.)

There is still some debate as to whether or not Titus actually ordered the destruction of the Temple complex. We are inclined to side with G. J. Goldberg's view expressed in his contrarian article *The Siege and Destruction of Jerusalem*.[4] He writes:

> *The Temple was destroyed despite Titus' order that it be preserved, and despite his attempts to put out the fire once it started. So writes Josephus, and so this is how Titus wished to be seen. But a later historian, Sulpicius Severus (apparently based on Tacitus' lost history) says the opposite – that Titus ordered the destruction. It is difficult to know the truth, but a glaring piece of evidence is the calendar: Titus held the decisive council to determine the Temple's fate on the Ninth of Av, and the fire began the next day, the Tenth. The Tenth corresponding exactly to the date of the destruction of the First Temple by Nebuchadnezzar of Babylon (Jeremiah 52:12; but 2 Kings 25:8 places it on the Seventh of Av). Titus' Jewish advisers, including Josephus, would have made him aware of that fact. We can be all but certain that Titus chose the meeting date for its historical significance, and attack on the Temple on the Tenth would have been auspicious for Roman success and a fateful signal for the Judeans.*
>
> *But for Josephus, the date of the fire was not due to Roman choice. He had been trying his hardest to obtain the peaceful surrender of the rebels and in this way preserve the Temple and the city. The long, long sermon he claims to have given before the walls is surely a fabrication.*
>
> *It is easy to imagine that after the destruction he would have tormented himself: "Is there something I could have said that would have saved the Temple? If I had only found the right words..." The idealized speeches can be seen as an intellectual way to handle this guilt, as indeed, perhaps, is his entire writing of the War. In these speeches he finds solace by explicitly identifying*

---

4   See http://www.josephus.org/FlJosephus2/warChronology7Fall.html.

himself with Jeremiah, another prophet who failed to save his city. There was nothing, he realizes, that he or any human could have done:

The Deity, indeed long since, had sentenced the Temple to the flames; but now in the revolution of the years had arrived the fated day, the Tenth of the Month of Lous [Av]. [...] Deeply as one must mourn for the most marvelous edifice which we have ever seen or heard of, yet may we draw very great consolation from the thought that there is no escape from Fate, for works of art and places, any more than for living beings. And one may well marvel at the exactness of the cycle of Destiny; for, as I said, she waited until the very month and the very day on which in bygone times the Temple had been burnt by the Babylonians.[5]

His solution is simple. The destruction was not Josephus' fault, nor was it the decision of Titus: the date was not the choice of Rome, but the decision of Fate. Josephus is required to praise Titus, as he did Vespasian before him, because these were chosen by Destiny. By doing so, he was able to relinquish any idea of his own guilt, and live in a kind of peace.

Luke 21:21-24

[21]Then those in Judea must flee to the mountains, those inside the city must leave it, and those in the countryside must not go into it, [22]because these are the days of vengeance when all that is written will be fulfilled.
[23]"How terrible it will be for those women who are pregnant or who are nursing babies in those days!—because there will be great distress in the land and wrath against this people. [24]They will fall by the edge of the sword and be carried off as captives among all the nations, and Jerusalem will be trampled on by unbelievers until the times of the unbelievers are fulfilled."

The destruction predicted by Jesus in Luke 21:21-24 was fulfilled with astonishing brutality and literalness. Consistent with a prediction recorded by the prophet Daniel, the Temple was not to be destroyed until the Messiah was "cut down," (Daniel 9:24-26) as the Bible records Gabriel warning Daniel about the future of Israel:

[24]*Seventy weeks have been decreed concerning your people and your holy city: to restrain transgression, to put an end to sin,*

---
5 Cf. War 250, 267-270

to make atonement for lawlessness, to establish everlasting righteousness, to conclude vision and prophecy, and to anoint the Most Holy Place. ²⁵ So be informed and discern that seven weeks and 62 weeks will elapse from the issuance of the command to restore and rebuild Jerusalem until the Anointed Commander. The plaza and moat will be rebuilt, though in troubled times. ²⁶ Then after the 62 weeks, the anointed one will be cut down (but not for himself). Then the people of the Coming Commander will destroy both the city and the Sanctuary. Its ending will come like a flood, and until the end there will be war, with desolations having been decreed.

Daniel 9:24-26

The pro-Roman Jewish historian Josephus described some of the circumstances surrounding the fall of Jerusalem in chapters eight and nine of Book Six of his famous treatise, *War of the Jews*:[6]

(403) So the Romans being now become masters of the wars, they both placed their ensigns upon the towers, and made joyful acclamations for the victory they had gained, as having found the end of this war much lighter than its beginning; for when they had gotten upon the last was, without any bloodshed, they could hardly believe what they found to be true; but seeing nobody to oppose them, they stood in doubt what such an unusual solitude could mean. (404) But when they went in numbers into the lanes of the city, with their swords drawn, they slew those whom they overtook, without mercy, and set fire to the houses wither the Jews were fled, and burnt every soul in them, and laid waste a great many of the rest; (405) and when they were come to the houses to plunder them, they found in them entire families of dead men, and the upper rooms full of dead corpses, that is of such as died by the famine; they then stood in a horror at this sight, and went out without touching anything. (406) But although they had this commiseration for such as were

---

6   Cited in http://www.pbs.org/wgbh/pages/frontline/shows/religion/maps/primary/josephussack.html.

destroyed in that manner, yet had they not the same for those that were still alive, but they ran every one through whom they met with, and obstructed the very lanes with their dead bodies, and made the whole city run down with blood, to such a degree indeed that the fire of many of the houses was quenched with these men's blood. (407) And truly so it happened, that though the slayers left off at the evening, yet did the fire greatly prevail in the night, and as all was burning, came that eighth day of the month Gorpieus [Elul] upon Jerusalem; (408) a city that had been liable to so many miseries during the siege, that, had it always enjoyed as much happiness from its first foundation, it would certainly have been the envy of the world. Nor did it on any other account so much deserve these sore misfortunes, as by producing such a generation of men as were the occasions of this its overthrow.

CHAPTER 9

1. (409) Now, when Titus was come into this [upper] city, he admired not only some other places of strength in it, but particularly those strong towers which the tyrants, in their mad conduct, had relinquished; (410) for when he saw their solid altitude, and the largeness of their several stones, and the exactness of their joints, as also how great was their breadth, and how extensive their length, he expressed himself after the manner following:-(411) "We have certainly had God for our assistant in this war, and it was no other than God who ejected the Jews out of these fortifications; for what could the hands of men, or any machines, do towards overthrowing these towers!" (412) At which time he had many such discourses to his friends; he also let such go free as had been bound by the tyrants, and were left in the prisons. (413) To conclude, when he entirely demolished the rest of the city, and overthrew its wars, he left these towers as a monument of his good fortune, which had proved his auxiliaries, and enabled him to take what could not otherwise have been taken by him.

2. (414) And now, since his soldiers were already quite tired with killing men, and yet there appeared to be a vast multitude still remaining alive, Caesar gave orders that they should kill none but those that were in arms, and opposed them, but should take the rest alive. (415) But, together with those whom they had orders to slay, they slew the aged and the infirm; but for those that were in their flourishing age, and who might be useful to them, they drove them together into the temple, and shut them up within the walls of the court of the women; (416) over which Caesar set one of his freed men, as also Fronto, one of his own friends; which last was to determine every one's fate, according to his merits. (417) So this Fronto slew all those that had been seditious and robbers, who were impeached one by another; but of the young men he chose out the tallest and most beautiful, and reserved them for the triumph; (418) and as for the rest of the multitude that were above seventeen years old, he put them into bonds, and sent them to the Egyptian mines. Titus also sent a great number into the provinces, as a present to them, that they might be destroyed upon their theaters, by the sword and by the wild beasts; but those that were under seventeen years of age were sold for slaves. (419) Now during the days wherein Fronto was distinguishing these men, there perished, for want of food, eleven thousand; some of whom did not taste any food, through the hatred their guards bore to them; and others would not take in any when it was given them. The multitude also was so very great, that they were in want even of corn for their sustenance.

3. (420) Now the number of those that were carried captive during this whole war was collected to be ninety-seven thousand, as was the number of those that perished during the whole siege eleven hundred thousand, (421) the greater part of whom were indeed of the same nation [with the citizens of Jerusalem], but not belonging to the city itself; for they were come up from all the country to the feast of unleavened bread, and were on a sudden shut up by an army, which, at the very first, occasioned

so great a traitness among them that there came a pestilential destruction upon them, and soon afterward such a famine, as destroyed them more suddenly.[7]

CHRONOLOGY OF THE SIEGE[8]

Reference	Action	Action Detail
4.658-663; Life 416	*Dec 69 - Early 70* Vespasian dispatches Titus to Judea.	Vespasian, the new Emperor, dispatches son Titus from Alexandria to finish the war in Judea. Titus marches to Caesarea with 2000 Alexandrian troop and 3000 Euphrates guards under command of Tiberius Alexander (Jewish apostate). Josephus accompanies them.
5.40-66	Titus nears Jerusalem; first fight.	Legion XV and XII join Titus; and encamp at Gibeah of Saul, 30 stadia (3.5 mi, 5.5 km) north of Jerusalem. While Titus reconnoiters with 600 horsemen, the Judean fighters attack, but Titus bravely plunges through them to safety.
5.67	The Legions assemble and camp at Jerusalem.	Legion V joins Titus by way of Emmaus. The camp is moved to Mt. Scopus, overlooking Jerusalem. Legion X soon joins them, making a separate camp on the Mt. of Olives, east of the city across the Kidron valley.
5.25; 5.71	The factions awake to the danger.	In Jerusalem, the factions have continued fighting. Nearly all of the grain stored in the city has been burnt during the conflict. When confronted with the reality of the three Roman camps, the factions at last make an uneasy alliance among themselves.
5.72-97	Daring Judean attack on Titus.	A group of Judean soldiers dash across Kidron in a surprise attack on the 10th Legion. Titus and picked troops come to the rescue, driving the Judeans back down the ravine, Titus at times singlehandedly keeping them from advancing. "Thus, if without a syllable added in flattery or withheld from envy, the truth must be told, Caesar personally twice rescued the entire legion when in jeopardy..." (5.97)
5.98 ff; 5.248-257	John of Gischala controls the Temple.	John of Gischala (Josephus' old rival in Galilee) defeats Eleazar's Zealots and gains control of the inner court of the Temple. The factions are reduced to two. Simon son of Gioras (the popular leader from the countryside) has 10,000 Judeans plus 5,000 Idumeans, John has 6,000 of his original men plus 2,400 of Eleazar's that have joined him. Simon controls the Upper City and the Third Wall to the Kidron valley at the southeast corner, and part of the Lower City. John controls the Temple and environs and the Kidron valley. The region between has been reduced to ashes.

7 *The Works of Josephus,* translated by William Whiston (Hendrickson Publishers, 1987)
8 See http://www.josephus.org/FlJosephus2/warChronology7Fall.html.

Reference	Action	Action Detail
5.114	Josephus begins negotiations.	Josephus conveys to the rebels Titus' invitation to peace negotiations, but receives no response.
5.106-130	Approach to the city walls levelled.	Titus orders the leveling of gardens, walls, plantations of the suburbs, flattening the space from Scopus almost to the city walls. A Judean pretense at negotiations ends in an ambush of several Roman soldiers.
5.133; 5.567	May 1, 70 Nissan/ Xanthicus 14 Titus moves camp to NW Jerusalem.	Titus and three legions move camp to the northwest corner of Jerusalem, two stadia (1/4 mile) from the tower Psephinus. The 10th Legion remains on the Mt. of Olives.
5.261	Titus, Josephus and Nicanor reconnoiter.	Titus circles the walls to select an assault point, accompanied by Nicanor and Josephus in an attempt to negotiate with the rebels. Nicanor (an old friend from Galilee) is wounded by a rebel arrow in the left shoulder.
5.260	Assault point chosen.	Titus decides to make assault "opposite the tomb of John Hyrcanus" in the northwest in order to capture the Upper City and the Antonia fortress. The Legions are ordered to build earthworks.
5.262-274	Both sides begin artillery fire.	Simon places previously captured Roman artillery on the walls opposite the works, but his men are inexperienced with their use. Titus positions artillery in front of his engineers for protection. The 10th Legion has the best artillery, capable of sending a one-talent (75 pound/34 kg) stone a distance of two stadia (one-quarter mile/370 meters). The Judeans place observers on the walls to warn of the incoming missiles, which are clearly visible white stones, allowing time for their men to take cover. The Romans respond with stealth technology: they paint the stones black.
5.275-289	The battering rams begin to act on the walls.	The ramps having been completed to within ramming distance, Titus orders the battering rams into action. The tremendous noise of the battering spurs the rival Judean factions into a truce, and they jointly attack the rams from the walls with fire and projectiles. In a ground sortie, Judeans set fire to the Roman works – "Jewish daring outstripped Roman discipline" – but Titus drives off the attackers and the fire is extinguished. In this attack one Jewish prisoner is taken and crucified in sight of the walls to frighten the populace. An Idumean general, John, is killed by an arrow.

Reference	Action	Action Detail
5.292	Roman tower collapses.	The next night a fifty-cubit-high Roman siege tower collapses; the troops panic, believing the rebels had invaded. Titus calms them.
5.300-302	May 25 Artemisius/ Iyyar 7 Outermost wall breaks.	After 15 days of battering, Jerusalem's outer (Third) wall begins to break from the rams. The insurgents abandon the wall without much concern, in favor of defending the other two. The Romans raze a large part of the wall and the northern quarter of the city.
5.303-315	Romans move camp to the Second Wall.	Titus moves the camp to within the Third Wall. Among the Judeans, John defends the Antonia fortress and the north portico of the Temple, Simon occupies the approach to the tomb of John Hyrcanus and the wall near the Herodian tower Hippicus. They stage quick sorties against the Romans and "still cherish hopes of salvation;" Simon in particular is revered. Judeans "thought only of the injury which they could inflict, and death seemed to them a trivial matter if it involved the fall of one of the enemy. Titus, on the other hand, cared as much for his soldiers' safety as for success...he ordered his troops to prove their manhood without running personal risks."
5.317-330	False negotiations by Castor.	Titus brings the battering ram against the central tower of the north portion of the Second Wall. The Judean deceiver Castor delays Titus with false peace negotiations, but a suspicious Josephus refuses to take part. Castor attacks one of the negotiators; when the battering is resumed, Castor sets fire to the tower and escapes.
5.331-347	May 30 The Second Wall cracks. Titus enters but is forced back.	Jerusalem's Second Wall is breached five days after the Third Wall. Titus with picked troops recklessly enters the breach in the Second Wall and into a crowded market district, asking the citizens to surrender peacefully so as to preserve the city. But the Judean militants attack, many soldiers are wounded, "and the entire invading force would probably have been annihilated, had not Titus come to their relief, covering them as the soldiers are forced back through the wall."
5.347	June 4 The Second Wall is razed.	After battling four more days, the Romans finally master the Second Wall and raze its northern portion.
5.348	A pause in the siege.	Titus suspends the siege and dramatically lines the soldiers up to receive their pay in sight of the wall, a process that takes four days, impressing upon the rebels the numbers and arms of the Romans. The rebels do not surrender.

Reference	Action	Action Detail
5.356; 5.466	Early June (c. Artemesius 12) Romans begin building earthen banks at two locations, Antonia and the Hyrcanus monument.	Titus splits his forces to build four embankments: Legions V and XII build earthworks against the Antonia Fortress so as to attack the Temple, and Legions X and XV build works in the northern part of this city across from John Hyrcanus' monument in order to take the Upper City. The rebels fire on them with hundreds of artillery pieces.
5.361-419; Life 1-7, Life 414-417	Josephus appeals to the rebels to surrender.	Titus, seeking to avoid the destruction of the city, delegates Josephus to speak to the rebels in their native language and persuade them to surrender. Josephus circles the walls as he speaks to the rebels. He implores them to spare themselves, the people, the country and the Temple. The Romans, he says, have done more to protect the Temple than they. It is rational to give in to superior arms, and the Romans were masters of the world because, clearly, the will of the Deity was with them. The city's forefathers had surrendered to the Romans knowing this. The Romans knew that famine was raging in the city, its fall was inevitable, yet they would be treated well if they surrendered now, while none would be spared if all offers were rejected. The Bible demonstrates that when the Deity supports the Jews, success is obtained without warfare, while if war is waged against superior powers the result is always defeat and destruction for the Jews. "Thus invariably have arms been refused to our nation, and warfare has been the sure signal for defeat." Josephus compares himself directly to Jeremiah: "For, though Jeremiah boldly proclaimed that they were hateful to God…and would be taken captive unless they surrendered the city" they did not put Jeremiah to death, but in contrast the rebels now "assail me with abuse and missiles, while I exhort you to save yourselves." Miracles, moreover, greeted the Romans: the pool at Siloam, which had been dried up, now filled with water at Titus' approach. In the end, Josephus makes a personal appeal: "I have a mother, a wife, a not ignoble family, and an ancient and illustrious house involved in these perils; and maybe you think it is on their account that my advice is offered. Slay them, take my blood as the price of your own salvation! I, too, am prepared to die, if my death will lead to your learning wisdom."

Jesus and Bible History

Reference	Action	Action Detail
5.420-445	Horrific famine seizes Jerusalem.	Although Josephus "with his tears thus loudly appealed to them," the insurgents do not yield. However, non-combatants are inspired to desert; they sell their possessions for gold, then swallow the gold coins to hide them as they escape to the Romans. The deserters give the Romans pitiful reports of increasing famine in the city and attacks by insurgents performing house-to-house searches for food, beating and torturing those within. The wealthy are robbed and murdered by the forces of John and Simon. "To narrate their enormities in detail is impossible; but, to put it briefly, no other city every endured such miseries, nor since the world began has there been a generation more prolific in crime."
5.446-451	Mass crucifixions.	As the construction of the embankments proceeds the Romans capture escapees from the city, as many as 500 a day. Prisoners are tortured, killed, and then crucified before the walls to intimidate the populace. Titus is saddened by the necessity of the crucifixions. "So great was their number, that space could not be found for the crosses nor crosses for the bodies."
5.458-459	The Judeans swear to fight Romans with their last breath, even if it means the destruction of the Temple.	The cruelty of the Romans has the reverse effect of discouraging desertion. Titus continues to exhort the rebels to surrender peacefully and thus save the city and the Temple. The Judeans reply by expressing negative opinions of Titus and the Emperor, and declare they prefer death to slavery, will fight the Romans with their last breath, and "that the world was a better Temple for the Deity than this one." [A radical concept too shocking for Josephus to contemplate: that the Temple might not be necessary.] The result of the conflict, they say, in any case is up to the divine will, not to them.
5.466-490; 5.522-526	June 16 Artemesius 29 The rebels destroy the earthworks.	On the seventeenth day of the building of the works, John undermines the Antonia earthworks built by the Vth Legion and sets fire to the supporting timbers, causing the tunnels to collapse and the whole works to burn. Two days later Simon's men set fire to the other works and battering engines. The Roman soldiers are dispirited at the loss of so much hard work and also at the lack of timber to rebuild, for all the trees around the city had been cut down for a distance of 90 stadia (10mi / 16 km).

Reference	Action	Action Detail
5.491-534	Titus decides to starve the city.	Titus holds a difficult consultation with his officers. Unable to rebuild the works, but unwilling to wait indefinitely, Titus decides to blockade the city completely to prevent food supplies entering. At the same time he will rebuild the embankments at one position only, against Antonia. Enthusiastic troops build an earthen wall (or trench) completely around the city in three days. All hope of escape being cut off, the famine within the city intensifies. Burials are neglected, bodies pile up. Insurgents continue the trials of prominent persons, execute eminent men and imprison Josephus' father.
5.541-547	Josephus knocked unconscious by a rebel missile.	As Josephus continues his exhortations at the wall, he is struck in the head with a stone and knocked unconscious. The Romans rescue him. Militants think him dead and rejoice. Josephus' mother, in prison, laments his death. But Josephus quickly recovers and appears before the walls, vowing revenge. "The sight of him animated the people and filled the rebels with dismay."
5.548-561	Deserters cut open for their gold.	Syrian troops discover some deserters have swallowed gold coins. The rumor spreads that all deserters are filled with gold. Arabs and Syrians cut open all who escape the city. "In one night no less than two thousand were ripped up." Josephus interprets this as another example of divine retribution.
5.562-566	John plunders the Temple.	John melts down the Temple vessels for gold and distributes sacred wine and oil to his men. He reasons they can employ "divine things on behalf of the Divinity."
5.567-572	Hundreds of thousands dead.	Deserter Mannaeus ben Lazarus is assigned by the Romans to watch a city gate. He counts 115,880 bodies carried through the gate during the siege, in the period from Xanthicus 14 to Panemus 1 (May 1 to July 20). Reports from within the city give the total dead among the lower classes at 600,000.
6.1-22	July 20 Panemus/ Tammuz 1 New earthworks ready.	The Antonia earthworks are completed in 21 days. These are heavily guarded, as all timber had been used within 10 miles of the city. John makes a strong attempt to destroy the constructions but fails.
6.23-32	Antonia is breached, but to no effect.	The Romans, under heavy fire, bring siege-engines against the Antonia Fortress. Armored engineers undermine the foundation. Suffering the pounding of the battering rams, a portion of the wall collapses. It has been weakened by the tunnel previously dug by John's men to attack the earlier works. But the Romans are dismayed to discover John has built another wall behind it.

Reference	Action	Action Detail
6.33-53	Titus encourages the soldiers.	Titus exhorts the dispirited troops, saying: The Deity is on their side—it is more glorious to die in battle than of disease—fallen warriors immediately—take their place among the stars rather than reside in the underworld—the new wall will be easily overthrown and once Antonia is taken the city is theirs.
6.54-67	July 22 Panemus/ Tammuz 3 First attack fails.	Inspired by Titus, Sabinus of Syria leads an impressive attack to scale the wall, but at the summit trips and is killed.
6.68-92	July 24 Romans take Antonia.	Two dozen soldiers, acting on their own initiative, lead a daring night attack and seize Antonia. The rebels fall back into the Temple grounds, battle fiercely and prevent further Roman advances.
6.93-129	August 5 Panemus/ Tammuz 17 Temple sacrifices end.	The daily sacrifices in the Temple are halted.
6.93	Josephus argues with John to restore the sacrifices.	Josephus delivers a message from Titus to the rebels, within hearing of all the populace: John may leave the Temple so that it will be no longer polluted, and the sacrifices may be restored. John enters into a heated argument with Josephus, John stating the city was God's and so could not be captured, Josephus replying that John had driven the divine presence away by stopping the sacrifices. John is unmoved, but great numbers of upper-class citizens, especially priests, desert at this point to the Romans.
6.130-149	Battle for the Temple.	A major battle for the Temple between the Romans and Judeans ends in a draw. Josephus records the names of a number of Judean heroes.
6.150-157	Earthworks built around the First Wall.	The legions build several embankments to approach the First Wall: one at the northwest corner of the inner Temple, one at the northern hall between two gates, one opposite the west portico of the outer court, and one opposite the north portico. The work is exhausting, timber having to be carried from a great distance.
6.158-163	Assault on the 10th Legion.	The rebels attempt an assault on the 10th Legion on the Mount of Olives, but are repulsed after a sharp battle.

Reference	Action	Action Detail
6.165	August 10 Panemus/ Tammuz 22 Rebels set fire to Temple porticoes.	The rebels set fire to the northwest portico that is connected to Antonia, to begin to separate the Temple from the occupied fortress.
6.166; 6.311	August 12 Panemus/ Tammuz 24 Temple severed from Antonia.	Romans set fire to the adjoining portico. The rebels cut away the rest. Antonia becomes completely disconnected from Temple. (This causes the Temple to become 'four-square', fulfilling an oracle predicting the city's fall.) Conflicts around the Temple rage incessantly.
6.177-190	August 15 Panemus/ Tammuz 27 Romans killed in west portico trap.	When the rebels feign retreat, a number of Romans leap onto the west portico, but find it is a trap: the portico has been filled with incendiary materials. It is set ablaze, killing nearly all of the soldiers (except for one clever Artorius). The west portico is cut away by the rebels. The Romans destroy the north portico up to the Kidron ravine.
6.193-219	Horrible famine. The news of Mary provokes hatred and despair.	The victims of famine are dying in countless numbers. Hungry rebels like mad dogs stagger from house to house searching for food. Shoe leather and grass is gnawed on. Famine reaches its ultimate depth: the tale of Mary daughter of Eleazar shocks the rebels and Romans alike. "For fear of being regarded as fabricator, I would gladly have omitted this tragedy, had I not innumerable witnesses among my contemporaries." Titus vows to bury this abomination beneath the ruins of the city.
6.220-228	August 27 Lous/Av 8 Romans fail to breach the wall of the Temple court.	Two legions complete their earthworks. Titus orders rams opposite the western hall of the outer Temple court. Siege-engines and mines having little effect, Romans scale the porticoes with ladders, but suffer heavy losses.
6.233-237	Titus orders the Temple gates set on fire.	"Now that Titus saw that his endeavor to spare a foreign Temple led only to the injury and slaughter of his troops," he orders the gates set on fire. The silver melts and the fire enters the woodwork and spreads to the porticoes. After a day, Titus orders the fire extinguished and a road built to the gates for the ascent of the Legions, but fires continue to burn. Two important officers of Simon's desert to the Romans.

Jesus and Bible History

Reference	Action	Action Detail
6.229-243	August 28 Lous/Av 9 War council on whether to destroy the Temple. Titus decides to save it.	Titus holds a council to decide what to do with the Temple. This council consists of his six chief staff officers: Tiberius Alexander (prefect of the forces and of Jewish descent), the commanders of Legions V, X, and XV, the prefect of the two Alexandrian legions, and the procurator of Judea. The tribunes and procurators also are called in. Some commanders recommend it be destroyed, others that it be preserved unless the rebels used it as a fortress. Titus states he would preserve the Temple at all costs, even if used as a fortress, because its beauty should be preserved as a possession of Rome.
6.244-264; Jeremiah 52:12 (contra 2 Kings 25:8)	August 29 Lous/Av 10 Roman soldier sets fire to the interior of the rooms surrounding the sanctuary.	The Judeans attack the guards in the outer court through the east gate, are forced back to the inner court after a three hour battle. Titus withdraws to Antonia, resolving to attack the next day. But the rebels again attack and are routed back to the sanctuary. At that moment one of the soldiers, without orders "but moved by some supernatural impulse," snatches a burning timber from a fire and throws it through a golden door on the north side of the chambers surrounding the sanctuary.
6.265	Interior of the holy house set on fire.	Titus is given the news. He attempts to order the fire extinguished, but is either not heard or is ignored. Battle rages around the altar. Titus enters the sanctuary to view its contents. The interior is not yet on fire, and seeing that the building can still be saved, Titus makes a second attempt to have the fire put out. But when he exits the building, one who had entered with him thrusts a firebrand through the hinges of the gate. The interior of the sanctuary is now on fire. "Thus, against Caesar's wishes, was the Temple set on fire."
6.271 ff	The Temple is consumed by fire.	Josephus provides an eyewitness account of the destruction, the fire and the noise. "You would indeed have thought that the Temple-hill was boiling over from its base, being everywhere one mass of flame, yet the stream of blood was more copious than the flames." He observes that this was on the very day and month that the First Temple had been burnt by the Babylonians.
6.281-288	Crowds of people burned alive on the porticoes following a false prophet.	The Romans burn all the buildings in the Temple complex, destroying the treasure chambers of the wealthy. The populace, especially poor women and children, are persuaded by a "false prophet" to go up to the Temple court to receive deliverance from the Deity. The crowd of about 6,000 climbs onto the porticoes, which are set on fire by the Romans. All perish.

Reference	Action	Action Detail
6.315	Genuine signs had predicted the destruction.	There were many false prophets at the time, says Josephus, yet people had not paid attention to the genuine signs of destruction: a star resembling a sword standing over the city, a comet, a brilliant light around the altar, a vision of armed battalions in the sky, and voices in the Temple, along with the prophecies of a peasant crying 'Woe to Jerusalem.' "It is impossible for men to escape their fate, even though they foresee it."
6.316-322	Roman sacrifices performed in the Temple.	Romans carry standards into the sanctuary at the east gate and sacrifice to them. So much gold has been taken from Temple that the price of gold throughout Syria is halved. The priests are executed by Titus.
6.323-355	Rebels in the city refuse to surrender.	The rebels flee into the city and ask for council with Titus. Titus lectures them and offers to spare their lives if they surrender. The rebels reply they cannot accept his offer, having sworn never to do so. Instead they ask to be freed into the desert. An angry Titus ends the talks, orders troops to burn and sack the city.
6.358-364	Lower City burned.	The rebels gather all their plunder and flee to the Upper City. The entire Lower City is burned to the pool of Siloam.
6.365	Josephus negotiates.	Josephus still attempts to talk the rebels into surrendering, or at least to give up the holy relics.
6.379	Rebels in tunnels.	Rebel leaders hide in the underground passages.
6.374	September 7 Lous/Av 19 Siege of the Upper City.	Titus orders new earthworks built to attack the Upper City. Four legions work on the west side of the city opposite the royal palace. Syrian auxiliaries build embankments to the east of the Upper City.
6.379-6.383	Rebels and their families sold as slaves.	The chiefs of the Idumaeans send emissaries to surrender to Titus, but Simon discovers the plot and executes the conspirators. There are masses of deserters to the Romans, most of whose lives are spared by Titus. Over 40,000 captured citizens are released by the Romans, but the rebels, including women and children, are sold as slaves. Due to the excess of supply, they are priced low.
6.387-391; 7.162	Temple treasures recovered.	Priest Jesus ben Thebuthi delivers some of the Temple treasures to Titus in exchange for protection. Included are two candelabra, solid gold and massive tables, bowls, and platters, the veils, the high-priests garments including the precious stones, and many other items. The Temple treasurer Phineas provides more, including priestly clothing and incense. The treasures are eventually displayed by Vespasian in Rome in the newly constructed Temple of Peace.

Jesus and Bible History

Reference	Action	Action Detail
Life 418-421	Josephus frees his brother and acquaintances, including taking down three who are crucified.	Josephus gains permission from Titus to release his brother and 50 friends. Josephus enters the Temple compound and liberates 190 captive women and children he knows, and receives sacred books (from the temple?). He recognizes three acquaintances who had been crucified, and Titus allows them to be taken down – two die, one survives.
6.392-402; 6.409-413	September 25 Gorpiaeus/ Elul 7 Romans take the Upper City.	The earthworks against the Upper City are completed after 18 days. The rebels panic, fleeing or surrendering without a fight despite their superior position in the massive Herodian towers. Many hide in the ravine below Siloam and then in the underground passages.
6.403-408	September 26 Gorpiaeus/ Elul 8 Jerusalem is sacked and set ablaze.	The Romans now command the whole city, plant standards on the walls, and loot the city. All Jerusalem is in flames.
6.414-419	All people in Jerusalem enslaved or killed.	Everyone in Jerusalem is made a prisoner; any that are armed are put to death, as are the old and feeble. Fronto is appointed to determine the fate of the rest: those under age seventeen are sold, the strong are sent to the work camps, others to the games.
6.420-422	1,000,000 dead.	Number of prisoners taken in the entire war: 97,000. Died during siege: 1,100,000. This large number during the siege was due to the Passover celebration, as Jews from many countries had been in the city for the festival when the siege began. Josephus tells skeptical readers this number is consistent with Cestius' population estimate under Nero.
6.430-43; 7.26-36	Simon and John captured.	Simon hides in the underground passages with his close followers. He attempts to tunnel his way out, but eventually gives up and arises out of the ground at the site of the Temple wearing a royal purple robe. He surrenders quietly to General Terentius Rufus. This alerts the Romans to the passages, which are then searched; 2,000 bodies are found. John gives up from starvation. John is sentenced to life in prison, while Simon is to be executed at the triumph in Rome.
6.434	The walls of Jerusalem are razed.	Romans set fire to the outlying quarters of the city and tear the walls to the ground.

Reference	Action	Action Detail
7.1-4	Jerusalem and the Temple demolished.	Titus orders the whole city and Temple to be razed to the ground, leaving only the tallest towers and a small portion of the wall on the west. The Xth legion is left to garrison Jerusalem. *Figure 13: The Arch of Titus in Rome. Depicts the Menorah taken from the Jerusalem temple as displayed during the triumphal march. Photo by G. J. Goldberg*
7.19	Titus departs to Alexandria.	The 12th Legion, which had been defeated by the Jews under Cestius, is banished to the Armenian border. The 5th and 15th legions accompany Titus to Caesarea and then to Alexandria.

CLAIM #27: JESUS' PUBLICLY STATED BELIEF THAT NOAH EXISTED AND THAT THE FLOOD OF HIS DAY AFFECTED THE ENTIRE WORLD FORMED THE BASIS OF HIS WARNING ABOUT HOW HIS RETURN TO EARTH WOULD AFFECT THE ENTIRE WORLD.

In his *Olivet Discourse*, in which Jesus the Messiah provides to his followers an executive briefing on the end of the world, Jesus took it for granted that Noah was a historical figure and that the flood described in the book of Genesis actually happened. The Gospels written by Matthew and Luke describe the event:

> [36]*"No one knows when that day and hour will come — neither the heavenly angels nor the Son, but only the Father,* [37]*because just as it was in Noah's time, so it will be when the Son of Man comes.* [38]*In those days before the flood, people were eating and drinking, marrying and giving in marriage*

right up to the day when Noah went into the ark. ³⁹ They were unaware of what was happening until the flood came and swept all of them away. That's how it will be when the Son of Man appears."

Matthew 24:36-39

²⁶ "Just as it was in Noah's time, so it will be in the Son of Man's time. ²⁷ People were eating, drinking, marrying, and being given in marriage right up to the day when Noah went into the ark. Then the flood came and destroyed all of them.

Luke 17:26-27

CLAIM #28: JESUS' PUBLICLY STATED BELIEF THAT ABRAHAM, ISAAC, AND JACOB ACTUALLY LIVED FORMED THE BASIS OF HIS WARNING TO AND REBUKE OF ISRAEL'S LEADERS ABOUT THEIR THREATENED *EXCLUSION* FROM ETERNAL LIFE.

One of the rebukes by Jesus to Israel's leaders during one of his meetings with a Roman centurion presents a solemn warning about the coming *exclusion* of certain Jewish religious leaders from eternal life. But notice, if you would, please, that Jesus does this by crafting his argument on the foundation of his assumption that Abraham, Isaac, and Jacob lived at some time during the history of national Israel. Matthew 8:5-12 records the incident:

> *⁵ When Jesus returned to Capernaum, a centurion came up to him and begged him repeatedly, ⁶ "Sir, my servant is lying at home paralyzed and in terrible pain."*
> *⁷ Jesus told him, "I will come and heal him."*
> *⁸ The centurion replied, "Sir, I am not worthy to have you come under my roof. But just say the word, and my servant will be healed, ⁹ because I, too, am a man under authority and I have soldiers under me. I say to one of them 'Go' and he goes, to another 'Come' and he comes, and to my servant 'Do this' and he does it."*

> [10] *When Jesus heard this, he was amazed and told those who were following him, "I tell all of you with certainty, not even in Israel have I found this kind of faith!* [11] *I tell all of you, many will come from east and west and will feast with Abraham, Isaac, and Jacob in the kingdom from heaven.* [12] *But the unfaithful heirs of that kingdom will be thrown into the darkness outside. In that place there will be wailing and gnashing of teeth."*
>
> Matthew 8:5-12

Claim #29: Jesus' publicly stated belief that Abraham, Isaac, and Jacob actually lived formed the basis of his defense of the resurrection of the dead.

One of the rebukes by Jesus to Israel's leaders concerned their sophomoric views about marriage, whether in the present age or in the age to come. Notice, if you would, please, how Jesus links their ignorance of the truth about marriage to his views on the resurrection from the dead. And then he links the validity of the future resurrection from the dead by mentioning Abraham, Isaac, and Jacob, whom he declares are *still alive* with God in heaven. Matthew 22:29-32, Mark 12:24-27, and Luke 20:37 mention this:

> [29] *Jesus answered them, "You are mistaken because you don't know the Scriptures or God's power,* [30] *because in the resurrection, people neither marry nor are given in marriage but are like the angels in heaven.* [31] *As for the resurrection from the dead, haven't you read what was spoken to you by God when he said,* [32] *'I am the God of Abraham, the God of Isaac, and the God of Jacob'? He is not the God of the dead, but of the living."*
>
> Matthew 22:29-32

> [24] *Jesus answered them, "Aren't you mistaken because you don't know the Scriptures or God's power?* [25] *When people rise from the dead, they neither marry nor are given in marriage but are like the angels in heaven.* [26] *As for the dead being raised,*

haven't you read in the book of Moses, in the story about the bush, how God said, 'I am the God of Abraham, the God of Isaac, and the God of Jacob'? ²⁷ *He is not the God of the dead, but of the living. You are badly mistaken!"*

Mark 12:24-27

³⁷ *Even Moses demonstrated in the story about the bush that the dead are raised, when he calls the Lord, 'the God of Abraham, the God of Isaac, and the God of Jacob.'* ³⁸ *He is not the God of* **the** *dead, but of the living, because he considers all people to be alive to him.*

Luke 20:37

CLAIM #30: JESUS' MATTER-OF-FACT MENTION OF ABRAHAM IN HIS DIALOGUE WITH ZACCHAEUS DEMONSTRATED THAT HE TOOK IT FOR GRANTED THAT ABRAHAM HAD BEEN A REAL PERSON.

One day a notoriously corrupt Jewish tax collector entertained Jesus of Nazareth at a meal. After the meal, Jesus affirmed the reality of the man's repentance by mentioning the man's association with Abraham, whom Jesus presumed actually had lived on the earth. Luke 19:8-10 records the conversation:

⁸ *Later, Zacchaeus stood up and announced to the Lord, "Look! I'm giving half of my possessions to the destitute, and if I have accused anyone falsely, I'm repaying four times as much as I owe."*
⁹ *Then Jesus told him, "Today salvation has come to this home, because this man is also a descendant of Abraham,* ¹⁰ *and the Son of Man has come to seek and to save the lost."*

Luke 19:8-10

³⁷ *"I know that you are Abraham's descendants. Yet you are trying to kill me because you've not received what I've told you.* ³⁸ *I declare what I've seen in my Father's presence, and you're doing what you've heard from your father."*
³⁹ *They replied to him, "Our father is Abraham!"*

Jesus told them, "If you were Abraham's children, you would be doing what Abraham did."

John 8:37-39

⁵⁶Your father Abraham rejoiced that he would see my day, and he saw it and was glad."
⁵⁷Then the Jewish leaders asked him, "You are not even 50 years old, yet you have seen Abraham?"
⁵⁸Jesus told them, "Truly, I tell all of you emphatically, before there was an Abraham, I AM!"

John 8:56-58

We invite the reader to pay particular attention to what Jesus said in John 8:56: the Pharisees understood the implications of Jesus well enough to express their *absolute disbelief* in the implications of what he was claiming. Specifically, while the Pharisees had enough confidence in the credibility of the book of Genesis to believe that Abraham had existed, they could not believe that Jesus was claiming to have known Abraham personally. But Jesus *leveraged* his previous statement recorded in John 8:56 to add fuel to the fire of the debate: he claimed to have existed as God before Abraham when he said, "Before there was an Abraham, I AM!"

CLAIM #31: JESUS PUBLICLY STATED AND BELIEVED THAT THE DESTRUCTION OF SODOM AND GOMORRAH WAS A REAL, HISTORICAL EVENT AND REFERRED TO IT AS THE FOUNDATION OF HIS WARNING ABOUT THE COMING JUDGMENT AT THE END OF THE WORLD.

Matthew 10:11-15 describes Jesus' instructions to his disciples about their communication of the Gospel to the world. In doing so, he reminds them about what will happen to those individuals who reject obedience to his demands that people believe in him.

¹¹"Whatever town or village you enter, find out who is receptive in it and stay there until you leave. ¹²As you enter the house, greet its occupants. ¹³If the household is receptive, let your blessing of peace come on it. But if it isn't receptive, let your blessing of peace return to you. ¹⁴ *If no one welcomes you or listens to your words, as you leave that house or town, shake its dust off your feet.* ¹⁵ *I tell all of you with certainty, it will be more bearable for the region of Sodom and Gomorrah on the day of judgment than for that town.'"*

Matthew 10:11-15

⁸ *"Whenever you go into a town and the people welcome you, eat whatever they serve you,* ⁹ *heal the sick that are there, and tell them, 'The kingdom of God is near you!'* ¹⁰ *But whenever you go into a town and people don't welcome you, go out into its streets and say,* ¹¹ *'We're wiping off your town's dust that clings to our feet in protest against you! But realize this: the kingdom of God is near!'* ¹² *I tell you, on the last day it will be easier for Sodom than for that town!"*

Luke 10:8-12

²⁸ *So it was in Lot's time. People were eating and drinking, buying and selling, planting and building.* ²⁹ *But on the very day when Lot left Sodom, fire and sulfur rained down from heaven and destroyed all of them.* ³⁰ *The day when the Son of Man is revealed will be like that.*

Luke 17:28-30

Jesus' high reliability of the book of Genesis' account of the destruction of Sodom and Gomorrah was also mentioned in the Messiah's rebuke to Capernaum. Matthew 11:23-24 tells us:

²³ *"And you, Capernaum! You won't be lifted up to heaven, will you? You'll go down to Hell! Because if the miracles that happened in you had taken place in Sodom, it would have remained to this day.* ²⁴ *Indeed I tell you, it will be more bearable for the land of Sodom on Judgment Day than for you!"*

Matthew 11:23-24

Claim #32: Jesus believed that Moses and Elijah were real figures in the history of Israel, and claimed to have spoken with both of them.

Mark 9:2-6 describes one of the most dramatic incidents in the life of Jesus when he took three of his disciples on a hike up a nearby mountain to be with him on a short, but very private retreat. Mark tells us:

> ² ...Jesus took Peter, James, and John and led them up a high mountain to be alone with him. His appearance was changed in front of them, ³ and his clothes became dazzling white, whiter than anyone on earth could bleach them. ⁴ Then Elijah appeared to them, accompanied by Moses, and they were talking with Jesus.
> ⁵ Then Peter told Jesus, "Rabbi, it's good that we're here! Let's set up three shelters—one for you, one for Moses, and one for Elijah." ⁶ (Peter didn't know how to respond, because they were terrified.)
>
> Mark 9:2-6

The account transmitted to us regarding this incident is striking in its simplicity and sheer humanity of the drama that played out on that mountain top. For one thing, it's abundantly clear from the narrative that the incident **was no mere vision**. For a brief few minutes, Jesus the Messiah manifested the *Shekinah* glory of God, which he always possessed, but which he veiled for all other times in his

*Figure 14: The fragmentary Tel Dan stela inscription
Photo: The Israel Museum, Jerusalem/Israel Antiquities Authority (photograph by Meidad Suchowolski).*

earthly, mortal existence. During those few minutes, the New Testament record claims that Jesus met with Moses and Elijah, and engaged in an extended dialogue with them both.

CLAIM #33: JESUS DEMONSTRATED THAT HE BELIEVED KING DAVID EXISTED BY AFFIRMING THE MAN'S EXISTENCE AND BY CITING MANY PSALMS, ALL THE WHILE ATTRIBUTING THEIR AUTHORSHIP TO DAVID.

Few modern Biblical archaeology discoveries have attracted as much attention as the Tel Dan inscription—also called the "House of David" inscription—that was discovered in writing on a ninth-century B.C. stone stela. That's because the inscription furnished the first historical evidence that the man named King David in the *Tanakh* really existed. Well now, at least that's how the liberal *Biblical Archaeology Review* assesses its 1993 discovery at the site of Tel Dan in northern Israel in an excavation directed by Israeli archaeologist Avraham Biran.

Then again, if these enemies of the historical validity of the Hebrew Scriptures would only take a good look at the statements attributed to Jesus the Messiah in the New Testament, they would learn that Jesus' own words furnish abundant evidence that King David not only was a real historical person, but that he authored the Psalms attributed to him in the Hebrew Scriptures.

The broken and fragmentary inscription commemorates the victory of an Aramean king over his two southern neighbors: the "king of Israel" and the "king of the House of David." In the carefully incised text written in Aramaic characters, the king boasts that he vanquished several thousand Israelite and Judahite horsemen and charioteers before personally dispatching both of his royal opponents. Unfortunately, the recovered fragments of the "House of David" inscription do not preserve the names of the specific kings involved in this brutal encounter, but most scholars believe the stela recounts a campaign of Hazael of Damascus in which he defeated both Jehoram of Israel and Ahaziah of Judah.[9]

---

9   Cited from http://www.biblicalarchaeology.org/daily/biblical-artifacts/artifacts-and-the-bible/-the-tel-dan-inscription-the-first-historical-evidence-of-the-king-david-bible-story/?mqsc=-E3824550.

One notable example of Jesus tendency to assume the historical validity of the record of David's existence and reign over Israel may be read in Matthew 12:1-8:

> *¹At that time, Jesus walked through the grain fields on a Sabbath. His disciples became hungry and began picking heads of grain to eat. ²When the Pharisees saw this, they told him, "Look! Your disciples are doing what is not lawful to do on the Sabbath!"*
> *³But he told them, "Haven't you read what David did when he and his companions were hungry? ⁴How is it that he went into the house of God and ate the Bread of the Presence, which was not lawful for him and his companions to eat but was reserved for the priests? ⁵Or haven't you read in the Law that on every Sabbath the priests in the Temple violate the Sabbath and yet are innocent? ⁶But I tell you, something greater than the Temple is here! ⁷If you had known what 'I want mercy and not sacrifice' means, you would not have condemned the innocent, ⁸for the Son of Man is Lord of the Sabbath."*
>
> Matthew 12:1-8

Matthew's edition of this incident also affirms the canonicity of the writings of the prophet Hosea, which are part of the *Nevi'im*. Hosea 6:6 is quoted by Jesus in his response to the Jewish leaders. This verse is part of a larger context containing an exhortation by Hosea for the ancient Israelis to return to God. Hosea 6:1-7 reads:

> *¹"Come, let us return to the* LORD*;*
> *even though he has torn us,*
> *he will heal us.*
> *Even though he has wounded us,*
> *he will bind our wounds.*
> *²After two days, he will restore us to life,*
> *on the third day he will raise us up,*
> *and we will live in his presence.*
> *³Let us know,*

let us pursue knowledge of the Lord;
his coming is as certain as the dawn.
He will come to us like the rain,
like the autumn and spring rains come on the earth.
⁴"What am I to do with you, Ephraim?
What am I to do with you, Judah?
Your love is like a morning rain cloud—
it passes away like the morning dew.
⁵ Therefore I cut them to pieces by the prophets,
killing them by the words from my mouth.
The verdict against you shines like a beacon.
⁶ For it is love that I seek,
and not sacrifice;
knowledge of God more than burnt offerings.
⁷"But like Adam, they broke the covenant;
in this they have acted deceitfully against me.

Hosea 6:1-7

A slightly different version of this episode may be read in Mark 2:23-28:

²³ Jesus happened to be going through the grain fields on a Sabbath. As they made their way, his disciples began picking the heads of grain. ²⁴ The Pharisees asked him, "Look! Why are they doing what is not lawful on Sabbath days?"

²⁵ He asked them, "Haven't you read what David did when he and his companions were hungry and in need? ²⁶ How was it that he went into the House of God during the lifetime of Abiathar the high priest and ate the Bread of the Presence, which was not lawful for anyone but the priests to eat, and gave some of it to his companions?"

²⁷ Then he told them, "The Sabbath was made for people, not people for the Sabbath. ²⁸ Therefore, the Son of Man is Lord even of the Sabbath."

Mark 2:23-28

Luke also records this pronouncement in Luke 6:1-5:

¹One time Jesus was walking through some grain fields on a Sabbath. His disciples were picking the heads of grain, rubbing them in their hands, and eating them. ²Some of the Pharisees asked, "Why are you doing what isn't lawful on Sabbath days?"
³Jesus answered them, "Haven't you read what David did when he and his companions became hungry? ⁴How was it that he went into the house of God, took the Bread of the Presence and ate it, which was not lawful for anyone but the priests to eat, and then gave some of it to his companions?" ⁵Then he told them, "The Son of Man is Lord of the Sabbath."

Luke 6:1-5

In each of these three passages from the *Synoptic Gospels*, Jesus the Messiah is referring to a passage in the *Chetubim* (Historical Writings) portion of the Hebrew Scriptures recorded in First Samuel 21:1-6:

¹David came to Nob to Ahimelech the priest, and Ahimelech was trembling as he came to meet David. Ahimelech told him, "Why are you alone, and no one with you?"
²David told Ahimelech the priest, "The king commanded me about a matter, saying to me, 'Don't let anyone know anything about the matter I'm sending you to do and about which I've commanded you. I've directed the young men to a certain place.' ³Now, what do you have available? Give me five loaves of bread or whatever you have."
⁴The priest answered David: "There is no ordinary bread available; only consecrated bread, provided that the young men have kept themselves from women."
⁵David answered the priest, saying to him, "Indeed, women were kept from us as is usual whenever I go out on a mission, and the equipment of the young men is consecrated even when it's an ordinary journey, so how much more is their equipment consecrated today?" ⁶so the priest gave him consecrated bread

*because no bread was there except the Bread of the Presence
that had been removed from the* LORD's *presence and replaced
with hot bread on the day it was taken away.*
1 Samuel 21:1-6

In citing this portion of First Samuel to answer his critics, Jesus affirms the historical reality of David, of Ahimelech the priest, and the accuracy of the account recorded in First Samuel regarding King Saul's pursuit of David and the after effects of that pursuit.

CLAIM #34: JESUS QUOTED PSALM 8:2 AS A BASIS FOR HIS REBUKE TO THE HIGH PRIESTS AND SCRIBES OF JERUSALEM.

All too often in life, children recognize what their parents and other adults miss. In the simplicity of their young minds, when they see miracles happen, they instinctively know that God is at work. In Matthew 21:14-16, the Apostle records an incident in the Temple when the high priests and scribes "couldn't see the forest for the trees," so to speak.

> [14] *Blind and lame people came to him in the Temple, and he healed them.* [15] *But when the high priests and the scribes saw the amazing things that he had done and the children shouting in the Temple, "Hosanna to the Son of David," they became furious* [16] *and asked him, "Do you hear what these people are saying?"*
> *Jesus told them, "Yes! Haven't you ever read, 'From the mouths of infants and nursing babies you have created praise'?"*
Matthew 21:14-16

The passage that Jesus quotes here is a paraphrase of Psalm 8:1-2, which reads:

> [1] LORD, *our Lord,*
> *how excellent is your name in all the earth!*
> *You set your glory above the heavens!*
> [2] *Out of the mouths of infants and nursing babies*
> *you have established strength*

on account of your adversaries,
in order to silence the enemy and vengeful foe.

Psalm 8:1-2

Claim #35: Jesus quoted Psalm 35:19 and Psalm 69:4 as referring to himself.

In the Gospel of John, the Apostle whom Jesus kept on loving cites Psalm 35:19 and Psalm 69:4, claiming that these psalms refer to himself. John 15:23-25 records Jesus the Messiah as saying:

> [23] *"The person who hates me also hates my Father.* [24] *If I hadn't done among them the actions that no one else did, they wouldn't have any sin. But now they have seen and hated both me and my Father.* [25] *But this happened so that what has been written in their Law might be fulfilled: 'They hated me for no reason.'"*

John 15:23-25

Claim #36: Jesus said that King David authored Psalm 41, using its authority to bolster his claim to be God incarnate.

Jesus depended on the fulfillment of Psalm 41:9 in his life to demonstrate that he was, in fact, God incarnate. John 13:18-19 tells us:

> [18] *"I'm not talking about all of you. I know the ones I have chosen. But the Scripture must be fulfilled: 'The one who ate bread with me has turned against me.'* [19] *I'm telling you this now, before it happens, so that when it does happen, you may believe that I AM."*

John 13:18-19

Claim #37: Jesus said that King David authored Psalm 110, and used a quotation from it to demonstrate how David's Messiah was also God incarnate.

Jesus attributed authorship of Psalm 110 to King David. Matthew 22:41-46 records a dialog in which he engaged the Pharisees in a debate so profound that his reply could not be rebutted:

⁴¹ While the Pharisees were still gathered, Jesus asked them,
⁴² "What do you think about the Messiah? Whose son is he?"
They told him, "David's."
⁴³ He asked them, "Then how can David by the Spirit call him
'Lord' when he says,
⁴⁴ 'The Lord told my Lord,
"Sit at my right hand,
until I put your enemies under your feet."'?
⁴⁵ If David calls him 'Lord', how can he be his son?"
⁴⁶ No one could answer him at all, and from that day on no
one dared to ask him another question.

Matthew 22:41-46

Mark's Gospel records the event, also. Mark 12:35-37 tells us:

³⁵ While Jesus was teaching in the Temple, he asked,
"How can the scribes say that the Messiah is David's son?
³⁶ David himself said by the Holy Spirit,
'The Lord told my Lord,
"Sit at my right hand,
until I put your enemies under your feet."'
³⁷ David himself calls him 'Lord,' so how can he be his son?"
And the large crowd kept listening to him with delight.

Mark 12:35-37

Luke 20:41-43 sets forth an identical reference to Jesus the Messiah's claim that David is the author of Psalm 110:

⁴¹ Then he asked them, "How can people say that the Messiah
is David's son? ⁴² Because David himself in the book of
Psalms says,

> 'The Lord told my Lord,
> "Sit at my right hand,
> ⁴³until I make your enemies a footstool for your feet."'
> ⁴⁴So David calls him 'Lord.' Then how can he be his son?"
>
> Psalm 110

CLAIM #38: JESUS DEMONSTRATED THAT HIS ADMISSION TO BE THE MESSIAH WAS LINKED TO STATEMENTS FROM KING DAVID AND THE PROPHET DANIEL CONTAINED IN THE HEBREW SCRIPTURES OF HIS DAY.

When the time came for Jesus to endure his trial before the religious authorities of first century Israel, Matthew 26:63-64 records how Jesus confessed to being the Messiah by citing the Hebrew Scriptures. He cited a portion of the *Chetubim* (the Psalms and the book of Daniel):

> ⁶³But Jesus was silent. Then the high priest told him, "I command you by the living God to tell us if you are the Messiah, the Son of God!"
> ⁶⁴Jesus told him, "You have said so. Nevertheless I tell you, from now on you will see 'the Son of Man seated at the right hand of Power' and 'coming on the clouds of heaven.'"
>
> Matthew 26:63-64

The reply of Jesus recorded by the Apostle Matthew consists of citations from the book of Psalms and from the book of Daniel. Both books were grouped together by the Jews as part of the Chetubim, the third division of the Hebrew Scriptures. The *Gospel of Mark* also contains these quotations. Mark 14:62 reads:

> ⁶¹But he kept silent and didn't answer at all. The high priest asked him again, "Are you the Messiah, the Son of the Blessed One?"
> ⁶²Jesus said, "I AM, and
> 'you will see the Son of Man
> seated at the right hand of the Power'
> ⁶²…and 'coming with the clouds of heaven.'"
>
> Mark 14:61-62

The first quotation is from Psalm 110:1. The larger context in which this quotation occurs is an extended set of promises from God to his Messiah about what will happen in the future when he comes to conquer the earth, as you can tell by reading the entirety of Psalm 110:1-7:

> *¹A declaration from the LORD to my Lord:*
> *"Sit at my right hand*
> *until I make your enemies your footstool."*
> *²When the LORD extends your mighty scepter from Zion,*
> *rule in the midst of your enemies.*
> *³Your soldiers are willing volunteers on your day of battle;*
> *in majestic holiness, from the womb,*
> *from the dawn, the dew of your youth belongs to you.*
> *⁴The LORD took an oath and will never recant:*
> *"You are a priest forever,*
> *after the manner of Melchizedek."*
> *⁵The Lord is at your right hand;*
> *he will utterly destroy kings in the time of his wrath.*
> *⁶He will execute judgment against the nations,*
> *filling graves with corpses.*
> *He will utterly destroy leaders far and wide.*
> *⁷He will drink from a stream on the way,*
> *then hold his head high.*
>
> Psalm 110:1-7

The first four verses of Psalm 110 describe God's promises to his Messiah. By ascribing David's psalm *to himself*, Jesus is confessing to the high priests of Israel at his trial that he is the priest who lives forever, after the manner of Melchizedek (verse 4). Frankly, this identification by Jesus of himself with God's Messiah is a claim that because he lives forever, he is, in fact, the eternal living God of Israel incarnate as the rightful descendant of David and the rightful heir to David's throne..

Verses 5-7 of this psalm consist of a promise from David's Lord, the Messiah, that as David's protector, he will remain at David's side (referred to as David's "right hand" in the psalm). The Messiah tells David that on a future day, acting as Messiah, he will "execute judgment against the nations," destroying the enemies of God "far and wide".

The second citation from the Hebrew Scriptures that Jesus provides by way of answer to the high priests is from Daniel 7:13:

> [13] *"I continued to observe the night vision—and look!—someone like the Son of Man was coming, accompanied by heavenly clouds. He approached the Ancient of Days and was presented before him.* [14] *To him dominion was bestowed, along with glory and a kingdom, so that all peoples, nations, and languages are to serve him. His dominion is an everlasting dominion—it will never pass away—and his kingdom is one that will never be destroyed."*
>
> Daniel 7:13

For Jesus to cite this portion of Daniel's prophecy about the culmination of world history is for Jesus to claim that he is the one whose "kingdom is one that will never be destroyed" (Daniel 7:14). But in order for his dominion to be everlasting, as Daniel 7:14 claims it will be, that ruler must live forever. It is this individual that Jesus claims to be as he stands before Israel's leaders. Therefore, not only does Jesus refer to Psalm 110:1 and Daniel 7:14's authority as referring to himself, he uses these verses to bolster his claim to be the Messiah of Israel's past great King David.

CLAIM #39: JESUS ATTRIBUTED AUTHORSHIP OF PSALM 118 TO KING DAVID.

Psalms 118:22-23 contains a reference to the rejection of the Messiah, according to a rather embarrassing question asked by Jesus to the Jewish leadership of his day in Matthew 21:42-44:

> [42] *Jesus asked them, "Have you never read in the Scriptures,*
> *'The stone that the builders rejected*
> *has become the cornerstone.*
> *This was the Lord's doing,*
> *and it is amazing in our eyes.'?*
> [43] *That is why I tell you that the kingdom of God will be taken*

away from you and given to a people who will produce fruit for it. ⁴⁴ The person who falls over this stone will be broken to pieces, but it will crush anyone on whom it falls."

Matthew 21:42-44

The statement is repeated in Mark 12:10-11's version of the event:

*¹⁰ Haven't you ever read this Scripture:
'The stone that the builders rejected
has become the cornerstone.
¹¹ This was the Lord's doing,
and it is amazing in our eyes'?"*

Mark 12:10-11

Luke 20:17-18 also records Jesus as having made this statement:

*¹⁷ But Jesus looked at them and asked, "What does this text mean:
'The stone that the builders rejected
has become the cornerstone'?
¹⁸ Everyone who falls on that stone will be broken to pieces, and it will crush anyone on whom it falls."*

Luke 20:17-18

Claim #40: Jesus cites Psalm 118, claiming that King David's psalm is predictive of his second coming.

Matthew 23:37-39 and Luke 13:35 record Jesus citing Psalm 118:26:

³⁷ "O Jerusalem, Jerusalem, who kills the prophets and stones to death those who have been sent to her! How often I wanted to gather your children together as a hen gathers her chicks under her wings, but you were unwilling! ³⁸ Look! Your house is left abandoned! ³⁹ I tell you, you will not see me again until you say, 'How blessed is the one who comes in the name of the Lord!'"

Matthew 23:37-39

> ³⁵*Look! Your house is left vacant to you. I tell you, you will not see me again until you say, 'How blessed is the one who comes in the name of the Lord!'"*
>
> Luke 13:35

Claim #41: Jesus cites Psalm 118, claiming that King David's psalm is predictive of his rejection by Israel and subsequent exaltation.

Luke 20:17-18 shows Jesus citing Psalm 118:22:

> ¹⁷*But Jesus looked at them and asked, "What does this text mean:*
> *'The stone that the builders rejected*
> *has become the cornerstone'?*
> ¹⁸*Everyone who falls on that stone will be broken to pieces, and it will crush anyone on whom it falls."*
>
> Luke 20:17-18

Claim #42: Jesus believed that King Solomon and the Queen of Sheba were real figures in the history of Israel, and that they both would have a place with him at the resurrection of the dead.

Jesus of Nazareth defended the future reality of the coming resurrection of the dead by citing the historical reality of King Solomon and the Queen of Sheba. He claimed that they would have a part in the resurrection of the dead. Matthew 12:42 records the admonition:

> ⁴²*The queen of the south will stand up and condemn the people living today, because she came from so far away to hear the wisdom of Solomon. But look! Something greater than Solomon is here!"*
>
> Matthew 12:42

The Queen of Sheba's visit to King Solomon is discussed in First Kings 10:1-10 and Second Chronicles 9:1-12:

Jesus and Bible History

¹*When the queen of Sheba heard about Solomon's reputation with the* LORD, *she came to test him with difficult questions.* ²*She brought along a large retinue, camels laden with spices, and lots of gold and precious stones. Upon her arrival, she spoke with Solomon about everything that was on her mind.* ³*Solomon answered all of her questions. Nothing was hidden from Solomon that he did not explain to her.* ⁴*When the queen of Sheba had seen all of Solomon's wisdom for herself, the palace that he had built,* ⁵*the food set at his table, his servants who sat with him, his ministers in attendance and how they were dressed, his personal staff and how they were dressed, and even his personal stairway by which he went up to the* LORD's *Temple, she was breathless!*

⁶*"Everything I heard about your wisdom and what you have to say is true!" she gasped,* ⁷*"but I didn't believe it at first! But then I came here and I've seen it for myself! It's amazing! I wasn't told half of what's really great about your wisdom. You're far better in person than what the reports have said about you!* ⁸*How blessed are your staff! And how blessed are your employees, who serve you continuously and get to listen to your wisdom!* ⁹*And blessed be the* LORD *your God, who is delighted with you! He set you in place on the throne of Israel because the Lord loved Israel forever. That's why he made you to be king, so you could carry out justice and implement righteousness."*

¹⁰*Then she gave the king 120 talents of gold, a vast quantity of spices, and precious stones. No spices ever came again that were comparable to those that the queen of Sheba gave to King Solomon.*

Kings 10:1-10

¹*When the queen of Sheba heard about Solomon's reputation, she traveled to Jerusalem and tested him with difficult questions. She brought along a large retinue, camels laden with spices, and lots of gold and precious stones. Upon her*

arrival, she spoke with Solomon about everything that was on her mind. ²Solomon answered all of her questions. Because nothing was hidden from Solomon, he hid nothing from her. ³When the queen of Sheba had seen Solomon's wisdom for herself, the palace that he had built, ⁴the food set at his table, his servants who waited on him, his ministers in attendance and how they were dressed, his personal staff and how they were dressed, and even his personal stairway by which he went up to the Lord's Temple, she was breathless!

⁵"Everything I heard about your wisdom and what you have to say is true!" she gasped, ⁶"but I didn't believe it at first! But then I came here and I've seen it for myself! It's amazing! I wasn't told half of what's really great about your wisdom. You're far better in person than what the reports have said about you! ⁷How blessed are your staff! And how blessed are your employees, who serve you continually and get to listen to your wisdom! ⁸Blessed be the Lord your God, who is delighted with you! He set you in place on his throne to be king for the Lord your God. He made you king over them so you could carry out justice and implement righteousness, because your God loves Israel and intends to establish them forever."

⁹Then she gave the king 120 talents of gold, a vast quantity of spices, and precious stones. There were no spices comparable to those that the queen of Sheba gave to King Solomon.

¹⁰Hiram's servants and Solomon's servants, who brought gold from Ophir, also presented algum wood and other precious stones. ¹¹The king used the algum wood to have steps made for the Lord's Temple and for the royal palace, as well as lyres and harps for the choir, and nothing like that wood had been seen before in the territory of Judah. ¹²In return, King Solomon gave the queen of Sheba everything she wanted and requested in addition to what she had brought for the king. Afterward, she returned to her own land, accompanied by her servants.

2 Chronicles 9:1-12

Jesus and Bible History

The accounts recorded in the Hebrew Scriptures are filled with extraordinary detail, and both passages are assumed by Jesus the Messiah to be accurate and dependable records of an event that actually occurred during the lifetime of King David's son Solomon. The Queen of Sheba is known in non-biblical history as *Makeda* (Ethiopian), *Nicaula* (Roman), and *Bilquis* (Arabic). She ruled an ancient kingdom that was located in the area of the Middle East that today we call Ethiopia and Yemen.

She remains unnamed in the biblical accounts, and Jesus does not refer to her by name. She is mentioned by the famous Jewish historian Flavius Josephus as the queen of both Egypt and Ethiopia. Recent archaeological discoveries in the Mahram Bilqis (*Mahram Bilkees*, "Temple of the Moon Deity") in Mareb, Yemen, support the view that the Queen Sheba ruled over southern Arabia, with evidence suggesting the area to be the capital of the Kingdom of Sheba.[10]

> *Virtually all modern scholars agree that Sheba was the South Arabian kingdom of Saba, centered around the oasis of Marib, in present-day Yemen. Sheba was quite known in the classical world, and its country was called Arabia Felix.*[11] *Around the middle of the first millennium B.C., there were Sabaeans also in the Horn of Africa, in the area that later became the realm of Aksum.*[12] *There are five places in the Bible where the writer distinguishes the apparently Yemenite Sheba (שְׁבָא), the Yemenite Sabaeans, from Seba (סְבָא), the African Sabaeans. In Psalm 72:10b they are mentioned together: "May ... the kings of Sheba and Seba offer tribute."*[13] *This spelling differentiation, however, may be purely factitious; the indigenous inscriptions make no such difference, and both Yemenite and African Sabaeans are spelled identically.*[14]

Despite all of the above evidence, liberal higher critics and non-evangelical archaeologists deny the existence of the Queen of Sheba

---

10 For further reading, see http://www.newworldencyclopedia.org/entry/Queen_of_Sheba.
11 See Yosef Tobi (2007), "QUEEN OF SHEBA", Encyclopaedia Judaica 16 (2nd ed.), Gale, p. 765.
12 F. L. Beeston (1995), "SABA", The Encyclopaedia of Islam 8 (2nd ed.), Brill, pp. 663–665
13 John McClintock; James Strong, eds. (1894), "Seba", Cyclopaedia of Biblical, Theological and Ecclesiastical Literature 9, Harper & Brothers, pp. 495–496
14 Beeston, pp. 663-665.

163

and of her kingdom. Furthermore, liberal bias denying the historicity of the Queen of Sheba and of the kingdom of Sheba pervades today's research media. For example, the common on-line encyclopedia *Wikipedia* rather confidently declares:

> *Israel Finkelstein and Neil Asher Silberman write that "the Sabaean kingdom began to flourish only from the eighth century BCE onward" and that the story of Solomon and Sheba is "an anachronistic seventh-century set piece meant to legitimize the participation of Judah in the lucrative Arabian trade."*[15] *The British Museum states that there is no archaeological evidence for such a queen but that the kingdom described as hers was Saba, "the oldest and most important of the South Arabian kingdoms"* [16] [17]

In rebuttal to these liberal higher critical views, Dr. Robert Dick Wilson said this:

> *My readers will note, also, that the correctness of the English version of the original text of all these passages cannot be denied; and that the manuscripts and versions agree as to the accuracy of the text that has been transmitted to us. Then, let my readers bestir themselves and think what they would decide, if they were serving on a jury, as to the evidence of documents, regarding whose text and obvious meaning there could be no doubt on the ground of evidence except only that suggested by the lawyer who wanted to impugn the veracity of the documents. We know that these passages of the Old Testament were the same in the time of Jesus that they are now... No textual variants of any moment are found in any of the manuscripts. or versions. There is no serious dispute as to the meaning of any clause in any of the passages.*[18]

---

15 Israel Finkelstein, Neil Asher Silberman, David and Solomon: In Search of the Bible's Sacred Kings and the Roots of the Western Tradition p. 171
16 "The kingdoms of ancient South Arabia". Britishmuseum.org. Retrieved 2013-02-22.
17 Cf. https://en.wikipedia.org/wiki/Sheba.
18 Robert Dick Wilson. Jesus and the Old Testament. Princeton Theological Review Vol. 24 No. 4 (1926), p. 635

6 | JESUS AND THE BIBLICAL PROPHETS

That Jesus of Nazareth demonstrated high confidence in the authenticity, reliability, and accuracy of the Hebrew Scriptures can be seen in how he referred to the historicity of various biblical characters and in his citations of the prophetic literature We invite the reader to consider, for example, the following direct quotes from the New Testament:

CLAIM #43: JESUS BELIEVED THAT JONAH EXISTED AND WAS SWALLOWED BY A SEA CREATURE. HE EMPLOYED THAT HISTORICAL FACT AS A COMPARATIVE TO EXPLAIN HIS COMING RESURRECTION.

Jesus of Nazareth defended the reality of his coming resurrection of the dead by citing the historical reality of the prophet Jonah. By extension, his reference to the historical existence of Jonah and the validity of Jonah's time in the sea creature requires that he also recognized the historical reality of Jonah's admonition to Nineveh and the historical existence of the city of Nineveh itself. Luke 11:29-32 recounts the incident:

> [29] *Now as the crowds continued to throng around Jesus, he went on to say, "This people living today are an evil generation. It craves a sign, but no sign will be given to it except the sign of Jonah,* [30] *because just as Jonah became a sign to the people of Nineveh, so the Son of Man will be a sign to this generation.* [31] *The queen of the south will stand up at the judgment and condemn the people living today, because she came from the ends of the earth to hear the wisdom of Solomon. But look, something greater than Solomon is here!* [32] *The men of Nineveh will stand up at the judgment and condemn the people living today, because they repented at the preaching of Jonah. But look, something greater than Jonah is here!"*
>
> Luke 11:29-32

Matthew 12:38-41 also contains a version of this incident:

> [38] *Then some of the scribes and Pharisees told Jesus, "Teacher, we want to see a sign from you."*
> [39] *But he replied to them, "An evil and adulterous generation craves a sign. Yet no sign will be given to it except the sign of the prophet Jonah,* [40] *because just as Jonah was in the stomach of the sea creature for three days and three nights, so the Son of Man will be in the heart of the earth for three days and three nights.* [41] *The men of Nineveh will stand up at the judgment and condemn the people living today, because they repented at the preaching of Jonah. But look—something greater than Jonah is here!*
>
> Matthew 12:38-41

Later in Matthew's Gospel, a secondary incident is recorded in which Jesus rather unceremoniously comments to the Pharisees and Sadducees that their request for a miraculous sign from God

Jesus and the Biblical Prophets

to vindicate Jesus' claims will be refused, except for his resurrection from the dead, in keeping with Jonah's time in the great fish.

> ¹*When the Pharisees and Sadducees arrived, in order to test Jesus they asked him to show them a sign from heaven.*
> ²*He replied to them, "You say,*
> *'Red sky at night,*
> *what a delight!*
> ³*Red sky in the morning,*
> *cloudy and storming.'*
> *You know how to interpret the appearance of the sky, yet you can't interpret the signs of the times?* ⁴*An evil and adulterous generation craves a sign, but no sign will be given to it except the sign of Jonah." Then he left them and went away.*
>
> Matthew 16:1-4

ON THE HISTORICITY OF JONAH AND NINEVEH

Jesus asserted that Jonah was a real person. He assumed that the man visited the city of Nineveh, which during Jonah's lifetime was the capital of the ancient Assyrian empire. And he used the three days of Jonah's time inside the great sea creature[1] as a comparative to predict his own resurrection from the dead. In doing so, he assumed that the man's three day experience paralleled *exactly* the duration of Jesus' own time in the tomb of Joseph of Arimathea.

Jewish tradition suggests that when he was just a young lad, Jonah

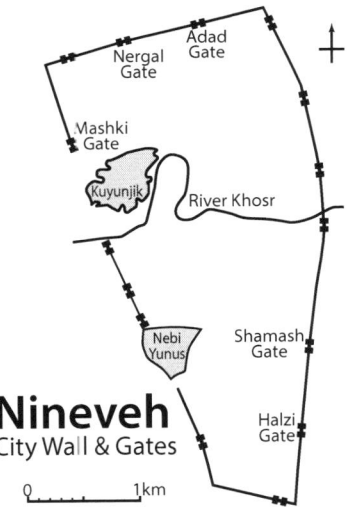

Figure 15: Simplified plan of Nineveh ruins, including location of tomb of Jonah (Nebi Yunus).

---

1 Hebrew: דג גדול, *dag gadol*; Greek Septuagint: κῆτος μέγα, *kētos mega*. The words refer to any large sea creature. Ancient Hebrews did not distinguish between species of fish or whales. This linguistic ambiguity makes it impossible in our modern era to identify the specific genus of the creature involved.

was the little boy who was brought back to life by Elijah the prophet, who is described in First Kings 17 as having been a guest in the household of his mother, the single parent of Zarephath, but this tradition is not supported by any textual evidence within the *Tanakh*, and Jesus himself never commented one way or another regarding this tradition. Even to this day, the canonicity of the book of Jonah is so highly respected that all four chapters of the work are read in the original Hebrew (!) as the *Haftarah* Bible reading portion at the afternoon *mincha* prayer on *Yom Kippur* (the Day of Atonement).

Figure 16: Tomb of Jonah in 1999 before its destruction by ISIS.

The Hebrew Scriptures mention the ancient city of Nineveh several times outside of the book of Jonah. For example, the first mention of the city may be found in Genesis 10:11, where Nineveh is described as having been founded by Nimrod. King Sennacherib reigned over Assyria from Nineveh, according to Second Kings 19:39 and Isaiah 37:37. The entire book written by the prophet Nahum is devoted to prophetic statements regarding its dismal future. Zephaniah 2:13 describes its destruction, as well. Nineveh was located near the junction of the Tigris and the Khosr Rivers on a set of ruins measuring approximately 1,900 acres, circumscribed by a 7.5 mile long brick rampart located near the modern city of Mosul, Iraq.

Under King Sennacherib, who located his capital city in Nineveh, the region became one of the most important cities. For many years, though, liberal higher critics of the Bible maintained that the city never existed. This denial sprang from a deliberate *ignoring* of the archaeological evidence. As early as the mid-1700's the Danish explorer Carsten Niebuhr had visited the area.

A century later, French Consul General Paul-Émile Botta began to excavate the area, as did British adventurer Sir Austen Henry Layard, who discovered the lost palace of Sennacherib, with its 71 rooms, and the library of Ashurbanipal, with its 22,000 cuneiform tablets. Unfortunately, many of the ruins of ancient Nineveh were destroyed in late 2014 and early 2015 by the Islamic State of Iraq and Syria (ISIS), who considered those ruins to be idolatrous.

The book of Jonah is named after the person whose experiences are the subject of its historical record. Jonah is one of only a few individuals whose ministry and message was solely to non-Jews. His book contains no direct claim of authorship, either by the prophet Jonah or by anyone else. Even Jesus never quite gets around to saying the book was authored by Jonah. But he does cite the man's experiences as having actually occurred during the history of Israel.

The only biblical clue about Jonah or the historical context of his ministry is contained in Second Kings 14:25. The clearly miraculous preservation of Jonah inside the marine creature for three days has led some to suggest that the record of Jonah's ill-fated journey was a late-dated allegorical myth.

However, no history of textual transmission, rabbinic tradition, or early Christian tradition supports this presumption. Furthermore, as we have noted above, because Jesus himself referred to Jonah's experiences inside the creature as an actual event that occurred in history, and because Jesus claimed that those experiences were a precursor to his own death and return from the tomb, there's no reason not to doubt Jesus' high view of the man's book.

At any rate, no chronological setting that could assist the reader in dating the book appears anywhere in the text of Jonah's work. The earliest possible date for the events described in this book would be during the first half of the eighth century BC, judging by a reference to the time of Jonah's ministry recorded in Second Kings 14:25. A number of modern scholars favor an exilic or post-exilic date (i.e., between the sixth and fourth centuries BC) for the composition of this work.

To sum up, Jesus the Messiah cited Jonah's experiences as *authentic history*.

CLAIM #44: JESUS' MATTER-OF-FACT MENTION OF JEREMIAH THE PROPHET AND HIS QUOTE FROM HIS BOOK DEMONSTRATED THAT HE TOOK IT FOR GRANTED THAT JEREMIAH HAD BEEN A REAL PERSON AND THAT HIS BOOK WAS AUTHORITATIVE.

Jesus of Nazareth cited the book of Jeremiah in a quiet discussion with his disciples one day. Matthew 13:10-13 recounts the incident in which this occurred.:

> [10] *Then the disciples came and asked Jesus, "Why do you speak to people in parables?"*
> [11] *He answered them, "You have been given knowledge about the secrets of the kingdom from heaven, but it hasn't been given to them,* [12] *because to anyone who has something, more will be given, and he will have more than enough. But from the one who doesn't have anything, even what he has will be taken away from him.* [13] *That's why I speak to them in parables, because*
> *'they look but don't see,*
> *and they listen but don't hear or understand.'*
>
> Matthew 13:10-13

This quotation is a direct citation from Jeremiah 5:21. Here's how the passage reads in the *Nevi'im* portion of the *Tanakh*:

> [20] *"Declare this to the descendants of Jacob,*
> *and proclaim it in Judah:*
> [21] *'Hear this, you foolish and stupid people:*
> *They have eyes, but don't see;*
> *they have ears, but don't hear.*
> [22] *'You don't fear me, do you?' declares the Lord.*
> *'You don't tremble before me, do you?*
> *I'm the one who put the sand as a boundary for the sea,*
> *a perpetual barrier that it cannot cross.*
> *Though the waves toss, they cannot prevail against it,*

though they roar, they cannot cross it.'
²³ But these people have stubborn and rebellious hearts.
²⁴ They don't say to themselves,
'Let's fear the Lord our God,
who gives rain in its season,
both the autumn and the spring rain.
He sets aside for us the weeks appointed for the harvest.'
²⁵ Your iniquities have turned these things away,
and your sins have held back from you what is good.
²⁶ "Evil men are found among my people.
They lie in wait like someone who traps birds.
They set a trap,
but they do so to catch people.
²⁷ Like a cage full of birds,
so their houses are filled with treachery.
This is how they have become prominent and rich,
²⁸ and have grown fat and sleek.
There is no limit to their evil deeds.
They don't argue the case of the orphan to secure justice.
They don't defend the rights of the poor.
²⁹ 'Should I not punish them for this?'
asks the Lord.
'Should I not avenge myself
on a nation like this?'
³⁰ "An appalling and horrible thing
has happened in the land:
³¹ The prophets prophesy falsely,
the priests rule by their own authority,
and my people love it this way.
But what will you do in the end?"

Jeremiah 5:20-31

By citing Jeremiah's salient rebuke to national Israel of that prophet's generation, Jesus assumes that the man actually lived and that he was the author of the prophetic book that bears his name.

Also, Jesus is citing the rebuke of God himself, thus identifying *himself* as the same speaker who called Israel to return to him. In citing Jeremiah, Jesus the Messiah was letting his disciples know that from his own standpoint, just as God rebuked ancient Israel, Jesus was rebuking first century Israel. Furthermore, as we'll see below with respect to what Jesus said about how he quoted Isaiah, Jesus is claiming to be the same God who inspired Jeremiah back in the years before the exile to Babylon occurred.

The book that Jeremiah wrote is named after the ministry and prophetic messages of the priest who recorded them over a period of more than 40 years. Rabbinic and conservative Christian tradition assign authorship to this book to Jeremiah, whose father Hilkiah may have been the same person who played a significant role under Judah's reformation (ca. 621 BC) described in Second Chronicles 34:9.

Jeremiah's prophetic ministry and writing career extended from his early teenage years, commencing in the thirteenth year of King Josiah (ca. 627 BC) and continuing through the beginning of the Babylonian captivity of Nebuchadnezzar (c 586 BC). Jeremiah continued his predictive and exhortative ministry well into his forced exile to Tahpanez, Egypt, which is recorded in Jeremiah 44:7.

By citing Jeremiah's work, Jesus authenticated the man's historical existence and the validity of his prophetic ministry.

CLAIM #45: **JESUS' MATTER-OF-FACT MENTION OF ISAIAH THE PROPHET AND HIS EXTENSIVE QUOTES FROM HIS BOOK DEMONSTRATE THAT HE TOOK IT FOR GRANTED THAT ISAIAH HAD BEEN A REAL PERSON AND THAT HIS WRITTEN WORKS WERE AUTHORITATIVE.**

Jesus of Nazareth cited the book of Isaiah with astonishing regularity during his public ministry. Matthew 13:10-15 recounts an incident in which this occurred:

> [10] *Then the disciples came and asked Jesus, "Why do you speak to people in parables?"*
> [11] *He answered them, "You have been given knowledge about*

the secrets of the kingdom from heaven, but it hasn't been given to them, ¹² because to anyone who has something, more will be given, and he will have more than enough. But from the one who doesn't have anything, even what he has will be taken away from him. ¹³ That's why I speak to them in parables, because
'they look but don't see,
and they listen but don't hear or understand.'
¹⁴ "With them the prophecy of Isaiah is being fulfilled, which says:
'You will listen and listen but never understand.
You will look and look but never comprehend,
¹⁵ for this people's heart has become dull,
and their ears are hard of hearing.
They have shut their eyes
so that they might not see with their eyes,
and hear with their ears,
and understand with their heart and turn,
and I would heal them.'

Matthew 13:10-15

The prophecy by Isaiah to which Jesus the Messiah refers in verses 14-15, above, is found in Isaiah 6:9-10:

⁹ "Go!" he responded. "Tell this people:
" 'Keep on hearing, but do not understand;
keep on seeing, but do not perceive.'
¹⁰ Dull the mind of this people,
deafen their ears,
and blind their eyes.
By doing so, they won't see with their eyes,
hear with their ears,
understand with their minds,
turn back,
and be healed."

Isaiah 6:9-10

An observant reader will note that Jesus' quote from Isaiah 9:6-10 is not, strictly speaking a direct citation from the Hebrew language original of Isaiah's work. It reads more like a paraphrase. I believe there were two reasons why Jesus did not quote the original Hebrew of Isaiah's prediction in this particular instance.

Jesus' use of Targums in teaching

First, it's highly likely that Jesus was employing the Jewish equivalent of a *targum* of this passage. The *Encyclopedia Britannica* provides this information about *targums*:

> **Targum**, *(Aramaic: "Translation," or "Interpretation"), any of several translations of the Hebrew Bible or portions of it into the Aramaic language. The word originally indicated a translation of the Old Testament in any language but later came to refer specifically to an Aramaic translation.*
>
> *The earliest Targums date from the time after the Babylonian Exile when Aramaic had superseded Hebrew as the spoken language of the Jews in Palestine. It is impossible to give more than a rough estimate as to the period in which Hebrew was displaced by Aramaic as a spoken language. It is certain, however, that Aramaic was firmly established in Palestine by the 1st century AD, although Hebrew still remained the learned and sacred language. Thus the Targums were designed to meet the needs of unlearned Jews to whom the Hebrew of the Old Testament was unintelligible.*
>
> *The status and influence of the Targums became assured after the Second Temple was destroyed in AD 70, when synagogues replaced the Temple as houses of worship. For it was in the synagogue that the practice of reading from the Old Testament became widely observed, along with the custom of providing these readings with a translation into Aramaic. When Scripture was read aloud in the synagogue, it was translated aloud by a meturgeman, or professional interpreter (hence the name*

Jesus and the Biblical Prophets

Targum), for the benefit of the congregation. The translator tried to reproduce the original text as closely as possible, but since his object was to give an intelligible rendering of the biblical text, the Targums eventually took on the character of paraphrase and commentary, leaving literal translation behind.

To prevent misconceptions, a meturgeman expanded and explained what was obscure, adjusted the incidents of the past to the ideas of later times, emphasized the moral lessons to be learned from the biblical narratives, and adapted the rules

Figure 17: 11th century Hebrew Bible with Targum, probably from Tunisia originally. Part of the Schøyen Collection.

175

and regulations of the Scriptures to the conditions and requirements of the current age. The method by which the text was thus utilized as a vehicle for conveying homiletic discourses, traditional sayings, legends, and allegories is abundantly illustrated by the later Targums, as opposed to the more literal translations of the earlier Targums.

Though written Targums gradually came into being, it was the living tradition of oral translation and exposition that was recognized as authoritative throughout the Talmudic period of the early centuries of the Christian Era. The official recognition of a written Targum, and therefore the final fixing of its text, belongs to the post-Talmudic period of the 5th century ad. The best known, most literal, and possibly the earliest Targum is the Targum of Onkelos on the Pentateuch, which appeared in its final revision in the 3rd century ad. Other Targums include the Targum of Pseudo-Jonathan, the Samaritan Targum, and the Targum of Jonathan ben Uzziel.

In other words, by the first century, AD, Hebrew had been eclipsed by Aramaic as the common lingua franca of Jesus day. Since he knew the common people were hanging on every word of Jesus' rebuttal to the Jewish leaders who were constantly attempting to oppose him, it's probable that Jesus, at least in this instance, cited his own off-the-cuff translation of the Hebrew into Aramaic so his general audience could follow his logic.

Jesus' use of paraphrase to highlight his divine nature

But there's a *second* possibility regarding why Jesus may have paraphrased Isaiah 6:9-10, and there's no particular reason why Jesus may have had both possibilities in mind while speaking to the Jewish leaders. That reason can be clearly seen when you compare Isaiah 9:10 as Isaiah wrote the words with how Jesus quoted Isaiah's prophetic writing. Take a good look, if you would, please, at the not-so-subtle difference between Isaiah's original and Jesus' quote:

Isaiah's original:
"understand with their minds,
turn back, and be healed."
Jesus' paraphrase:
"and understand with their heart and turn,
and I would heal them."

In Isaiah's original prophecy, the actual speaker is God himself. Isaiah is communicating to unrepentant Israel on behalf of God. But in Jesus' paraphrase, he changes the voice of the verb from the passive "be healed" to the active "I would heal them". In other words, Jesus is using the quote from Isaiah to accomplish *three* objectives:

- *First, to rebuke the Jewish leaders; and,*
- *Second, to show that Isaiah wrote about him; and,*
- *Third, to equate himself with God.*

And it's not like Jesus didn't know what the Hebrew original actually said, like some liberal higher critics contend. Isaiah 6:9-10 is quoted by Jesus, and ***not*** as a paraphrase, in Mark 4:10-12:

[10] *When he was alone with the Twelve and those around him, they began to ask him about the parables.* [11] *He told them, "The secret about the kingdom of God has been given to you. But to those on the outside, everything comes in parables* [12] *so that*
'they may see clearly but not perceive,
and they may hear clearly but not understand,
otherwise they might turn around and be forgiven.'"

Mark 4:10-12

Notice, if you would please, how closely Jesus' citation of Isaiah 9:6-10 adheres to the Hebrew, since on this occasion Jesus isn't emphasizing his divine nature:

Isaiah's original:
"turn back, and be healed."
Jesus' paraphrase:
"and turn around and be forgiven."

The main difference between Jesus' quotation and Jeremiah's Hebrew is that Jesus uses the Aramaic *synonym* for repentance, emphasizing the *effect* of the turning back rather than the action.

Luke's edition of this incident, apparently given on another occasion, cites Isaiah without making any reference to his deity. Luke 8:4-10 presents the larger context of Jesus the Messiah's explanation to his disciples.

> ⁴*Now while a large crowd was gathering and people were coming to Jesus from every city, he said in a parable:*
> ⁵*"A farmer went out to sow his seed. As he was sowing, some seeds fell along the path, were trampled on, and birds from the sky ate them up.* ⁶*Others fell on stony ground, and as soon as they came up, they dried up because they had no moisture.* ⁷*Others fell among thorn bushes, and the thorn bushes grew with them and choked them.* ⁸*But others fell on good soil, and when they came up, they produced 100 times as much as was planted." As he said this, he called out, "Let the person who has ears to hear, listen!"*
> ⁹*Then his disciples began to ask him what this parable meant.* ¹⁰*So he said, "You have been given knowledge about the secrets of the kingdom of God. But to others they are given in parables, so that*
> *'they might look but not see,*
> *and they might listen but not understand.'"*
>
> Luke 8:4-10

ON THE *UNITY* OF ISAIAH'S BOOK: THE APOSTLE JOHN'S VIEW

Many liberal higher critics of Scripture claim that Isaiah wasn't the real author of the book that is attributed to him in the *Tanakh*. These doubters of the claimed authors of the Hebrew Scriptures have posited the existence of at least two different writers. The usual division is that the first author of Isaiah, who is usually called *Proto-Isaiah*, wrote chapters 1-39 of the book, while chapters 40-66 were penned by an unknown writer whom the critics have labeled *Deutero-Isaiah*. Over the years, other scholars have suggested that there were *three* different Isaiahs, not two. The basis upon which these theories of diverse authorship was crafted is the *a priori* assumption that predictive prophecy is *impossible* and that all allegations of these phenomena were *vaticinia ex eventu*, or prophecies created *after the fact* to create the deceptive illusion that biblical prophets such as Isaiah were prognosticators with credibility. There exists, of course, absolutely *no* textual or manuscript evidence for this theory. Neither the Masoretic Text, the Dead Sea Scrolls, nor any extant editions of the Greek language Septuagint demonstrate even the slightest heritage of dual authorship of the book of Isaiah.

Instead, the overwhelming testimony of the New Testament is that all 66 chapters of the book of Isaiah were written by a single author. His name was Isaiah. Notice, if you would please, how the Apostle John in John 12:37-38 describes the ministry and life of Jesus the Messiah as having been fulfilled by and mentioned in the writings of Isaiah:

> [37] *Although he had performed numerous signs in their presence, they did not believe in him,* [38] *so that what the prophet Isaiah spoke might be fulfilled when he said:*
> *"Lord, who has believed our message,*
> *and to whom has the Lord's power been revealed?"*
>
> John 12:37-38

In making these citations, notice how the statement is made from Isaiah 53:1, commonly called by the liberal higher critics "Deutero-Isaiah":

> [1] *"Who has believed our message,*
> *and to whom has the arm of the Lord been revealed?*
> [2] *For he grew up before him like a tender plant,*
> *and like a root out of a dry ground;*
> *he had no form and he had no majesty that we should look at him, and there is no attractiveness that we should desire him.*
>
> Isaiah 53:1-2

Notice also the second statement made by the Apostle John:

>[39] This is why they could not believe: Isaiah also said,
>[40] "He has blinded their eyes
> and hardened their heart,
> so that they might not perceive with their eyes,
> and understand with their mind and turn,
> and I would heal them."
>[41] Isaiah said this when he saw his glory and spoke about him.
>[42] Yet many people, even some of the authorities, believed in him, but because of the Pharisees they did not admit it so they would not be thrown out of the synagogue. [43] For they loved the praise of human beings more than the praise of God.
>
> John 12:39-43

Verse 40 is a direct citation from Isaiah 6:9, which is commonly called by the liberal higher critics "Proto-Isaiah". The writer of this Gospel says that a single Isaiah wrote both chapters of his book. Furthermore, the Apostle John *specifically* claims that Isaiah saw his glory and spoke about him. This incident to which Matthew referred is described only a few verses earlier in Isaiah 6:2-5:

>[1] In the year that King Uzziah died, I saw the Lord sitting upon his throne, high and exalted. The train of his robe filled the Temple. [2] The seraphim stood above him. Each had six wings: with two he covered his face, and with two he covered his feet, and with two he was flying. [3] They kept on calling to each other:
> "Holy, holy, holy is the Lord of the Heavenly Armies!
> The whole earth is full of his glory!"
>[4] The foundations of the thresholds quaked at the sound of those who kept calling out, and the Temple was filled with smoke.
>[5] "How terrible it will be for me!" I cried, "because I am ruined! I'm a man with unclean lips, and I live among a people with unclean lips! And my eyes have seen the King, the Lord of the Heavenly Armies!"
>
> Isaiah 6:1-5

This vision is commonly considered by conservative scholars to be a reference to the pre-Incarnate Jesus the Messiah, seen by Isaiah as he was being called by God to be a prophet to eighth century Israel. To sum up our thoughts regarding the multiple author view of Isaiah, we cite Darren Slade's excellent work, *The Unity and Authorship of Isaiah*:

> ...the literary context of Isaiah does not provide evidence that pseudo-writers compiled the text centuries after the "predicted" events. Likewise, it is apparent that critics take an undue prejudice against predictive prophecy on account of its relevancy to the historical context. Those who deny a single author approach the book with a presupposition regarding Isaiah's geographical location. They do not consider the fact that predictive prophecy can occur outside the context of the prophet's contemporary audience and was used to reveal God's supremacy over other deities.
>
> It can be adequately demonstrated that the book of Isaiah is thoroughly similar in style, word length, literary devices, and vocabulary. Any literary differences are likely the result of a change in topic and theme. More persuasively, however, is that all historical and archaeological evidence confirms the book of Isaiah has been copied and transmitted as a single unit. The critics are left with no physical evidence to support their claims. They rely purely on historical conjecture and assumption based on selective differences in literary style without any real proof for their claims. Therefore, the traditional view that Isaiah was written by a single author in the eighth century should still be maintained.

Arguably the most elegant and beautifully composed prophetic writings of the entire Bible, this book that Jesus quotes so authoritatively derives its name from its primary author and prophet whose materials are recorded in it. Many see this book as naturally divided into two sections. The longer section (chapters 1-39) may be studied in six parts:

1. God's Complaint against His People (1:1-31)
2. A Rebuke for Trusting in Human Resources apart from God (2:1-12:6)
3. God's Sovereignty over the Nations (13:1-23:18)
4. Exhortations to Trust God's Rule (24:1-27:13)
5. The Certain Defeat of the Enemies of God's People (28:1-35:10)
6. A record of certain events in the life of Hezekiah (36:1-39)

The book's shorter section (chapters 40-66) may be studied in three parts:

1. God's Dealings with Cyrus (40:1-48:22)
2. The Suffering Servant (49:1-57:21)
3. Prophecies of Future Glory (58:1-66:24)

Rabbinic and early church tradition assign authorship to the prophet Isaiah. The distinct differences in literary style between these two major sections described above, coupled with Isaiah's supernatural prediction (made ca. 710 BC) about King Cyrus of Persia (cf. 44:28-45:6), whom the prophet identified by name about 150 years before he was born, has led some modern critics to suggest that chapters 40-66 of the book were composed (or, at the very least, edited) by a different individual who lived at a later time.

However, conservative scholars suggest that the stylistic variances are explained by differences in purpose and target audience and that Isaiah's forecast about of the coming of Cyrus was a genuine, supernatural prediction. The Gospel of Matthew attributes its citations from the two allegedly different sections Isaiah 9:1-2 (cf. Matthew 4:16) and Isaiah 40:3 (cf. Matthew 3:3) as having been written by Isaiah himself without attributing the quotations to different authors, as does the Gospel of John's citations from Isaiah 6:9-10 (cf. John 12:40) and Isaiah 53:1 (cf. John 12:38).

Isaiah's prophecies touch upon the administrations of Jotham, Ahaz, and Hezekiah over a period of about 60 years, during the ascendency of the Assyrian empire and predicting both its demise and also the rise of the Chaldeans and Persians as successors. He also served as a historiographer of King Uzziah "from first to last" (2 Chronicles 26:22), though Isaiah 6:1 records that his prophetic ministry began the same year in which Uzziah died (i.e., ca. 739 BC). He appears to have been martyred early in the reign of the wicked King Manasseh. Some see an allusion to Isaiah's martyrdom in Heb. 11:37.

At any rate, the last dated event in the book of Isaiah was the fourteenth year of Hezekiah (ca. 701 BC). The Assyrian King Esarhaddon (ca. 681–669 BC) is mentioned in Isaiah 37:38.

EVIDENCE OF THE UNITY OF ISAIAH FROM NEW TESTAMENT QUOTATIONS

That Jesus believed the entire collection of 66 chapters that comprise this work were written by a single author—Isaiah himself—is evident by examining all 21 citations from the book.

NEW TESTAMENT QUOTES FROM ISAIAH 1-39

1. MATTHEW 4:14 CITES ISAIAH 9:1-2

In Matthew 4:12-14, the writer cites Isaiah 9:1-2 as evidence of Jesus' qualifications to serve as the Messiah:

> ¹²*Now when Jesus heard that John had been arrested, he went back to Galilee.* ¹³*He left Nazareth and settled in Capernaum by the sea, in the regions of Zebulun and Naphtali,* ¹⁴*in order to fulfill what was declared by the prophet Isaiah when he said,*
> ¹⁵*"O Land of Zebulun and Land of Naphtali,*
> *on the road to the sea, across the Jordan,*
> *Galilee of the unbelievers!*
> ¹⁶*The people living in darkness have seen a great light,*
> *and for those living in the land and shadow of death,*
> *a light has risen."*
>
> Matthew 4:12-14

Here's how the citation is rendered in the *Holy Bible: International Standard Version,* which was made from the Great Isaiah Scroll found in Qumran Cave 1 of the Dead Sea Scrolls:[2]

> [1] But there will be no gloom for her who was in distress.
> Formerly, he brought contempt to the region of Zebulun and
> the region of Naphtali, but in the future he will have made
> glorious the way of the sea, the territory beyond the Jordan—
> Galilee of the nations.
> [2] The people who walked in darkness
> have seen a great light;
> for those living in a land of deep darkness,
> a light has shined upon them.
>
> Isaiah 9:1-2

2. MATTHEW 13:14-15, JOHN 12:39-41, AND ACTS 28:25-27 CITE ISAIAH 6:9-10

In Matthew 13:14-15, Jesus cites Isaiah 6:9-10 to bolster his condemnation of the religious leaders of first century Israel:

> [14] "With them the prophecy of Isaiah is being fulfilled,
> which says:
> 'You will listen and listen but never understand.
> You will look and look but never comprehend,
> [15] for this people's heart has become dull,
> and their ears are hard of hearing.
> They have shut their eyes
> so that they might not see with their eyes,
> and hear with their ears,
> and understand with their heart and turn,
> and I would heal them.'
>
> Matthew 13:14-15

---

[2] This ancient scroll dates from about the second century, BC. The two oldest surviving Masoretic Text editions of the Hebrew Scriptures date from about 900-1000 AD.

John 12:39-41 also cite the text of Isaiah 6:9:

³⁷*Although he had performed numerous signs in their presence, they did not believe in him,* ³⁸*so that what the prophet Isaiah spoke might be fulfilled when he said:*
"Lord, who has believed our message,
and to whom has the Lord's power been revealed?"
³⁹*This is why they could not believe: Isaiah also said,*
⁴⁰*"He has blinded their eyes*
and hardened their heart,
so that they might not perceive with their eyes,
and understand with their mind and turn,
and I would heal them."
⁴¹*Isaiah said this when he saw his glory and spoke about him.*

John 12:37-41

In Acts 28:25-27, the Apostle Paul cites Isaiah 6:9:

²⁵*...Paul added this statement: "The Holy Spirit was so right when he spoke to your ancestors through the prophet Isaiah!* ²⁶*He said,*
'Go to this people and say,
"You will listen and listen
but never understand,
and you will look and look
but never see!
²⁷*For this people's minds have become stupid,*
and their ears can barely hear,
and they have shut their eyes
so that they may never see with their eyes,
and listen with their ears,
and understand with their heart
and turn and let me heal them."'

Acts 28:25b-27

The original source text recorded in Isaiah 6:9-10 reads as follows:

⁹ᵇKeep on hearing, but do not understand;
keep on seeing, but do not perceive.
¹⁰Dull the mind of this people,
deafen their ears,
and blind their eyes.
By doing so, they won't see with their eyes,
hear with their ears,
understand with their minds,
turn back,
and be healed.

Isaiah 6:9b-10

3. MATTHEW 15:7 AND MARK 7:6-7 CITE ISAIAH 29:13

In Matthew 15:7, Jesus cites Isaiah 29:13 during his rebuke of the religious leaders of first century Israel for their religious hypocrisy:

⁷You hypocrites! How well did Isaiah prophesy of you when he said,
⁸'These people honor me with their lips,
but their hearts are far from me.
⁹Their worship of me is empty,
because they teach human rules as doctrines.'"

Matthew 15:7-9

In Mark 7:6-7, Jesus is once again quoted as citing Isaiah 29:13 during his rebuke of the religious leaders of first century Israel for their religious hypocrisy:

⁶He told them, "Isaiah was right when he prophesied about you hypocrites. As it is written,
'These people honor me with their lips,
but their hearts are far from me.
⁷Their worship of me is worthless,
because they teach human rules as doctrines.'

The text of Isaiah 29:13 reads as follows in the ISV:

> [13] *Then the Lord said:*
> *"Because these people draw near with their mouths*
> *and honor me with their lips,*
> *but their hearts are far from me,*
> *worship of me has become*
> *merely like rules taught by human beings.*
>
> Mark 7:6-7

4. ROMANS 9:29 CITE ISAIAH 1:9

In Romans 9:29, the Apostle Paul cites Isaiah 1:9:

> [29] *It is just as Isaiah predicted:*
> *"If the Lord of the Heavenly Armies*
> *had not left us some descendants,*
> *we would have become like Sodom*
> *and would have been compared to Gomorrah."*
>
> Romans 9:29

The source of Paul's citation from Isaiah 1:9 reads:

> [9] *If the LORD of the Heavenly Armies*
> *hadn't left us a few survivors,*
> *we would be like Sodom;*
> *we would be like Gomorrah.*
>
> Isaiah 1:9

5. ROMANS 15:12 CITES ISAIAH 11:10

In Romans 15:12, the Apostle Paul cites Isaiah 11:10:

> [12] *And again, Isaiah says,*
> *"There will be a Root from Jesse.*
> *He will rise up to rule the gentiles,*
> *and the gentiles will hope in him."*
>
> Romans 15:12

In doing so, he attributes authorship of the so-called "Proto-Isaiah" to the man Isaiah himself. The original passage in Isaiah 11:10 reads in the ISV:

¹⁰At that time, as to the root of Jesse, who will be standing as a banner for the peoples, the nations will rally to him, and his resting place is glorious.

Isaiah 11:10

Notice, if you would please, the clear evidence observable when comparing these two citations that Paul utilized a *Targum* method of creating a Greek language rendering of the Hebrew language text as recorded in the Great Isaiah Scroll from which the ISV translated the book of Isaiah.

New Testament quotes from Isaiah 40-60

1. Matthew 3:3, Luke 3:4, and John 1:23 cites Isaiah 40:3-5

In Matthew 3:3, John the Baptizer cites Isaiah 40:3 as having been fulfilled by the ministry and life of Jesus the Messiah:

He is a voice calling out in the wilderness:
'Prepare the way for the Lord!
Make his paths straight!'"

Matthew 3:3b

In Luke 3:4, the writer Luke cites this passage as well, speaking of both John the Baptizer and Jesus the Messiah:

³John went throughout the entire Jordan region, proclaiming a baptism about repentance for the forgiveness of sins, ⁴as it is written in the book of the words of the prophet Isaiah,
"He is a voice calling out in the wilderness:
'Prepare the way for the Lord! Make his paths straight!
⁵Every valley will be filled,
and every mountain and hill will be leveled.
The crooked ways will be made straight,

and the rough roads will be made smooth.
⁶Everyone will see the salvation
that God has provided."'

Luke 3:4-6

John 1:23 repeats these words by John the Baptizer:

²³He replied, "I am
'...a voice crying out in the wilderness,
*"Prepare the L*ORD*'s highway,"'*
as the prophet Isaiah said."

John 1:23

The full, original context of this passage from the so-called "Deutero-Isaiah" reads in the ISV (citing the Great Isaiah Scroll) as follows:

³A voice cries out:
*'In the wilderness prepare the way for the L*ORD*;*
and in the desert a straight highway for our God.'
⁴Every valley will be lifted up,
and every mountain and hill will be lowered;
the rough ground will become level,
and the mountain ridges made a plain.
*⁵Then the glory of the L*ORD *will be revealed,*
and all humanity will see it at once;
for the mouth of the Lord has spoken."

Isaiah 40:3-5

Notice, if you would please, how the original context of John the Baptizer's quote from the book of Isaiah is the prophet's description of the public manifestation of the direct, visible presence of the glory of the Creator God who has come to visit his people. Isaiah's original prophecy continuing through verse five is not cited by John the Baptizer, however. Fulfillment of that prophecy will not take place until the Second Coming, which Jesus predicted would be visible to the entire world, all at the same time.

2. Matthew 8:16-17, John 12:37-38, Acts 8:28-30, and Romans 10:16 cite Isaiah 53:1-17

In Matthew 8:16-17, Matthew cites Isaiah 53:4 as being fulfilled in the healing ministry of Jesus the Messiah:

> [16]…He drove out the spirits by speaking a command and healed everyone who was sick. [17] This was to fulfill what was declared by the prophet Isaiah when he said,
> "It was he who took our illnesses away
> and removed our diseases."
>
> Matthew 8:16b-17

In John 12:37-38, Jesus cites Isaiah 53:1 during his rebuke of the religious leaders of first century Israel for their religious hypocrisy:

> [37]Although he had performed numerous signs in their presence, they did not believe in him, [38]so that what the prophet Isaiah spoke might be fulfilled when he said:
> "Lord, who has believed our message,
> and to whom has the Lord's power been revealed?"
>
> John 12:37-38

Acts 8:27-35 records the instance of the Ethiopian eunuch's visit to Jerusalem and what happened to him during his journey back to Ethiopia:

> [27]Now there was an Ethiopian eunuch, who was a member of the court of Candace, queen of the Ethiopians. He was in charge of all her treasures and had come up to Jerusalem to worship. [28]Now he was returning home, seated in his chariot, and reading from the prophet Isaiah.
> [29]The Spirit told Philip, "Approach that chariot and stay near it." [30]So Philip ran up to it and heard him reading the prophet Isaiah out loud.
> Philip asked, "Do you understand what you're reading?"
> [31]The man replied, "How can I unless someone guides me?" So he invited Philip to get in and sit with him. [32]This was the

> *passage of Scripture he was reading:*
> *"Like a sheep he was led away to be slaughtered,*
> *and like a lamb is silent before its shearer,*
> *so he does not open his mouth.*
> *³³ In his humiliation, justice was denied him.*
> *Who can describe his descendants?*
> *For his life is taken away from the earth."*
> *³⁴ The eunuch asked Philip, "I ask you, who is the prophet talking about? Himself? Or someone else?" ³⁵ Then Philip began to speak, and, starting from this Scripture, he told him the good news about Jesus.*
>
> Acts 8:27-35

Romans 10:15-17 records the tendency of non-believes to remain opposed to their own salvation when he cites a portion of this passage from Isaiah:

> *¹⁵ And how can people preach unless they are sent? As it is written, "How beautiful are those who bring the good news!" ¹⁶ But not everyone has obeyed the gospel, for Isaiah asks, "Lord, who has believed our message?" ¹⁷ Consequently, faith results from listening, and listening results through the word of the Messiah.*
>
> Romans 10:15-17

The original context of Isaiah's prophecy is a lengthy poetic description of the Suffering Servant in Isaiah 52-53. The immediate context is Isaiah 53:3-4:

> *¹ "Who has believed our message,*
> *and to whom has the arm of the* LORD *been revealed?*
> *² For he grew up before him like a tender plant,*
> *and like a root out of a dry ground;*
> *he had no form and he had no majesty that we should look at him,*
> *and there is no attractiveness that we should desire him.*
> *³ "He was despised and rejected by others,*

and a man of sorrows,
intimately familiar with suffering;
and like one from whom people hide their faces;
and we despised him
and did not value him.
⁴ "Surely he has borne our sufferings
and carried our sorrows;
yet we considered him stricken,
and struck down by God,
and afflicted.
⁵ But he was wounded for our transgressions,
and he was crushed for our iniquities,
and the punishment that made us whole was upon him,
and by his bruises we are healed.
⁶ All we like sheep have gone astray,
we have turned, each of us, to his own way;
and the LORD has laid on him
the iniquity of us all.
⁷ He was oppressed and he was afflicted,
yet he didn't open his mouth;
like a lamb that is led to the slaughter,
as a sheep that before its shearers is silent,
so he did not open his mouth.
⁸ "From detention and judgment he was taken away—
and who can even think about his descendants?
For he was cut off from the land of the living,
he was stricken for the transgression of my people.
⁹ Then they made his grave with the wicked,
and with rich people in his death,
although he had committed no violence,
nor was there any deceit in his mouth."
¹⁰ "Yet the Lord was willing to crush him,
and he made him suffer.
Although you make his soul an offering for sin,
he will see his offspring,

and he will prolong his days,
and the will of the Lord will triumph in his hand.
[11] Out of the suffering of his soul he will see light
and find satisfaction.
And through his knowledge his servant, the righteous one,
will make many righteous,
and he will bear their iniquities.
[12] Therefore I will allot him a portion with the great,
and he will divide the spoils with the strong;
because he poured out his life to death,
and was numbered with the transgressors;
yet he carried the sins of many,
and made intercession for their transgressions."

Isaiah 53:1-12

3. Matthew 12:17 cites Isaiah 42:1-3

In Matthew 12:15-21, Jesus is described by Matthew, the writer of this Gospel, as fulfilling Isaiah 42:1-3 with respect to his ministry:

[15b] Many crowds followed him, and he healed all of them,
[16] ordering them not to make him known. [17] This was to fulfill
what was declared by the prophet Isaiah when he said,
[18] "Here is my Servant whom I have chosen,
whom I love, and with whom I am pleased!
I will put my Spirit on him,
and he will proclaim justice to unbelievers.
[19] He will not quarrel or shout,
and no one will hear him shouting in the streets.
[0] He will not snap off a broken reed
or snuff out a smoldering wick
until he has brought justice through to victory.
[21] And in his name unbelievers will hope."

Matthew 12:15b-21

The original context of Isaiah 42:1-4 discusses the unstoppable victory of God's Servant:

> [1] *"Here is my servant, whom I support,*
> *my chosen one, in whom I delight.*
> *I've placed my Spirit upon him;*
> *and he'll deliver his justice throughout the world.*
> [2] *He won't shout,*
> *or raise his voice,*
> *or make it heard in the street.*
> [3] *A crushed reed he will not break,*
> *and a fading candle he won't snuff out.*
> *He'll bring forth justice for the truth.*
> [4] *And he won't grow faint or be crushed*
> *until he establishes justice on the mainland,*
> *and the coastlands take ownership of his Law."*
>
> Isaiah 42:1-4

4. Luke 4:16-20 cites Isaiah 61:1, 2

In Luke 4:16-20, Luke writes about an incident that occurred one Sabbath day in a synagogue located in his own home town of Nazareth. Jesus cites Isaiah 61:1-2:

> [16] *Then Jesus came to Nazareth, where he had been raised. As was his custom, he went into the synagogue on the Sabbath day. When he stood up to read,* [17] *the scroll of the prophet Isaiah was handed to him. Unrolling the scroll, he found the place where it was written,*
> [18] *"The Spirit of the Lord is upon me;*
> *he has anointed me to tell*
> *the good news to the poor.*
> *He has sent me to announce release to the prisoners*
> *and recovery of sight to the blind,*
> *to set oppressed people free,*
> [19] *and to announce the year of the Lord's favor."*

²⁰ *Then he rolled up the scroll, gave it back to the attendant, and sat down.*

Luke 4:16-20

The original context of Isaiah 62:1-3 discusses the proclamation of the day of salvation by God's Servant, the Messiah:

¹ *"The Spirit of the Lord is upon me,*
　because the Lord has anointed me;
he has sent me to bring good news to the oppressed
　and to bind up the brokenhearted,
to proclaim freedom for the captives,
　and release from darkness for the prisoners;
² *to proclaim the year of the Lord's favor,*
　the day of vengeance of our God;
to comfort all who mourn;…"

Isaiah 62:1-3

5. Romans 10:20 cites Isaiah 65:1-3

In Romans 10:20, Isaiah 65:1-3 is cited by the Apostle Paul in his rebuke of the religious leaders of first century Israel willful failure to accept Jesus as their rightful Messiah:

²⁰ *And Isaiah boldly says,*
"I was found by those who were not looking for me;
I was revealed to those who were not asking for me."

Romans 10:20

The context of Isaiah's prophecy that is being quoted is a prediction that God will extend his grace to non-Jews:

¹ *"I let myself be sought by those who didn't ask for me;*
I let myself be found by those who didn't seek me.
I said, 'Here I am! Here I am!'
to a nation that didn't call on my name.
² *I held out my hands all day long*
to a disobedient people,

> *who walk in a way that isn't good,*
> *following their own inclinations—*
> *³a people who continually provoke me to my face;*
>
> Isaiah 65:1-3

In addition to the direct citations from the book of Isaiah in the Gospels, Acts, and Romans, of the 27 books that make up the corpus of the text of the New Testament, allusions to the book of Isaiah can be found in all of them except for seven. All of these allusions assume that Isaiah's book is a single united work penned by a single individual. As E.W. Bullinger observes:

> *The eighty-five citations or allusions are distributed as follows: In Matthew there are nine; Mark, six; Luke, five; John, five; Acts, five; Romans, eighteen (eight from the "former" part, and ten from the "latter"); 1 Corinthians, six; 2 Corinthians, four; Galatians, one; Ephesians, two; Philippians, one; 1 Thessalonians, one; 2 Thessalonians, one; Hebrews, two; James, one; 1 Peter, five; 2 Peter, one; Revelation, twelve (five from the "former" part, and seven from the "latter").*
>
> *Twelve books give six direct quotations.*
>
> *Eighteen books contain eighty-five allusions to Isaiah.*
>
> *Only seven books out of twenty-seven have none.*
>
> *The greater part of the New Testament is concerned with establishing the genuineness and authority of the book of the prophet Isaiah, and its one authorship.*[3]

CLAIM #46: JESUS CITES ISAIAH THE PROPHET TO LINK THE APOSTASY OF HIS GENERATION TO ISAIAH'S MENTION OF HIM.

Jesus of Nazareth cited the authority of the book of Isaiah in one of his rebukes to the Pharisees in Matthew 15:7-9:

---

3 Cited from http://therain.org/appendixes/app80.html.

⁷You hypocrites! How well did Isaiah prophesy of you when he said,
⁸'These people honor me with their lips,
but their hearts are far from me.
⁹Their worship of me is empty,
because they teach human rules as doctrines.'"

Matthew 15:7-9

CLAIM #47: JESUS LINKS THE AUTHORITY OF THE PROPHETS ISAIAH AND JOEL AS PREDICTIONS RELATING TO HIS SECOND COMING.

Jesus of Nazareth also cited the authority of the book of Isaiah and the book of Joel in his Olivet Discourse regarding the end of the age. Matthew 24:29, Mark 13:24-25 record his statement where he quotes Isaiah 13:10, 34:4, and Joel 2:10:

²⁹"Now immediately after the troubles of those days,
'The sun will be darkened,
the moon will not reflect its light,
the stars will fall from the sky,
and the powers from the heavens will be disrupted.'

Matthew 24:29

²⁴"But after the troubles of those days,
'The sun will be darkened,
the moon will not reflect its light,
²⁵the stars will be falling out of the sky,
and the powers that are in the heavens will be disrupted.'

Mark 13:24-25

CLAIM #48: JESUS CITES THE PROPHET ISAIAH AS APPLYING TO THE REJECTION BY ISRAEL'S FIRST CENTURY LEADERS IN THEIR REJECTION OF THE RIGHTEOUS REQUIREMENTS OF THE LAW IN DEFERENCE TO THEIR ORAL TRADITIONS.

We've already noted earlier in this work how Jesus of Nazareth cited the authority of the book of Isaiah in referring to himself as the

Messiah of Israel. But he also cited the book of Isaiah in reference to the hypocritical leaders of Israel. Mark 7:5-8 records a rebuke to the Pharisees and the scribes regarding how their actions fulfill Isaiah 29:13:

> ⁵So the Pharisees and the scribes asked Jesus, "Why don't your disciples live according to the tradition of the elders? Instead, they eat with unclean hands."
> ⁶He told them, "Isaiah was right when he prophesied about you hypocrites. As it is written,
> 'These people honor me with their lips,
> but their hearts are far from me.
> ⁷Their worship of me is worthless,
> because they teach human rules as doctrines.'
> ⁸You abandon the commandment of God and hold to human tradition."
>
> Mark 7:5-8

The larger context of Isaiah's prophecy that is being quoted by Jesus the Messiah is God's rebuke to the hypocrites of eighth century BC Israel. Isaiah 29:13-21 reads like this:

> ¹³Then the LORD said:
> "Because these people draw near with their mouths
> and honor me with their lips,
> but their hearts are far from me,
> worship of me has become
> merely like rules taught by human beings.
> ¹⁴Therefore, watch out!
> "As for me, I will once again
> do amazing things with this people,
> wonder upon wonder.
> The wisdom of their wise men will perish,
> and the insights of their discerning men will stay hidden."
> ¹⁵"How terrible it will be for you who go to great depths
> to hide your plans from the Lord,
> you whose deeds have been done in the dark,

and who say, 'Who can see us?
Who has recognized us?'
¹⁶ *He has turned the tables on you—*
as if the potter were thought to be like heat.
Can what is made say of the one who made it,
'He did not make me?'
Or can what is formed say of the ones who formed it,
'He has no skill?'
¹⁷ *"In a very little while,*
will not Lebanon be turned into a garden of fruit,
and the garden of fruit seem like a forest?
¹⁸ *On that day the deaf will hear*
the words of a scroll,
and out of gloom and darkness
the eyes of the blind will see.
¹⁹ *The humble will again experience joy in the Lord,*
and the poorest people will rejoice in the Holy One of Israel.
²⁰ *For the ruthless will vanish,*
and mockers will disappear,
and all who have an eye for evil will be cut down—
²¹ *those who make a person appear to be the offender*
in a lawsuit,
who set a trap for someone
who is making his defense in court,
and push aside the innocent
with specious arguments.

                                                          Isaiah 29:13-21

CLAIM #49: **JESUS CITES THE AUTHORITY OF THE PROPHET ISAIAH TO EXPLAIN THE NECESSITY OF ALL PROPHECIES WRITTEN ABOUT HIM IN THE HEBREW SCRIPTURES BEING FULFILLED.**

Isaiah 53:12 contains a prophecy about how Messiah will be numbered among criminals and condemned. In writing about how Jesus reminded his disciples about the necessity of the biblical prophecies being fulfilled in his life, the Apostle Luke records the following warning to his followers in Luke 22:36:

> ³⁶ *Then he told them, "But now whoever has a wallet must take it along, and his traveling bag, too. And the one who has no sword must sell his coat and buy one.* ³⁷ *Because I tell you, what has been written about me must be fulfilled: 'He was counted among the criminals.' Indeed, what is written about me must be fulfilled."*
>
> Luke 22:36

The larger context of Isaiah 53:12 is the famous prediction by Isaiah of the Suffering Servant, who dies on behalf of his people. In describing the reward obtained by the Messiah from God the Father for accomplishing the redemption of his people, Isaiah 53:12 proclaims:

> ¹² *Therefore I will allot him a portion with the great,*
> *and he will divide the spoils with the strong;*
> *because he poured out his life to death,*
> *and was numbered with the transgressors;*
> *yet he carried the sins of many,*
> *and made intercession for their transgressions.*
>
> Isaiah 53:12

CLAIM #50: JESUS CITES THE AUTHORITY OF THE PROPHET ISAIAH TO EXPLAIN WHAT LIFE WILL BE LIKE UNDER HIS REIGN DURING HIS MILLENNIAL KINGDOM.

Isaiah 54:13 contains a prophecy about how Messiah will be numbered among criminals and condemned. In writing about how Jesus reminded his disciples about the necessity of the biblical prophecies being fulfilled in his life, the Apostle Luke records the following warning to his followers in John 6:44-45:

> ⁴⁴ *No one can come to me unless the Father who sent me draws him, and I will raise him to life on the last day.* ⁴⁵ *It is written in the Prophets, 'And all of them will be taught by God.'*
>
> John 6:44-45

Jesus and the Biblical Prophets

This remarkable claim by Jesus the Messiah contains the startling promise by him that everyone who trusts in him will be raised to life on the last day. As proof of the reality of this promise, and the certainty of it coming to pass, Jesus cites a verse from Isaiah 54:10-14:

¹⁰ For the mountains may collapse
and the hills may reel,
but my gracious love will not depart from you,
neither will my covenant of peace totter,"
says the LORD, *who has compassion on you.*
¹¹ "O afflicted one, passed back and forth, and not comforted,
Look! I am about to set your stones in antimony,
and lay your foundations with sapphires.
¹² And I'll make your battlements of rubies,
and your gates of jewels,
and all your walls of precious stones.
¹³ Then all your children will be taught by the LORD,
and great will be your children's prosperity.
¹⁴ "In righteousness you'll be established;
you will be far from tyranny,
for you won't be afraid,
and from terror,
for it won't come near you.

Isaiah 54:10-14

CLAIM #51: JESUS CITES THE AUTHORITY OF THE PROPHETS ISAIAH AND JEREMIAH TO EXPLAIN WHY HE EXPELLED MERCHANTS FROM THE TEMPLE.

The Synoptic Gospels (the books of Matthew, Mark, and Luke) contain a record of an incident late in Jesus' ministry during which he expelled various merchants and their customers from the grounds of the Temple in Jerusalem. Here are their records, which demonstrate how Jesus used the authority of Isaiah and Jeremiah to explain why he did this:

15 When they came to Jerusalem, he went into the Temple and began to throw out those who were selling and those who were buying in the Temple. He overturned the moneychangers' tables and the chairs of those who sold doves. 16 He wouldn't even let anyone carry a vessel through the Temple. 17 Then he began to teach them: "It is written, is it not, 'My house is to be called a house of prayer for all nations'? But you've turned it into a hideout for bandits!"

Mark 11:15-17

12 Then Jesus went into the Temple, threw out everyone who was selling and buying in the Temple, and overturned the moneychangers' tables and the chairs of those who sold doves. 13 He told them, "It is written, 'My house is to be called a house of prayer,' but you are turning it into a hideout for bandits!"

Matthew 21:12-13

45 Then Jesus went into the Temple and began to throw out those who were selling things. 46 He told them, "It is written, 'My house is to be called a house of prayer,' but you have turned it into a hideout for bandits!"

Luke 19:45-46

Each of these three accounts cite the authority of Isaiah 56:7 and Jeremiah 7:11. Jesus' quotation that "My house is to be called a house of prayer" is a direct allusion to Isaiah 56:7, the larger context of which reads:

> *6 "Also, the foreigners who join themselves to the* LORD,
> *to minister to him,*
> *to love the name of the Lord,*
> *to be his servants,*
> *and to bless the* LORD'*s name,*
> *observing the Sabbath without profaning it,*
> *and who hold fast my covenant—*

⁷these I will bring to my holy mountain,
and make them joyful in my house of prayer.
Their burnt-offerings and their sacrifices
will rise up to be accepted on my altar;
for my house will be called a house of prayer
for everyone."

Isaiah 56:6-7

By citing this verse from Isaiah, Jesus is citing a section of the prophecies of Isaiah that deal with the future inclusion into Israel's covenant with God of the *Gentiles*. Furthermore, one of the more subtle implications of this citation from Isaiah 56 is that it is the LORD himself who is speaking as the covenant God of Israel to his stubborn nation in the eighth century, BC. Yet in this citation of the verse, Jesus is unmistakably identifying himself as being that God.

Jesus' citation of Jeremiah 7:11 as the basis for his authority and reason for expelling the merchants and their customers from the Temple is the more ominous of the two quotes that he makes from the Hebrew Scriptures. By reading the larger context of Jeremiah 7:11, which is Jeremiah 7:8-15, you can see why this is so:

⁸"Look, you're trusting in deceptive words that cannot benefit. ⁹Will you steal, murder, commit adultery, swear by false gods, burn incense to Baal, follow other gods that you don't know, ¹⁰and then come to stand before me in this house that is called by my name and say, 'We're delivered' so we can continue to do all these things that are repugnant to God? ¹¹Has this house that is called by my name become a hideout for bandits in your eyes? Look, I'm watching," declares the LORD.
¹²"Go to my place that was in Shiloh, where I first caused my name to dwell. See what I did to it because of the evil of my people Israel. ¹³Now, because you have done all these things," declares the LORD, *"I spoke to you over and over again, but you didn't listen. I called to you, but you didn't answer. ¹⁴Just as I did to Shiloh, I'll do to the house in which you trust and*

which is called by my name, the place that I gave to you and your ancestors. ¹⁵I'll cast you out of my sight, just as I cast out all your brothers, all the descendants of Ephraim.

Jeremiah 7:8-15

The immediate context of Jeremiah 7:11, which Jesus quotes *word for word* from the Hebrew text, is a threat to destroy the Temple in Jerusalem. "Just as I did to Shiloh, I'll do to the house in which you trust and which is called by my name." As a point of historical fact, as we noted in our section entitled *The Destruction of Jerusalem* on page 121, above, the same generation that witnessed the death of Jesus also witnessed the destruction of the Temple and the city of Jerusalem under Roman General Titus Vespasian in 70 AD.

John's Gospel contains a record of an earlier similar incident that occurred a few years earlier, right at the beginning of Jesus the Messiah's ministry:

¹³The Jewish Passover was near, and Jesus went up to Jerusalem. ¹⁴In the Temple he found people selling cattle, sheep, and doves, as well as moneychangers sitting at their tables. ¹⁵After making a whip out of cords, he drove all of them out of the Temple, including the sheep and the cattle. He scattered the coins of the moneychangers and knocked over their tables.
¹⁶Then he told those who were selling the doves, "Take these things out of here! Stop making my Father's house a marketplace!" ¹⁷His disciples remembered that it was written, "Zeal for your house will consume me."

John 2:13-17

This incident from the early ministry of Jesus does not, strictly speaking, record him as citing Psalm 69:9 as explaining what motivated him to clear the Temple of merchants, their merchandize, and their customers. But it does record the disciples as understanding why he did the expelling.

Jesus and the Biblical Prophets

Claim #52: Jesus quoted the work of the prophet Isaiah, proclaiming to his generation that he was the fulfillment of Isaiah 58:6 and 61:1-2.

The Synoptic Gospels each contain a record of an incident when Jesus the Messiah returned to his home town of Nazareth where he had grown up following his family's return from Egypt. The New Testament record is clear that he was rejected in his hometown by those who heard him. Here is how Matthew and Mark record the incident:

⁵³When Jesus had finished these parables, he left that place. ⁵⁴He went to his hometown and began teaching the people in their synagogue in such a way that they were amazed and asked, "Where did this man get this wisdom and these miracles? ⁵⁵This is the builder's son, isn't it? His mother is named Mary, isn't she? His brothers are James, Joseph, Simon, and Judas, aren't they? ⁵⁶And his sisters are all with us, aren't they? So where did this man get all these things?" ⁵⁷And they were offended by him.
But Jesus told them, "A prophet is without honor only in his hometown and in his own home." ⁵⁸He did not perform many miracles there because of their unbelief.

Matthew 13:53-58

¹Jesus left that place and went back to his hometown, and his disciples followed him. ²When the Sabbath came, he began to teach in the synagogue, and many who heard him were utterly amazed. "Where did this man get all these things?" they asked. "What is this wisdom that has been given to him? What great miracles are being done by his hands! ³This is the builder, the son of Mary, and the brother of James, Joseph, Judas, and Simon, isn't it? His sisters are here with us, aren't they?" And they were offended by him.
⁴Jesus had been telling them, "A prophet is without honor only in his hometown, among his relatives, and in his own home."

> ⁵*He couldn't perform a miracle there except to lay his hands on a few sick people and heal them. ⁶He was amazed at their unbelief. Then he went around to the villages and continued teaching.*
>
> Mark 6:1-6

We invite you to notice, however, that neither Matthew's nor Mark's rendition of this event give the reader even the slightest hint as to *why* Jesus was rejected by them. We're only told *that* he was rejected, and we're told in Mark's version (at verse 6) that Jesus was surprised by their unbelief. We don't find out the reason why he was rejected in his hometown until we read through Luke's edition of the incident. This inclusion of the reasons for the Messiah's rejection is to be expected, given how Luke's focus in his writings is on the relationship people had with Jesus and the reactions they had to him. You'll find his record of the encounter at Nazareth in Luke 4:16-21:

> ¹⁶*Then Jesus came to Nazareth, where he had been raised. As was his custom, he went into the synagogue on the Sabbath day. When he stood up to read, ¹⁷the scroll of the prophet Isaiah was handed to him. Unrolling the scroll, he found the place where it was written,*
> ¹⁸*"The Spirit of the Lord is upon me;*
> *he has anointed me to tell*
> *the good news to the poor.*
> *He has sent me to announce release to the prisoners*
> *and recovery of sight to the blind,*
> *to set oppressed people free,*
> ¹⁹*and to announce the year of the Lord's favor."*
> ²⁰*Then he rolled up the scroll, gave it back to the attendant, and sat down. While the eyes of everyone in the synagogue were fixed on him, ²¹he began to say to them, "Today this Scripture has been fulfilled, as you've heard it read aloud."*
> ²²*All the people began to speak well of him and to wonder at the gracious words that flowed from his mouth. They said, "This is Joseph's son, isn't it?"*

Jesus and the Biblical Prophets

²³ So he told them, "You will probably quote this proverb to me, 'Doctor, heal yourself! Do everything here in your hometown that we hear you did in Capernaum.'"
²⁴ He added, "I tell all of you with certainty, a prophet is not accepted in his hometown. ²⁵ I'm telling you the truth—there were many widows in Israel in Elijah's time, when it didn't rain for three years and six months and there was a severe famine everywhere in the land. ²⁶ Yet Elijah wasn't sent to a single one of those widows except to one at Zarephath in Sidon. ²⁷ There were also many lepers in Israel in the prophet Elisha's time, yet not one of them was cleansed except Naaman the Syrian."
²⁸ All the people in the synagogue became furious when they heard this. ²⁹ They got up, forced Jesus out of the city, and led him to the edge of the hill on which their city was built, intending to throw him off. ³⁰ But he walked right through the middle of them and went away.

Luke 4:16-30

CLAIM #53: JESUS' MATTER-OF-FACT MENTION OF DANIEL THE PROPHET AND HIS QUOTE FROM HIS BOOK DEMONSTRATED THAT HE TOOK IT FOR GRANTED THAT DANIEL HAD BEEN A REAL PERSON AND THAT HIS BOOK WAS AUTHORITATIVE.

The book of Daniel is a favorite of the liberal higher critics. So striking are its prophecies of the coming centuries after Daniel's time that the enemies of conservative biblical truth naturally *assumed* that no one has the ability to predict the future. Therefore the majority of Daniel's work not only had to have been written after the man died, but the book had to have been composed centuries later, perhaps about the mid-second century, BC. Of course, the higher critics didn't consider that there is not a *shred of textual evidence* that the book of Daniel was written after the time of Daniel. Furthermore, we have the testimony of Jesus the Messiah as to who wrote the prophetic book that bears his name: Daniel. Notice, if you would please, how Jesus assumes that Daniel was a historic figure, taking it for granted that the man lived just as the Hebrew Scriptures testify that he did. Consider, for example, the following citations from Daniel's writings:

> [15] *"So when you see the destructive desecration, mentioned by the prophet Daniel, standing in the Holy Place (let the reader take note),* [16] *then those who are in Judea must flee to the mountains.* [17] *Anyone who's on the housetop must not come down to get what is in his house,* [18] *and anyone who's in the field must not turn back to get his coat.*
>
> Matthew 24:15-18

Citing Daniel 9:27; 11:31; and 12:1, Mark 13:14-19 reads:

> [14] *"So when you see the destructive desecration standing where it should not be (let the reader take note), then those who are in Judea must flee to the mountains.* [15] *Anyone who's on his housetop must not come down and go into his house to take anything out of it,* [16] *and the one who's in the field must not turn back to get his coat.*
> [17] *"How terrible it will be for women who are pregnant or who are nursing babies in those days!* [18] *Pray that it may not be in winter,* [19] *because those days will be a time of suffering, a kind that has not happened from the beginning of creation—which God himself created—until now, and certainly will never happen again.*
>
> Mark 13:14-19

Mark 13:26 reads:

> [26] *Then people will see 'the Son of Man coming in clouds' with great power and glory.*
>
> Mark 13:26

Jesus the Messiah's citation of the book of Daniel, which is named after its author (who was taken captive to Babylon while he was a teenager by King Nebuchadnezzar in ca. 605 BC), contains some of the most strikingly *supernatural* prophecies of the entire *Tanakh*.

Rabbinic and conservative Christian tradition assign authorship to this book to Daniel, viewing the prophecies contained within it as supernatural, accurate, and historically trustworthy. Some modern scholars, who deny that the remarkable details contained in the work's prophetic corpus could have been the product of supernatural revelation, claim that the book was produced in its present form during the second century, BC, (i.e., after the events predicted came to pass).

However, modern conservative scholars point to Daniel's remarkably accurate prediction concerning the date of Messiah's appearance to Israel (9:1-27) and his foundation of the Church as the Rock that fills the earth (8:1-27) as incontrovertible evidence that the work was written many decades or centuries before their fulfillment. Daniel's prophetic ministry and writing career of about 70 years encompassed the captivity administrations of both Babylon and Medo-Persia, stretching from the first years of Nebuchadnezzar's reign, through the fall of Babylon (ca. 539 BC), and into the early years of Darius the Mede (CA. 535 BC). Portions of this book were composed in Aramaic, a language with which first century Israeli were quite familiar.

CLAIM #54: JESUS' QUOTATION OF THE PROPHET MICAH FROM THE MAN'S BOOK DEMONSTRATE THAT HE TOOK IT FOR GRANTED THAT MICAH HAD BEEN A REAL PERSON AND THAT HIS BOOK WAS AUTHORITATIVE.

Jesus the Messiah quotes Micah 7:6 in Matthew 10:34-36:

34 "Do not think that I came to bring peace on earth. I did not come to bring peace but a sword! 35 I came to turn
'a man against his father,
a daughter against her mother,
and a daughter-in-law against her mother-in-law.
36 A person's enemies will include members of his own family.'

Matthew 10:34-36

The book of Micah that Jesus the Messiah quotes is named after its author, who was from Moresheth (Micah 1:1), which is probably Moresheth Gath (1:14), an obscure village located about six miles north-northeast of the ancient military fortress of Lachish and about 25 miles southwest of Jerusalem. By citing Micah 7:6 in this passage from Matthew's Gospel, Jesus declares that he believes the prophet's work to be authoritative and binding on his followers.

Some scholars who deny the possibility of supernatural, predictive prophecy reject the presuppositions contained in this book regarding the Assyrian and Babylonian captivity (cf. 1:8-16; 2:12-13; 4:10; 7:7-20) and thus deny authorship to this book to Micah. But the people of Jeremiah's day quoted Micah 3:12 exactly, ascribing its authorship to him and noting how King Hezekiah averted the wrath of God to save Jeremiah's life (Jeremiah 26:24).

Conservative scholars cite supernatural predictions in the Sinai Covenant (cf. Deuteronomy 28:31-53), claiming that Micah's prophecies are the culmination of God's righteous punishments set forth therein. Also, Micah's prophesied inclusion of non-Jews in the salvation plan of God (4:1-3; 7:12, 16-17) were as much in the future with respect to Micah's day as the Babylonian and Assyrian captivities were, but no serious scholar questions the prophetic nature of gentile inclusion in the plan of God. Also, prophecies regarding the future Messianic era (2:13; 4:1-8; 5:2-8) were likewise prophetic for Micah's day, as they are for ours, and the legitimacy of these predictions is not questioned except by those who deny the future literal reign on the earth by the Messiah.

The earliest possible dates for the prophecies contained in this book would have commenced during the early days of Isaiah's prophecies and continued throughout the reigns of the Judean Kings Jotham, Ahaz, and Hezekiah (1:1), who lived ca. 750-686 BC. Micah's ministry overlapped that of Hosea. As we'll see below, Jesus also cited Hosea's work to validate what he was telling his audience.

Claim #55: Jesus' mention of the prophet Zechariah and his quote from the man's book demonstrate that he took it for granted that Zechariah had been a real person and that his book was authoritative.

Jesus the Messiah quotes Zechariah 12:12 and Daniel 7:13 in Matthew 24:30:

³⁰ Then the sign that is the Son of Man will appear in the sky, and all 'the tribes of the land will mourn' as they see 'the Son of Man coming on the clouds of heaven' with power and great glory.

Matthew 24:30

Furthermore, Jesus quotes Zechariah 13:7 in Matthew 26:31:

³¹ Then Jesus told them, "All of you will turn against me this very night, because it is written,
'I will strike the shepherd,
and the sheep of the flock will be scattered.'"

Matthew 24:31

²⁷ Then Jesus told them, "All of you will turn against me, because it is written,
'I will strike the shepherd,
and the sheep will be scattered.'" ....
⁴⁸ Jesus asked them, "Have you come out with swords and clubs to arrest me as if I were a bandit? ⁴⁹ Day after day I was with you in the Temple teaching, yet you didn't arrest me. But the Scriptures must be fulfilled." ⁵⁰ Then all the disciples deserted Jesus and ran away.

Mark 14:27, 48-50

The book of Zechariah is named after the prophet who composed it. He is identified by this book introduction itself (1:1-6) as having been the son of Berechiah, who was the son of Iddo (cf. Matthew 23:35). Other than these references, the Bible contains virtually no other information about this individual (who is mentioned along with Haggai, in Ezra 5:1 and 6:14). Even extra-biblical writings say little about him.

Some scholars see the writer of this book as a successor to the older prophet Haggai, who is thought to have died before the Temple reconstruction project that he envisioned was completed. This book claims (1:1-6) that its introductory vision was received by Zechariah sometime during the eighth month of the second year of the reign of Darius the Great (i.e., ca. November – October 520 BC).

By citing Zechariah's works, Jesus asserts the fundamental veracity of the man's work and its authoritative reliability to serve as supporting arguments for his discourses.

CLAIM #56: JESUS' QUOTATION FROM THE PROPHET HOSEA'S BOOK DEMONSTRATE THAT HE TOOK IT FOR GRANTED THAT HOSEA HAD BEEN A REAL PERSON AND THAT HIS BOOK WAS AUTHORITATIVE.

Jesus the Messiah cites the writings of the prophet Hosea in Luke 22:30-31, taking it for granted that Hosea not only lived, but that his writings were authentic and authoritative:

> [29] *because the time is surely coming when people will say, 'How blessed are the women who couldn't bear children and the wombs that never bore and the breasts that never nursed!'* [30] *Then people will begin to say to the mountains, 'Fall on us!', and to the hills, 'Cover us up!'* [31] *And if they do this when the wood is green, what will happen when it is dry?"*
>
> Luke 23:29-31

According to the first verse of the first chapter of Hosea's book, Hosea's prophetic ministry and writing career encompassed the administrations of Uzziah (ca. 792-740 BC), Jotham (coregent with Uzziah ca. 750 BC), Ahaz and Hezekiah (ca. 753-683 BC), and Jeroboam (ca. 793-753 BC). The book is named after its author, and Jesus quoted from it, informing his hearers that those who will be calling out to the mountains to cover them in Hosea 10:8 are those living in the latter days.

Rabbinic and conservative Christian tradition assign authorship of this book to Hosea, who composed the work in one of the most complex Hebrew language styles of the Bible. Some argue that the book contains a significant number of later interpolations that have proved extraordinarily difficult to outline into a coherent structure. This complexity, when coupled with modern day ignorance of his regional dialect, and the deliberately obscure nature of the book, resulted in a few scholars concluding that this book sustained numerous redactions over the centuries.

However, no evidence of textual transmission supports such redactions or editing of the book of Hosea, and internal evidence within the text demonstrates that the writer of this book held the historicity of the *Torah* in high regard. Hosea's work does not address the reigns of Zechariah, Shallum, Menahem, Pekahiah, Pekah, or Hoshea. Some conservative scholars account for this omission on the grounds that Hosea considered these latter kings to be ambitious usurpers unworthy of address in the heritage of David's line (cf. 7:1-7).

CLAIM #57: JESUS' MENTION OF THE PROPHET MALACHI AND HIS QUOTE FROM THE MAN'S BOOK DEMONSTRATE THAT HE TOOK IT FOR GRANTED THAT MALACHI HAD BEEN A REAL PERSON AND THAT HIS BOOK WAS AUTHORITATIVE.

Jesus the Messiah refers to the prophet Malachi in his discussion with his disciples recorded in Mark 9:11-12:

¹¹ So they asked him, "Don't the scribes say that Elijah must come first?"
¹² He told them, "Elijah is indeed coming first and will restore all things..."

Mark 9:11-12

Jesus also quoted Malachi 3:1 and Exodus 23:20 in Luke 7:26-27:

²⁶ Really, what did you go out to see? A prophet? Yes, I tell you, and even more than a prophet! ²⁷ This is the man about whom it is written,

> *'See, I am sending my messenger ahead of you,
> who will prepare your way before you.'*
>
> Luke 7:26-27

This book, which is named after the prophet who composed it, is written in the form of a series of legal complaints by the God of Israel, who acts as a prosecuting attorney as he pursues justice in court:

- **First Complaint:** *His People's Despised Love (1:-1:5)*
- **God's Second Complaint:** *Despised Offerings by His Priests (1:6-14),*
- **Third Complaint:** *His Priests Fail to Honor Him (2:1-12),*
- **Fourth Complaint:** *Marital Abuses by His Priests (2:13-16),*
- **Fifth Complaint:** *People who Complain (2:17),*
- **The Coming of the Messenger** *(3:1-6),*
- **Sixth Complaint:** *Gifts and Offerings (3:7-12),*
- **Seventh Complaint:** *Slandering God (3:13-15),*
- **The Restoration of the Righteous** *(3:16-18),*
- **The Coming Day of the Lord** *(4:1-6).*

This book is named after its author (1:1), about whom nothing is known and whom Jesus makes no mention by name. However, Jesus the Messiah's citation of Malachi's book to authenticate the validity of John the Baptizer's public ministry demonstrates the seriousness with which he regarded the work. Rabbinic and Christian traditions hold that Malachi's book was the last book of the Hebrew Scriptures to have been written before the beginning of the 400 year silent period that came to a close with the ministry of John the Baptist.

7 | Summary and Conclusions

We have demonstrated in this work that Jesus the Messiah trusted the Hebrew Scriptures of his day. Christians have claimed for centuries that the collection of 66 books we call *The Bible* is reliable with respect to what it affirms, correct in its history of God's dealings with his universe and with humanity, historically accurate regarding its doctrinal teachings, and an utterly trustworthy guide for day-to-day life. But frankly, *every* generation has had its share of doubters. Maybe you're one of them…

So we've provided this book for your reading in order to demonstrate to you what Jesus the Messiah believed about the Bible. Specifically, we counted 57 separate claims he made about the Hebrew Scriptures that existed as of the early part of the first century AD. Here's our summary of each of them:

JESUS' HIGH VIEW OF THE HEBREW SCRIPTURES

Claim #1: Jesus claimed that Moses specifically mentioned him, even though the *Torah* had been written about 1,400 years before Jesus had been born.

Claim #2: Jesus linked his claim that he would judge the dead at the Day of Resurrection to him having been written about by Moses in the *Torah*.

Claim #3: Jesus claimed that the Hebrew Scriptures in general spoke of him, even though the last book of the *Tanakh* had been written about 430 years before he had been born.

Claim #4: Jesus endorsed the absolute reliability and enduring nature of the Hebrew Scriptures so emphatically that he claimed not a single letter or portion of a letter would fail.

Claim #5: Jesus considered the laws contained in the *Torah* to have been authored by Moses.

Claim #6: Jesus considered circumcision to have been handed down from the days of the Patriarchs through the authority of Moses.

Claim #7: Jesus had little respect for the *traditions* handed down about how to obey the *Torah*, but he had high respect for the authority of the *Torah* itself.

Claim #8: Jesus believed that the authority of the *Torah* originated from the earliest days of humanity, not merely from Mount Sinai.

Claim #9: Jesus believed that the book of Genesis was written by Moses.

Claim #10: Jesus believed that Moses also authored the books of Leviticus, Exodus, and Deuteronomy.

Claim #11: Jesus believed that the Ten Commandments were authoritative and binding upon national Israel.

Claim #12: Jesus linked his claim to have been the only person to have gone to heaven with the historical reality of the incident of the serpent in the wilderness.

Summary and Conclusions

Claim #13: Jesus assumed that the claim of ancient Israel that Moses delivered the Law to the nation had historical validity.

Claim #14: Jesus assumed that the *Torah* continued in full immutable force and effect through the completion of the life ministry of John the Baptizer.

Claim #15: Jesus claimed that throughout the entirety of the Hebrew Scriptures, its writers mentioned him.

Claim #16: Jesus certified that the feeding of national Israel in the wilderness with manna actually occurred.

Claim #17: Jesus believed and stated publicly that the Scripture cannot be disregarded or broken.

Claim #18: Jesus believed and stated publicly that the authority of Moses should be respected and obeyed.

Claim #19: Jesus believed and stated publicly that the suffering and betrayal that he would undergo was predicted in the Hebrew Scriptures by the Prophets.

Claim #20: Jesus held the books of Leviticus and Deuteronomy in such high esteem that he linked the entirety of the Law and the Prophets to their integrity.

Claim #21: Jesus held conversations from time to time with Satan, which demonstrated that he believed this creature existed and had influence in the world.

Claim #22: Jesus held the book of Deuteronomy in such high esteem that he used it to rebut the temptations of Satan during his time in the wilderness.

Claim #23: Jesus held Deuteronomy in such high esteem that he cited it as the basis for Church discipline.

Claim #24: Jesus' publicly stated belief that Adam and Eve existed formed the basis of his high view of marriage.

Claim #25: Jesus' publicly stated belief that Abel and Zechariah existed formed the basis of his rebuke and warning that judgment was coming to national Israel.

Claim #26: Jesus' publicly stated belief that Able and Zechariah existed formed the basis of his warning about how Israel would soon be destroyed as a nation, an event that occurred in 70 AD.

Claim #27: Jesus' publicly stated belief that Noah existed and that the flood of his day affected the entire world formed the basis of his warning about how his return to earth would affect the entire world.

Claim #28: Jesus' publicly stated belief that Abraham, Isaac, and Jacob actually lived formed the basis of his warning to and rebuke of Israel's leaders about their threatened *exclusion* from eternal life.

Claim #29: Jesus' publicly stated belief that Abraham, Isaac, and Jacob actually lived formed the basis of his defense of the resurrection of the dead.

Claim #30: Jesus' matter-of-fact mention of Abraham in his dialogue with Zacchaeus demonstrated that he took it for granted that Abraham had been a real person.

Claim #31: Jesus publicly stated and believed that the destruction of Sodom and Gomorrah was a real, historical event and referred to it as the foundation of his warning about the coming judgment at the end of the world.

Claim #32: Jesus believed that Moses and Elijah were real figures in the history of Israel, and claimed to have spoken with both of them.

Claim #33: Jesus demonstrated that he believed King David existed by affirming the man's existence and by citing many Psalms, all the while attributing their authorship to David.

Claim #34: Jesus quoted Psalm 8:2 as a basis for his rebuke to the high priests and scribes of Jerusalem.

Claim #35: Jesus quoted Psalm 35:19 and Psalm 69:4 as referring to himself.

Claim #36: Jesus said that King David authored Psalm 41, using its authority to bolster his claim to be God incarnate.

Claim #37: Jesus said that King David authored Psalm 110, and used a quotation from it to demonstrate how David's Messiah was also God incarnate.

Claim #38: Jesus demonstrated that his admission to be the Messiah was linked to statements from King David and the prophet Daniel contained in the Hebrew Scriptures of his day.

Claim #39: Jesus attributed authorship of Psalm 118 to King David.

Claim #40: Jesus cites Psalm 118, claiming that King David's psalm is predictive of his second coming.

Claim #41: Jesus cites Psalm 118, claiming that King David's psalm is predictive of his rejection by Israel and subsequent exaltation.

Claim #42: Jesus believed that King Solomon and the Queen of Sheba were real figures in the history of Israel, and that they both would have a place with him at the resurrection of the dead.

Claim #43: Jesus believed that Jonah existed and was swallowed by a sea creature. He employed that historical fact as a comparative to explain his coming resurrection.

Claim #44: Jesus' matter-of-fact mention of Jeremiah the prophet and his quote from his book demonstrated that he took it for granted that Jeremiah had been a real person and that his book was authoritative.

Claim #45: Jesus' matter-of-fact mention of Isaiah the prophet and his extensive quotes from his book demonstrate that he took it for granted that Isaiah had been a real person and that his written works were authoritative.

Claim #46: Jesus cites Isaiah the prophet to link the apostasy of his generation to Isaiah's mention of him.

Claim #47: Jesus links the authority of the prophets Isaiah and Joel as predictions relating to his second coming.

Claim #48: Jesus cites the prophet Isaiah as applying to the rejection by Israel's first century leaders in their rejection of the righteous requirements of the Law in deference to their oral traditions.

Claim #49: Jesus cites the authority of the prophet Isaiah to explain the necessity of all prophecies written about him in the Hebrew Scriptures being fulfilled.

Claim #50: Jesus cites the authority of the prophet Isaiah to explain what life will be like under his reign during his Millennial Kingdom.

Claim #51: Jesus cites the authority of the prophets Isaiah and Jeremiah to explain why he expelled merchants from the Temple.

Claim #52: Jesus quoted the work of the prophet Isaiah, proclaiming to his generation that he was the fulfillment of Isaiah 58:6 and 61:1-2.

Claim #53: Jesus' matter-of-fact mention of Daniel the prophet and his quote from his book demonstrated that he took it for granted that Daniel had been a real person and that his book was authoritative.

Claim #54: Jesus' quotation of the prophet Micah from the man's book demonstrate that he took it for granted that Micah had been a real person and that his book was authoritative.

Claim #55: Jesus' mention of the prophet Zechariah and his quote from the man's book demonstrate that he took it for granted that Zechariah had been a real person and that his book was authoritative.

Claim #56: Jesus' quotation from the prophet Hosea's book demonstrate that he took it for granted that Hosea had been a real person and that his book was authoritative.

Claim #57: Jesus' mention of the prophet Malachi and his quote from the man's book demonstrate that he took it for granted that Malachi had been a real person and that his book was authoritative.

Jesus of Nazareth trusted the historical validity of the *Tanakh*. Every single person, without exception, who is mentioned by Jesus as having lived during Israel's previous centuries is recorded in the

Hebrew Scriptures, and Jesus considered those records to be accurate and trustworthy accounts of actual events.

As we have demonstrated within this work, Jesus displayed an unwavering confidence in the historical reliability and internal integrity of the Hebrew Scriptures. His respect for the Word of God even extended to the regulations about divorce and Sabbath rests, as Robert Dick Wilson observed:

> *Jesus recognizes the verbal accuracy and the authority of the Biblical texts bearing upon the Sabbath and divorce; and, then, as the Lord of both Sabbath and of man, He makes known a higher and better Law.* [1]

Regarding Jesus' use of Old Testament quotations, Wilson also noted:

> *One of the most noteworthy facts in the consideration of the New Testament citations from the Old Testament is the marvelous manner in which the citations attributed by the evangelists to Jesus Himself agree with the Textus Receptus of our Hebrew Bibles. In most of these citations by Jesus, we have exactly the same text in the Gospels as we find in the Hebrew, e.g., Matt. iv. 4. 7, v. 5, 21, 27, 31, 38, 43, viii. 17, ix. 13 (?) , xv. 4. 27, xvii. 16, xix. 4. 7, 19, xxi. 13, 16, 42, xxii. 32, 44, xxvii. 46. In Matt. iv. 10 and Luke iv. 8 the word "only" is added in accordance with the Septuagint and with the sense. In Matt. xi. 10, xiii. 14. IS, 35, xxvi. 37 the text is substantially the same. In xv. 8, 9, there is a slight variation by way of adaptation and in xix. 5 an "unimportant variation." In xxvi. 31, there is an interpretation by way of adaptation; and in xxiv. 21 a "free citation."* [2]

> *How, then, is it with the statements of the Old Testament to which Jesus refers and which from the prima facie evidence of the Gospels He seems to have believed to be true? Can these statements be accepted as true or can they not?* [3]

---
1   *Op* cit. p. 637.
2   *Ibid.*, p. 638
3   *Ibid.*, p. 639

Furthermore, when it came time for Jesus to defend his person, nature, and his mission, he cited the Bible of his day to authenticate his own authority and identity. To Jesus, the Hebrew Scriptures were the inerrant, infallible, and plenary inspired Word of God. If Jesus displayed such unwavering confidence in the integrity and inerrancy of the Scriptures, considering every word, letter, and stroke of a letter to be valid and reliable, should not all of us express the very same confidence in the entire record of the completed Old and New Testaments, as well?

Let us, in closing, remember Dr. Robert Dick Wilson's summary of the issues involved in Jesus' use of and trust in the Hebrew Scriptures of his day:

> *Further, anyone who professes to believe that the New Testament teaches that the Scriptures of the Old Testament were "of divine origin and excellence", that every Scripture is inspired of God (2 Tim. iii. IS, 16), that Jesus found in the Law, the Prophets and the Psalms, things that concerned Himself (Luke xxiv. 27, 44), and that Jesus, the evangelists, and all the writers of the books of the New Testament, show their faith in the veracity of the Old Testament records, must hesitate to place his opinion over against that of the founders of Christianity. Lastly, those of us who believe that Jesus was the Messiah sent from God, the prophet that was to come into the world, the Logos, the only begotten Son of God, will be pardoned for thinking that it is little short of blasphemy for a professing Christian to assert that Jesus did not know. If we believe not Him when He has spoken of earthly things, which we can more or less investigate and test, how can we believe Him when He speaks of heavenly things?* [4]

---

4   *Ibid.* p. 661.

APPENDIX: EVIDENCE FOR BIBLICAL FIGURES

THE ONE FAITHFUL WITNESS OF THE SCRIPTURAL RECORD

We should like to suggest that those who question the historical reliability of the Scriptures are really questioning something that is of a far more serious nature than merely doubting whether or not the people mentioned in the Bible really lived or whether or not the events recorded actually happened. Summarized succinctly, what these doubters are actually saying is that they doubt the recollections of God himself as to who lived and as to what took place.

We make this rather bold claim because for centuries Christians have claimed that the creative agent behind the existence of the Universe was Jesus the Messiah in his pre-incarnate state.

We Christians have claimed that:

- It was Jesus in his pre-incarnate state who in the Garden of Eden fashioned Adam from the ground of the earth with his own pre-incarnate hands.
- It was Jesus in his pre-incarnate state who gave Adam the account of creation that later became the first few chapters of Genesis.
- It was Jesus in his pre-incarnate state who called Noah and his family to live for a season inside the ark with him while he destroyed the world by a cataclysmic flood.
- It was Jesus in his pre-incarnate state who called Abram and his wife to leave Ur of the Chaldees to travel with him to what would one day be known as Israel.
- It was Jesus in his pre-incarnate state who was with Jacob during his sojourn in Egypt as he reunited with his long-lost son Joseph after his rise to become the second most powerful man in the world.
- It was Jesus in his pre-incarnate state who appeared as the Angel of the Lord to Abraham and to Moses, and who empowered Joshua and all of the judges of pre-Davidic Israel to conquer the land from the Canaanites.
- It was Jesus in his pre-incarnate state who anointed Saul as King, and David after him, to rule Israel.
- It was Jesus in his pre-incarnate state who superintended the deteriorating kingdom administrations of every king after them.
- It was Jesus in his pre-incarnate state who called his prophets to minister words of rebuke and encouragement to ancient Israel.
- And it was Jesus in his pre-incarnate state who became "Immanuel," the God who visited his people in the conception by Mary of the Son of Man in that virgin's womb.

Appendix: Evidence for Biblical figures

To put things a bit bluntly, but clearly, it was Jesus himself who was an eyewitness, so to speak, of the events of Scripture. Therefore, for modern "biblical scholars" to doubt the trustworthiness of the Bible is, in effect, for to set their own wisdom above that of God himself. This arrogance is, in fact, more accurately describable as *hubris*, the sin of Lucifer. In contrast to all of this, we claim that because Jesus trusted the reliability of Scripture, we can do so today.

On the Existence of the Historic Figures of Scripture

As a general rule, I've been on record for a number of years now regarding my public stance regarding that certain "scholarly" publication called *Biblical Archaeology Review*. Frankly, I don't trust that magazine's views regarding the historical reliability of the Bible. Most of the time when I read their documents (I have a subscription to their regular email news), I come away from reading them with an unsettling feeling that they think that they know more about what "really" happened during biblical days than did the authors of Scripture who recorded the events. More often than not, their contributions as to what "really happened" turn out to be a denial of what a plain reading of the text claims. As a result, I don't trust the objectivity of that publication.

But I recently came across a delightful exception. That exception is a remarkably thorough and exacting bit of research undertaken by BAR contributor Dr. Lawrence Mykytiuk, who has served on the Libraries Faculty of Purdue University as a professor of Library Science.[1] In April 2014 he published a piece called "*Archaeology Confirms 50 Real People in the Bible*".[2] His work was subsequently expanded to add three more characters, to a total of 53 individuals, in April of 2017.

For the record, I should concede that Mykytiuk's opinion of the historical reliability of the New Testament claims about Jesus is shadowy at best. Richard Carrier, one reviewer of the man's work, has characterized Mykytiuk's view of "the historical Jesus" as "so

---
1 Cited from http://purdue.academia.edu/LawrenceMykytiuk.
2 This article is Copyright © 2014, 2017 by Dr. Lawrence Mykytiuk. Published by Biblical Archaeology Review (http://www.biblicalarchaeology.org). Used by permission and pursuant to Fair Use. Cited from http://www.biblicalarchaeology.org/daily/people-cultures-in-the-bible/people-in-the-bible/50-people-in-the-bible-confirmed-archaeologically/.

awful it hardly warrants a response."[3] But like a broken digital clock right once per day, Mykytiuk's recitation of 53 obscure characters mentioned in the biblical record is fascinating to study, and scrupulously thorough in its exactness. We've cited his research rather thoroughly, below, giving well-deserved credit for the research to him, as befits proper scholarship and ethics. Here, then, is Lawrence Mykytiuk's list. All text that follows in this Appendix is cited pursuant to Dr. Mykytiuk and quotes his excellent research almost word-for-word:[4]

Lawrence Mykytiuk's List of 53 Biblical Figures

Egypt

Person #1 | Pharaoh Shishak (Sheshonq I), 945–924 BC, 1 Kings 11:40 and 14:25

In his inscriptions, including the record of his military campaign in Palestine in his 924 B.C.E. inscription on the exterior south wall of the Temple of Amun at Karnak in Thebes. See *OROT*, pp. 10, 31–32, 502 note 1; many references to him in *Third*, indexed on p. 520; Kenneth A. Kitchen, review of *IBP*, *SEE-J Hiphil* 2 (2005), www.see-j.net/index.php/hiphil/article/viewFile/19/17, bottom of p. 3, which is briefly mentioned in "Sixteen," p. 43 n. 22. (Note: The name of this pharaoh can be spelled Sheshonq or Shoshenq.)

Sheshonq is also referred to in a fragment of his victory stele discovered at Megiddo containing his cartouche. See Robert S. Lamon and Geoffrey M. Shipton, *Megiddo I: Seasons of 1925–34, Strata I–V.* (Oriental Institute Publications no. 42; Chicago: University of Chicago Press, 1939), pp. 60–61, fig. 70; Graham I. Davies, *Megiddo* (Cities of the Biblical World; Cambridge: Lutterworth Press, 1986), pp. 89 fig. 18, 90; *OROT*, p. 508 n. 68; *IBP*, p. 137 n. 119. (Note: The name of this pharaoh can be spelled Sheshonq or Shoshenq.)

---

3   Richard Carrier, *"Biblical Archaeology Review = Crappy Christian Propaganda Mag"*. Cited from http://www.richardcarrier.info/archives/6862.
4   Cited from http://www.biblicalarchaeology.org/daily/people-cultures-in-the-bible/people-in-the-bible/50-people-in-the-bible-confirmed-archaeologically/.

Appendix: Evidence for Biblical figures

Egyptian pharaohs had several names, including a throne name. It is known that the throne name of Sheshonq I, when translated into English, means, "Bright is the manifestation of Re, chosen of Amun/Re." Sheshonq I's inscription on the wall of the Temple of Amun at Karnak in Thebes (mentioned above) celebrates the victories of his military campaign in the Levant, thus presenting the possibility of his presence in that region. A small Egyptian scarab containing his exact throne name, discovered as a surface find at Khirbat Hamra Ifdan, now documents his presence at or near that location. This site is located along the Wadi Fidan, in the region of Faynan in southern Jordan.

As for the time period, disruption of copper production at Khirbet en-Nahas, also in the southern Levant, can be attributed to Sheshonq's army, as determined by stratigraphy, high-precision radiocarbon dating, and an assemblage of Egyptian amulets dating to Sheshonq's time. His army seems to have intentionally disrupted copper production, as is evident both at Khirbet en-Nahas and also at Khirbat Hamra Ifdan, where the scarab was discovered.

As for the singularity of this name in this remote locale, it would have been notable to find any Egyptian scarab there, much less one containing the throne name of this conquering Pharaoh; this unique discovery admits no confusion with another person. See Thomas E. Levy, Stefan Münger, and Mohammad Najjar, "A Newly Discovered Scarab of Sheshonq I: Recent Iron Age Explorations in Southern Jordan. Antiquity Project Gallery," *Antiquity* (2014); online: http://journal.antiquity.ac.uk/projgall/levy341.[5]

PERSON # 2 | SO (PHARAOH OSORKON IV), 730–715, 2 KINGS *17:4*

Scripture calls him "So, king of Egypt" (*OROT*, pp. 15–16). K. A. Kitchen makes a detailed case for So being Osorkon IV in *Third*, pp. 372–375. See *Raging Torrent*, p. 106 under "Shilkanni."

---

5   *Op.* cit.

Person #3 | T*irhakah* (P*haraoh* T*aharqa*) *690–664, 2* K*ings 19:9*

In many Egyptian hieroglyphic inscriptions; *Third*, pp. 387–395. For mention of Tirhakah in Assyrian inscriptions, see those of Esarhaddon and Ashurbanipal in *Raging Torrent*, pp. 138–143, 145, 150–153, 155, 156; *ABC*, p. 247 under "Terhaqah." The Babylonian chronicle also refers to him (*Raging Torrent*, p. 187). On Tirhakah as prince, see *OROT*, p. 24.

Person #4 | N*echo* II P*haraoh* N*eco* II), *610–595, 2* C*hronicles 35:20*

In inscriptions of the Assyrian king, Ashurbanipal (*ANET*, pp. 294–297) and the Esarhaddon Chronicle (*ANET*, p. 303). See also *Raging Torrent*, pp. 189–199, esp. 198; *OROT*, p. 504 n. 26; *Third*, p. 407; *ABC*, p. 232.

Person #5 | H*ophra* (P*haraoah* A*pries*), *589–570,* J*eremiah 44:30*

In Egyptian inscriptions, such as the one describing his being buried by his successor, Aḥmose II (Amasis II) (*Third*, p. 333 n. 498), with reflections in Babylonian inscriptions regarding Nebuchadnezzar's defeat of Hophra in 572 and replacing him on the throne of Egypt with a general, Aḥmes (Amasis), who later rebelled against Babylonia and was suppressed (*Raging Torrent*, p. 222). See *OROT*, pp. 9, 16, 24; *Third*, p. 373 n. 747, 407 and 407 n. 969; *ANET*, p. 308; D. J. Wiseman, *Chronicles of Chaldaean Kings (626–556 B.C.) in the British Museum* (London: The Trustees of the British Museum, 1956), pp. 94-95. Cf. *ANEHST*, p. 402. (The index of *Third*, p. 525, distinguishes between an earlier "Wahibre i" [*Third*, p. 98] and the 26th Dynasty's "Wahibre ii" [= Apries], r. 589–570.)

Appendix: Evidence for Biblical figures

MOAB

PERSON # 6 | MESHA, KING, EARLY TO MID-9TH CENTURY, 2 KINGS 3:4–27,

In the Mesha Inscription, which he caused to be written, lines 1–2; Dearman, *Studies*, pp. 97, 100–101; *IBP*, pp. 95–108, 238; "Sixteen," p. 43.

ARAM-DAMASCUS

PERSON # 7 | HADADEZER, KING, EARLY 9TH CENTURY TO 844/842, 1 KINGS 22:3

In Assyrian inscriptions of Shalmaneser III and also, I am convinced, in the Melqart stele. The Hebrew Bible does not name him, referring to him only as "the King of Aram" in 1 Kings 22:3, 31; 2 Kings chapter 5, 6:8–23. We find out this king's full name in some contemporaneous inscriptions of Shalmaneser III, king of Assyria (r. 858–824), such as the Black Obelisk (*Raging Torrent*, pp. 22–24). At Kurkh, a monolith by Shalmaneser III states that at the battle of Qarqar (853 B.C.E.), he defeated "Adad-idri [the Assyrian way of saying Hadadezer] the Damascene," along with "Ahab the Israelite" and other kings (*Raging Torrent*, p. 14; RIMA 3, p. 23, A.0.102.2, col. ii, lines 89b–92). "Hadadezer the Damascene" is also mentioned in an engraving on a statue of Shalmaneser III at Aššur (RIMA 3, p. 118, A.0.102.40, col. i, line 14). The same statue engraving later mentions both Hadadezer and Hazael together (RIMA 3, p. 118, col. i, lines 25–26) in a topical arrangement of worst enemies defeated that is not necessarily chronological.

On the long-disputed readings of the Melqart stele, which was discovered in Syria in 1939, see "Corrections," pp. 69–85, which follows the closely allied readings of Frank Moore Cross and Gotthard G. G. Reinhold. Those readings, later included in "Sixteen," pp. 47–48, correct the earlier absence of this Hadadezer in *IBP* (notably on p. 237, where he is not to be confused with the tenth-century Hadadezer, son of Rehob and king of Zobah).

Person # 8 | Ben-hadad, son of Hadadezer, co-regent 844/842, 2 Kings 6:24

In the Melqart stele, following the readings of Frank Moore Cross and Gotthard G. G. Reinhold and Cross's 2003 criticisms of a different reading that now appears in *COS*, vol. 2, pp. 152–153 ("Corrections," pp. 69–85). Several kings of Damascus bore the name Bar-hadad (in their native Aramaic, which is translated as Ben-hadad in the Hebrew Bible), which suggests adoption as "son" by the patron deity Hadad. This designation might indicate that he was the crown prince and/or co-regent with his father Hadadezer. It seems likely that Bar-hadad/Ben-hadad was his father's immediate successor as king, as seems to be implied by the military policy reversal between 2 Kings 6:3–23 and 6:24. It was this Ben-Hadad, the son of Hadadezer, whom Hazael assassinated in 2 Kings 8:7–15 (quoted in *Raging Torrent*, p. 25). The mistaken disqualification of this biblical identification in the Melqart stele in *IBP*, p. 237, is revised to a strong identification in that stele in "Corrections," pp. 69–85; "Sixteen," p. 47.

Person # 9 | Hazael, king, 844/842–ca. 800, 1 Kings 19:15, 2 Kings 8:8

Is documented in four kinds of inscriptions: 1) The inscriptions of Shalmaneser III call him "Hazael of Damascus" (*Raging Torrent*, pp. 23–26, 28), for example the inscription on the Kurbail Statue (RIMA 3, p. 60, line 21). He is also referred to in 2) the Zakkur stele from near Aleppo, in what is now Syria, and in 3) bridle inscriptions, i.e., two inscribed horse blinders and a horse frontlet discovered on Greek islands, and in 4) inscribed ivories seized as Assyrian war booty (*Raging Torrent*, p. 35). All are treated in *IBP*, pp. 238–239, and listed in "Sixteen," p. 44. Cf. "Corrections," pp. 101–103.

Person # 10 | Ben-hadad, son of Hazael, king, early 8th century, 2 Kings 13:3

In the Zakkur stele from near Aleppo. In lines 4–5, it calls him "Bar-hadad, son of Hazael, the king of Aram" (*IBP*, p. 240; "Sixteen,"

p. 44; *Raging Torrent*, p. 38; *ANET*, p. 655: *COS*, vol. 2, p. 155). On the possibility of Ben-hadad, son of Hazael, being the "Mari" in Assyrian inscriptions, see *Raging Torrent*, pp. 35–36.

PERSON # 11 | REZIN (= RAHIANU), KING, MID-8TH CENTURY TO 732, 2 KINGS 15:37

In the inscriptions of Tiglath-pileser III, king of Assyria (in these inscriptions, *Raging Torrent* records frequent mention of Rezin in pp. 51–78); *OROT*, p. 14. Inscriptions of Tiglath-pileser III refer to "Rezin" several times, "Rezin of Damascus" in Annal 13, line 10 (*ITP*, pp. 68–69), and "the dynasty of Rezin of Damascus" in Annal 23, line 13 (*ITP*, pp. 80–81). Tiglath-pileser III's stele from Iran contains an explicit reference to Rezin as king of Damascus in column III, the right side, A: "[line 1] The kings of the land of Hatti (and of) the Aramaeans of the western seashore . . . [line 4] Rezin of Damascus" (*ITP*, pp. 106–107).

NORTHERN KINGDOM OF ISRAEL

PERSON # 12 | OMRI, KING, 884–873, 1 KINGS 16:16

In Assyrian inscriptions and in the Mesha Inscription. Because he founded a famous dynasty which ruled the northern kingdom of Israel, the Assyrians refer not only to him as a king of Israel (*ANET*, pp. 280, 281), but also to the later rulers of that territory as kings of "the house of Omri" and that territory itself literally as "the house of Omri" (*Raging Torrent*, pp. 34, 35; *ANET*, pp. 284, 285). Many a later king of Israel who was not his descendant, beginning with Jehu, was called "the son of Omri" (*Raging Torrent*, p. 18). The Mesha Inscription also refers to Omri as "the king of Israel" in lines 4–5, 7 (Dearman, *Studies*, pp. 97, 100–101; *COS*, vol. 2, p. 137; *IBP*, pp. 108–110, 216; "Sixteen," p. 43.

PERSON # 13 | AHAB, KING, 873–852, 1 KINGS 16:28

In the Kurkh Monolith by his enemy, Shalmaneser III of Assyria. There, referring to the battle of Qarqar (853 B.C.E.), Shalmaneser calls him "Ahab the Israelite" (*Raging Torrent*, pp. 14, 18–19; RIMA 3, p. 23, A.0.102.2, col. 2, lines 91–92; *ANET*, p. 279; *COS*, vol. 2, p. 263).

PERSON # 14 | JEHU, KING, R. 842/841–815/814, 1 KINGS 19:16

In inscriptions of Shalmaneser III. In these, "son" means nothing more than that he is the successor, in this instance, of Omri (*Raging Torrent*, p. 20 under "Ba'asha . . ." and p. 26). A long version of Shalmaneser III's annals on a stone tablet in the outer wall of the city of Aššur refers to Jehu in col. 4, line 11, as "Jehu, son of Omri" (*Raging Torrent*, p. 28; RIMA 3, p. 54, A.0.102.10, col. 4, line 11; cf. *ANET*, p. 280, the parallel "fragment of an annalistic text"). Also, on the Kurba'il Statue, lines 29–30 refer to "Jehu, son of Omri" (RIMA 3, p. 60, A.0.102.12, lines 29–30).

In Shalmaneser III's Black Obelisk, current scholarship regards the notation over relief B, depicting payment of tribute from Israel, as referring to "Jehu, son of Omri" (*Raging Torrent*, p. 23; RIMA 3, p. 149, A.0. 102.88), but cf. P. Kyle McCarter, Jr., "'Yaw, Son of 'Omri': A Philological Note on Israelite Chronology," *Bulletin of the American Schools of Oriental Research* 216 (1974): pp. 5–7.

PERSON # 15 | JOASH (JEHOASH), KING, 805–790, 2 KINGS 13:9

In the Tell al-Rimaḥ inscription of Adad-Nirari III, king of Assyria (r. 810–783), which mentions "the tribute of Joash [= Iu'asu] the Samarian" (Stephanie Page, "A Stela of Adad-Nirari III and Nergal-Ereš from Tell Al Rimaḥ," *Iraq* 30 [1968]: pp. 142–145, line 8, Pl. 38–41; RIMA 3, p. 211, line 8 of A.0.104.7; *Raging Torrent*, pp. 39–41).

PERSON # 16 | JEROBOAM II, KING, 790–750/749, 2 KINGS 13:13

In the seal of his royal servant Shema, discovered at Megiddo (*WSS*, p. 49 no. 2; *IBP*, pp. 133–139, 217; "Sixteen," p. 46).

PERSON # 17 | MENAHEM, KING, 749–738, 2 KINGS 15:14

In the Calah Annals of Tiglath-pileser III. Annal 13, line 10 refers to "Menahem of Samaria" in a list of kings who paid tribute

(*ITP*, pp. 68–69, Pl. IX). Tiglath-pileser III's stele from Iran, his only known stele, refers explicitly to Menahem as king of Samaria in column III, the right side, A: "[line 1] The kings of the land of Hatti (and of) the Aramaeans of the western seashore . . . [line 5] Menahem of Samaria." (*ITP*, pp. 106–107). See also *Raging Torrent*, pp. 51, 52, 54, 55, 59; *ANET*, p. 283.

PERSON # 18 | PEKAH, KING, 750(?)–732/731, 2 KINGS 15:25

In the inscriptions of Tiglath-pileser III. Among various references to "Pekah," the most explicit concerns the replacement of Pekah in Summary Inscription 4, lines 15–17: "[line 15] . . . The land of Bit-Humria . . . . [line 17] Peqah, their king [I/they killed] and I installed Hoshea [line 18] [as king] over them" (*ITP*, pp. 140–141; *Raging Torrent*, pp. 66–67).

PERSON # 19 | HOSHEA, KING, 732/731–722, 2 KINGS 15:30

In Tiglath-pileser's Summary Inscription 4, described in preceding note 18, where Hoshea is mentioned as Pekah's immediate successor.

PERSON # 20 | SANBALLAT "I", GOVERNOR OF SAMARIA UNDER PERSIAN RULE, CA. MID-FIFTH CENTURY, NEHEMIAH 2:10

In a letter among the papyri from the Jewish community at Elephantine in Egypt (A. E. Cowley, ed., *Aramaic Papyri of the Fifth Century B.C.* (Oxford: Clarendon, 1923; reprinted Osnabrück, Germany: Zeller, 1967), p. 114 English translation of line 29, and p. 118 note regarding line 29; *ANET*, p. 492.

Also, the reference to "[ ]ballat," most likely Sanballat, in Wadi Daliyeh bulla WD 22 appears to refer to the biblical Sanballat as the father of a governor of Samaria who succeeded him in the first half of the fourth century. As Jan Dušek shows, it cannot be demonstrated that any Sanballat II and III existed, which is the reason for the present article's quotation marks around the "I" in Sanballat "I"; see Jan Dušek, "Archaeology and Texts in the Persian Period: Focus on Sanballat," in Martti Nissinen, ed., *Congress Volume: Helsinki 2010* (Boston: Brill. 2012), pp. 117–132.

SOUTHERN KINGDOM OF JUDAH

PERSON # 21 | DAVID, KING, CA. 1010–970, 1 SAMUEL 16:13

In three inscriptions, most notable is the victory stele in Aramaic known as the "house of David" inscription, discovered at Tel Dan; Avraham Biran and Joseph Naveh, "An Aramaic Stele from Tel Dan," *IEJ* 43 (1993), pp. 81–98, and idem, "The Tel Dan Inscription: A New Fragment," *IEJ* 45 (1995), pp. 1–18. An ancient Aramaic word pattern in line 9 designates David as the founder of the dynasty of Judah in the phrase "house of David" (2 Sam 2:11 and 5:5; Gary A. Rendsburg, "On the Writing ביתדוד [BYTDWD] in the Aramaic Inscription from Tel Dan," *IEJ* 45 [1995], pp. 22–25; *Raging Torrent*, p. 20, under "Ba'asha . . ."; *IBP*, pp. 110–132, 265–77; "Sixteen," pp. 41–43).

In the second inscription, the Mesha Inscription, the phrase "house of David" appears in Moabite in line 31 with the same meaning: that he is the founder of the dynasty. There David's name appears with only its first letter destroyed, and no other letter in that spot makes sense without creating a very strained, awkward reading (André Lemaire, "'House of David' Restored in Moabite Inscription," *BAR* 20, no. 3 [May/June 1994]: pp. 30–37. David's name also appears in line 12 of the Mesha Inscription (Anson F. Rainey, "Mesha' and Syntax," in J. Andrew Dearman and M. Patrick Graham, eds., *The Land That I Will Show You: Essays on the History and Archaeology of the Ancient Near East in Honor of J. Maxwell Miller*. (JSOT Supplement series, no. 343; Sheffield, England:Sheffield Academic, 2001), pp. 287–307; *IBP*, pp. 265–277; "Sixteen," pp. 41–43).

The third inscription, in Egyptian, mentions a region in the Negev called "the heights of David" after King David (Kenneth A. Kitchen, "A Possible Mention of David in the Late Tenth Century B.C.E., and Deity *Dod as Dead as the Dodo?" *Journal for the Study of the Old Testament* 76 [1997], pp. 39–41; *IBP*, p. 214 note 3, which is revised in "Corrections," pp. 119–121; "Sixteen," p. 43).

Appendix: Evidence for Biblical figures

In the table on p. 46 of *BAR*, David is listed as king of Judah. According to 2 Samuel 5:5, for his first seven years and six months as a monarch, he ruled only the southern kingdom of Judah. We have no inscription that refers to David as king over all Israel (that is, the united kingdom) as also stated in 2 Sam 5:5.

PERSON # 22 | UZZIAH (AZARIAH), KING, 788/787–736/735, 2 KINGS 14:21

In the inscribed stone seals of two of his royal servants: Abiyaw and Shubnayaw (more commonly called Shebanyaw); *WSS*, p. 51 no. 4 and p. 50 no. 3, respectively; *IBP*, pp. 153–159 and 159–163, respectively, and p. 219 no. 20 (a correction to *IBP* is that on p. 219, references to *WSS* nos. 3 and 4 are reversed); "Sixteen," pp. 46–47. Cf. also his secondary burial inscription from the Second Temple era (*IBP*, p. 219 n. 22).

PERSON # 23 | AHAZ (JEHOAHAZ), KING, R. 742/741–726, 2 KINGS 15:38

In Tiglath-pileser III's Summary Inscription 7, reverse, line 11, refers to "Jehoahaz of Judah" in a list of kings who paid tribute (*ITP*, pp. 170–171; *Raging Torrent*, pp. 58–59). The Bible refers to him by the shortened form of his full name, Ahaz, rather than by the full form of his name, Jehoahaz, which the Assyrian inscription uses. Cf. the unprovenanced seal of 'Ushna', more commonly called 'Ashna', the name Ahaz appears (*IBP*, pp. 163–169, with corrections from Kitchen's review of *IBP* as noted in "Corrections," p. 117; "Sixteen," pp. 38–39 n. 11). Because this king already stands clearly documented in an Assyrian inscription, documentation in another inscription is not necessary to confirm the existence of the biblical Ahaz, king of Judah.

PERSON # 24 | HEZEKIAH, KING, R. 726–697/696, 2 KINGS 16:20

Initially in the Rassam Cylinder of Sennacherib (in this inscription, *Raging Torrent* records frequent mention of Hezekiah in pp. 111–123; *COS*, pp. 302–303). It mentions "Hezekiah the

Judahite" (col. 2 line 76 and col. 3 line 1 in Luckenbill, *Annals of Sennacherib*, pp. 31, 32) and "Jerusalem, his royal city" (ibid., col. 3 lines 28, 40; ibid., p. 33) Other, later copies of the annals of Sennacherib, such as the Oriental Institute prism and the Taylor prism, mostly repeat the content of the Rassam cylinder, duplicating its way of referring to Hezekiah and Jerusalem (*ANET*, pp. 287, 288). The Bull Inscription from the palace at Nineveh (*ANET*, p. 288; *Raging Torrent*, pp. 126–127) also mentions "Hezekiah the Judahite" (lines 23, 27 in Luckenbill, *Annals of Sennacherib*, pp. 69, 70) and "Jerusalem, his royal city" (line 29; ibid., p. 33).

PERSON # 25 | MANASSEH, KING, 697/696–642/641, 2 KINGS 20:21

In the inscriptions of Assyrian kings Esarhaddon (*Raging Torrent*, pp. 131, 133, 136) and Ashurbanipal (ibid., p. 154). "Manasseh, king of Judah," according to Esarhaddon (r. 680–669), was among those who paid tribute to him (Esarhaddon's Prism B, column 5, line 55; R. Campbell Thompson, *The Prisms of Esarhaddon and Ashurbanipal* [London: Trustees of the British Museum, 1931], p. 25; *ANET*, p. 291). Also, Ashurbanipal (r. 668–627) records that "Manasseh, king of Judah" paid tribute to him (Ashurbanipal's Cylinder C, col. 1, line 25; Maximilian Streck, *Assurbanipal und die letzten assyrischen Könige bis zum Untergang Niniveh's*, [Vorderasiatische Bibliothek 7; Leipzig: J. C. Hinrichs, 1916], vol. 2, pp. 138–139; *ANET*, p. 294.

PERSON # 26 | HILKIAH, HIGH PRIEST DURING JOSIAH'S REIGN, CA. 640/639–609, 2 KINGS 22:4

In the City of David bulla of Azariah, son of Hilkiah (*WSS*, p. 224 no. 596; *IBP*, pp. 148–151; 229 only in [50] City of David bulla; "Sixteen," p. 49). The oldest part of Jerusalem, called the City of David, is the location where the Bible places all four men named in the bullae covered in the present endnotes 26 through 29.

Analysis of the clay of these bullae shows that they were produced in the locale of Jerusalem (Eran Arie, Yuval Goren, and Inbal Samet, "Indelible Impression: Petrographic Analysis of Judahite Bullae," in *The Fire Signals of Lachish: Studies in the Archaeology and History of*

Israel in the Late Bronze Age, Iron Age, and Persian Period in Honor of David Ussishkin [ed. Israel Finkelstein and Nadav Na'aman; Winona Lake, Ind.: Eisenbrauns, 2011], p. 10, quoted in "Sixteen," pp. 48–49 n. 34).

PERSON # 27 | SHAPHAN, SCRIBE DURING JOSIAH'S REIGN, CA.IN 640/639–609, 2 KINGS 22:3

In the City of David bulla of Gemariah, son of Shaphan (*WSS*, p. 190 no. 470; *IBP*, pp. 139–146, 228). See endnote 26 above regarding "Sixteen," pp. 48–49 n. 34.

PERSON # 28 | AZARIAH, HIGH PRIEST DURING JOSIAH'S REIGN, CA. 640/639–609, 1 CHRONICLES 5:39

In the City of David bulla of Azariah, son of Hilkiah (*WSS*, p. 224 no. 596; *IBP*, pp. 151–152; 229). See endnote 26 above regarding "Sixteen," pp. 48–49 n. 34.

PERSON # 29 | GEMARIAH, OFFICIAL DURING JEHOIAKIM'S REIGN, CA. 609–598, JEREMIAH 36:10

In the City of David bulla of Gemariah, son of Shaphan (*WSS*, p. 190 no. 470; *IBP*, pp. 147, 232). See endnote 26 above regarding "Sixteen," pp. 48–49 n. 34.

PERSON # 30 | JEHOIACHIN (JECONIAH = CONIAH), KING, 598–597, 2 KINGS 24:5

In four Babylonian administrative tablets regarding oil rations or deliveries, during his exile in Babylonia (*Raging Torrent*, p. 209; *ANEHST*, pp. 386–387). Discovered at Babylon, they are dated from the tenth to the thirty-fifth year of Nebuchadnezzar II, king of Babylonia and conqueror of Jerusalem. One tablet calls Jehoiachin "king" (Text Babylon 28122, obverse, line 29; *ANET*, p. 308). A second, fragmentary text mentions him as king in an immediate context that refers to "[. . . so]ns of the king of Judah" and "Judahites" (Text Babylon 28178, obverse, col. 2, lines 38–40; *ANET*, p. 308). The third tablet calls him "the son of the king of Judah" and refers to "the five sons of the king of Judah" (Text Babylon 28186, reverse, col. 2, lines 17–18; *ANET*, p. 308). The fourth text, the most fragmentary of all, confirms "Judah" and part of Jehoiachin's name, but contributes no data that is not found in the other texts.

Person # 31 | Shelemiah, father of Jehucal the official, late 7th century, Jeremiah 37:3; 38:1

Person # 32 | Jehucal (Jucal), official during Zedekiah's reign, fl. ca. 597–586, Jeremiah 37:3; 38:1

Both referred to in a bulla discovered in the City of David in 2005 (Eilat Mazar, "Did I Find King David's Palace?" *BAR* 32, no. 1 [January/February 2006], pp. 16–27, 70; idem, *Preliminary Report on the City of David Excavations 2005 at the Visitors Center Area* [Jerusalem and New York: Shalem, 2007], pp. 67–69; idem, "The Wall that Nehemiah Built," *BAR* 35, no. 2 [March/April 2009], pp. 24–33,66; idem, *The Palace of King David: Excavations at the Summit of the City of David: Preliminary Report of Seasons 2005-2007* [Jerusalem/New York: Shoham Academic Research and Publication, 2009], pp. 66–71). Only the possibility of firm identifications is left open in "Corrections," pp. 85–92; "Sixteen," pp. 50–51; this article is my first affirmation of four identifications, both here in notes 31 and 32 and below in notes 33 and 34.

After cautiously observing publications and withholding judgment for several years, I am now affirming the four identifications in notes 31 through 34, because I am now convinced that this bulla is a remnant from an administrative center in the City of David, a possibility suggested in "Corrections," p. 100 second-to-last paragraph, and "Sixteen," p. 51. For me, the tipping point came by comparing the description and pictures of the nearby and immediate archaeological context in Eilat Mazar, "Palace of King David," pp. 66–70, with the administrative contexts described in Eran Arie, Yuval Goren, and Inbal Samet, "Indelible Impression: Petrographic Analysis of Judahite Bullae," in Israel Finkelstein and Nadav Na'aman, eds., *The Fire Signals of Lachish: Studies in the*

Archaeology and History of Israel in the Late Bronze Age, Iron Age, and Persian Period in Honor of David Ussishkin (Winona Lake, Ind.: Eisenbrauns, 2011), pp. 12–13 (the section titled "The Database: Judahite Bullae from Controlled Excavations") and pp. 23–24. See also Nadav Na'aman, "The Interchange between Bible and Archaeology: The Case of David's Palace and the Millo," *BAR* 40, no. 1 (January/February 2014), pp. 57–61, 68–69, which is drawn from idem, "Biblical and Historical Jerusalem in the Tenth and Fifth-Fourth Centuries B.C.E.," *Biblica* 93 (2012): pp. 21–42. See also idem, "Five Notes on Jerusalem in the First and Second Temple Periods," *Tel Aviv* 39 (2012): p. 93.

PERSON # 33 | PASHHUR, FATHER OF GEDALIAH THE OFFICIAL, LATE 7TH CENTURY, JEREMIAH 38:1

PERSON # 34 | GEDALIAH, OFFICIAL DURING ZEDEKIAH'S REIGN, FL. CA. 597–586, JEREMIAH 38:1

Both referred to in a bulla discovered in the City of David in 2008. See "Corrections," pp. 92–96; "Sixteen," pp. 50–51; and the preceding endnote 31 and 32 for bibliographic details on E. Mazar, "Wall," pp. 24–33, 66; idem, *Palace of King David*, pp. 68–71) and for the comments in the paragraph that begins, "After cautiously ... "

ASSYRIA

PERSON # 35 | TIGLATH-PILESER III (PUL), KING, 744–727, 2 KINGS 15:19

In his many inscriptions. See *Raging Torrent*, pp. 46–79; *COS*, vol. 2, pp. 284–292; *ITP*; Mikko Lukko, *The Correspondence of Tiglath-pileser III and Sargon II from Calah/Nimrud* (State Archives of Assyria, no. 19; Assyrian Text Corpus Project; Winona Lake, Ind.: Eisenbrauns, 2013); *ABC*, pp. 248–249. On Pul as referring to Tiglath-pileser III, which is implicit in *ABC*, p. 333 under "Pulu," see *ITP*, p. 280 n. 5 for discussion and bibliography.

On the identification of Tiglath-pileser III in the Aramaic monumental inscription honoring Panamu II, in Aramaic monumental inscriptions 1 and 8 of Bar-Rekub (now in Istanbul and Berlin, respectively), and in the Ashur Ostracon, see *IBP*, p. 240; *COS*, pp. 158–161.

Person # 36 | Shalmaneser V (= Ululaya), king, *726–722, 2 Kings 17:2*

In chronicles, in king-lists, and in rare remaining inscriptions of his own (*ABC*, p. 242; *COS*, vol. 2, p. 325). Most notable is the Neo-Babylonian Chronicle series, Chronicle 1, i, lines 24–32. In those lines, year 2 of the Chronicle mentions his plundering the city of Samaria (*Raging Torrent*, pp. 178, 182; *ANEHST*, p. 408). ("Shalman" in Hosea 10:14 is likely a historical allusion, but modern lack of information makes it difficult to assign it to a particular historical situation or ruler, Assyrian or otherwise. See below for the endnotes to the box at the top of p. 50.)

Person # 37 | Sargon II, king, *721–705, Isaiah 20:1*

In many inscriptions, including his own. See *Raging Torrent*, pp. 80–109, 176–179, 182; *COS*, vol. 2, pp. 293–300; Mikko Lukko, *The Correspondence of Tiglath-pileser III and Sargon II from Calah/Nimrud* (State Archives of Assyria, no. 19; Assyrian Text Corpus Project; Winona Lake, Ind.: Eisenbrauns, 2013); *ABC*, pp. 236–238; *IBP*, pp. 240–241 no. (74).

Person # 38 | Sennacherib, king, *704–681, 2 Kings 18:13*

In many inscriptions, including his own. See *Raging Torrent*, pp. 110–129; *COS*, vol. 2, pp. 300–305; *ABC*, pp. 238–240; *ANEHST*, pp. 407–411, esp. 410; *IBP*, pp. 241–242.

Person # 39 | Adrammelech (Ardamullissu = Arad-mullissu), son and assassin of Sennacherib, ca. *7th century, 2 Kings 19:37*

In a letter sent to Esarhaddon, who succeeded Sennacherib on the throne of Assyria. See *Raging Torrent*, pp. 111, 184, and *COS*, vol. 3, p. 244, both of which describe and cite with approval Simo Parpola, "The Murderer of Sennacherib," in *Death in Mesopotamia: Papers Read at the XXVie Rencontre Assyriologique Internationale*, ed. Bendt Alster (Copenhagen: Akademisk Forlag, 1980), pp. 171–182. See also *ABC*, p. 240.

An upcoming scholarly challenge is the identification of Sennacherib's successor, Esarhaddon, as a more likely assassin in Andrew Knapp's paper, "The Murderer of Sennacherib, Yet Again," to be read in a February 2014 Midwest regional conference in Bourbonnais, Ill. (SBL/AOS/ASOR).

On various renderings of the neo-Assyrian name of the assassin, see *RlA* s.v. "Ninlil," vol. 9, pp. 452–453 (in German). On the mode of execution of those thought to have been conspirators in the assassination, see the selection from Ashurbanipal's Rassam cylinder in *ANET*, p. 288.

PERSON # 40 | ESARHADDON, KING, 680–669, 2 KINGS 19:37

In his many inscriptions. See *Raging Torrent*, pp. 130–147; *COS*, vol. 2, p. 306; *ABC*, pp. 217–219. Esarhaddon's name appears in many cuneiform inscriptions (*ANET*, pp. 272–274, 288–290, 292–294, 296, 297, 301–303, 426–428, 449, 450, 531, 533–541, 605, 606), including his Succession Treaty (*ANEHST*, p. 355).

BABYLONIA

PERSON # 41 | MERODACH-BALADAN II (MARDUK-APLA-IDINNA II), KING, 721–710 AND 703, 2 KINGS 20:12

In the inscriptions of Sennacherib and the Neo-Babylonian Chronicles (*Raging Torrent*, pp. 111, 174, 178–179, 182–183. For Sennacherib's account of his first campaign, which was against Merodach-baladan II, see *COS*, vol. 2, pp. 300-302. For the Neo-Babylonian Chronicle series, Chronicle 1, i, 33–42, see *ANEHST*, pp. 408–409. This king is also included in the Babylonian King List A (*ANET*, p. 271), and the latter part of his name remains in the reference to him in the Synchronistic King List (*ANET*, pp. 271–272), on which see *ABC*, pp. 226, 237.

Person # 42 | *Nebuchadnezzar II, king, 604–562, 2 Kings 24:1*

In many cuneiform tablets, including his own inscriptions. See *Raging Torrent*, pp. 220–223; *COS*, vol. 2, pp. 308–310; *ANET*, pp. 221, 307–311; *ABC*, p. 232. The Neo-Babylonian Chronicle series refers to him in Chronicles 4 and 5 (*ANEHST*, pp. 415, 416–417, respectively). Chronicle 5, reverse, lines 11–13, briefly refers to his conquest of Jerusalem ("the city of Judah") in 597 by defeating "its king" (Jehoiachin), as well as his appointment of "a king of his own choosing" (Zedekiah) as king of Judah.

Person # 43 | *Nebo-sarsekim, chief official of Nebuchadnezzar II, fl. ca. 6th century, Jeremiah 39:3*

In a cuneiform inscription on Babylonian clay tablet BM 114789 (1920-12-13, 81), dated to 595 B.C.E. The time reference in Jeremiah 39:3 is very close, to the year 586. Since it is extremely unlikely that two individuals having precisely the same personal name would have been, in turn, the sole holders of precisely this unique position within a decade of each other, it is safe to assume that the inscription and the book of Jeremiah refer to the same person in different years of his time in office. In July 2007 in the British Museum, Austrian researcher Michael Jursa discovered this Babylonian reference to the biblical "Nebo-sarsekim, the Rab-saris" (*rab ša-rēši*, meaning "chief official") of Nebuchadnezzar II (r. 604–562). Jursa identified this official in his article, "Nabu-šarrūssu-ukīn, *rab ša-rēši*, und 'Nebusarsekim' (Jer. 39:3)," *Nouvelles Assyriologiques Breves et Utilitaires* 2008/1 (March): pp. 9–10 (in German). See also Bob Becking, "Identity of Nabusharrussu-ukin, the Chamberlain: An Epigraphic Note on Jeremiah 39,3. With an Appendix on the Nebu(!)sarsekim Tablet by Henry Stadhouders," *Biblische Notizen* NF 140 (2009): pp. 35–46; "Corrections," pp. 121–124; "Sixteen," p. 47 n. 31. On the correct translation of *ráb ša-rēši* (and three older, published instances of it having been incorrect translated as *rab šaqê*), see *ITP*, p. 171 n. 16.

PERSON # 44 | NERGAL-SHAREZER (NERGAL-SHARUSUR THE SIN-MAGIR = NERGAL-ŠARRU-USUR THE SIMMAGIR), OFFICER OF NEBUCHADNEZZAR II, EARLY SIXTH CENTURY, JEREMIAH 39:3

In a Babylonian cuneiform inscription known as Nebuchadnezzar II's Prism (column 3 of prism EŞ 7834, in the Istanbul Archaeological Museum). See ANET, pp. 307–308; Rocio Da Riva, "Nebuchadnezzar II's Prism (EŞ 7834): A New Edition," *Zeitschrift für Assyriologie und Vorderasiatische Archäologie*, vol. 103, no. 2 (2013): 204, Group 3.

PERSON # 45 | NEBUZARADAN (= NABUZERIDDINAM = NABÛ-ZER-IDDIN), A CHIEF OFFICER OF NEBUCHADNEZZAR II, EARLY SIXTH CENTURY, 2 KINGS 25:8; JEREMIAH 39:9

In a Babylonian cuneiform inscription known as Nebuchadnezzar II's Prism (column 3, line 36 of prism EŞ 7834, in the Istanbul Archaeological Museum). See ANET, p. 307; Rocio Da Riva, "Nebuchadnezzar II's Prism (EŞ 7834): A New Edition," *Zeitschrift für Assyriologie und Vorderasiatische Archäologie*, vol. 103, no. 2 (2013): 202, Group 1.

PERSON # 46 | EVIL-MERODACH (AWEL MARDUK = AMEL MARDUK), KING, R. 561–560, 2 KINGS 25:27

In various inscriptions (*ANET*, p. 309; *OROT*, pp. 15, 504 n. 23). See especially Ronald H. Sack, *Amel-Marduk: 562-560 B.C.; A Study Based on Cuneiform, Old Testament, Greek, Latin and Rabbinical Sources* (Alter Orient und Altes Testament, no. 4; Kevelaer, Butzon & Bercker, and Neukirchen-Vluyn, Neukirchener, 1972).

PERSON # 47 | BELSHAZZAR, SON AND CO-REGENT OF NABONIDUS, FL. CA. 543?–540, DANIEL 5:1, ETC.

In Babylonian administrative documents and the "Verse Account" (Muhammed A. Dandamayev, "Nabonid, A," *RlA*, vol. 9, p. 10; *Raging Torrent*, pp. 215–216; *OROT*, pp. 73–74). A neo-Babylonian text refers to him as "Belshazzar the crown prince" (*ANET*, pp. 309–310 n. 5).

Persia

Person # 48 | Cyrus II (Cyrus the Great), king, r. 559–530, 2 Chronicles 36:22

In various inscriptions (including his own), for which and on which see *ANEHST*, pp. 418–426, *ABC*, p. 214. For Cyrus' cylinder inscription, see *Raging Torrent*, pp. 224–230; *ANET*, pp. 315–316; *COS*, vol. 2, pp. 314–316; *ANEHST*, pp. 426–430; P&B, pp. 87–92. For larger context and implications in the biblical text, see *OROT*, pp. 70-76.

Person # 49 | Darius I (Darius the Great), king, r. 520–486, Ezra 4:5

In various inscriptions, including his own trilingual cliff inscription at Behistun, on which see P&B, pp. 131–134. See also *COS*, vol. 2, p. 407, vol. 3, p. 130; *ANET*, pp. 221, 316, 492; *ABC*, p. 214; *ANEHST*, pp. 407, 411. On the setting, see *OROT*, pp. 70–75.

Person # 50 | Tattenai (Tatnai), provincial governor of Trans-Euphrates, late sixth to early fifth century, Ezra 5:3

In a tablet of Darius I the Great, king of Persia, which can be dated to exactly June 5, 502 B.C.E. See David E. Suiter, "Tattenai," in David Noel Freedman, ed., *Anchor Bible Dictionary* (New York: Doubleday, 1992), vol. 6, p. 336; A. T. Olmstead, "Tattenai, Governor of 'Beyond the River,'" *Journal of Near Eastern Studies* 3 (1944): p. 46. A drawing of the cuneiform text appears in Arthur Ungnad, *Vorderasiatische Schriftdenkmäler Der Königlichen Museen Zu Berlin* (Leipzig: Hinrichs, 1907), vol. IV, p. 48, no. 152 (VAT 43560). VAT is the abbreviation for the series *Vorderasiatische Abteilung Tontafel*, published by the Berlin Museum. The author of the *BAR* article wishes to acknowledge the query regarding Tattenai from Mr. Nathan Yadon of Houston, Texas, private correspondence, 8 September 2015.

Appendix: Evidence for Biblical figures

PERSON # 51 | XERXES I (AHASUERUS), KING, 486–465, ESTHER 1:1

In various inscriptions, including his own (P&B, p. 301; *ANET*, pp. 316–317), and in the dates of documents from the time of his reign (*COS*, vol. 2, p. 188, vol. 3, pp. 142, 145. On the setting, see *OROT*, pp. 70–75.

PERSON # 52 | ARTAXERXES I LONGIMANUS, KING, 465-425/424, EZRA 4:6, 7

In various inscriptions, including his own (P&B, pp. 242–243), and in the dates of documents from the time of his reign (*COS*, vol. 2, p. 163, vol. 3, p. 145; *ANET*, p. 548).

PERSON # 53 | DARIUS II NOTHUS, KING, 425/424-405/404, NEHEMIAH 12:22

In various inscriptions, including his own (for example, P&B, pp. 158–159) and in the dates of documents from the time of his reign (*ANET*, p. 548; *COS*, vol. 3, pp. 116–117).

"ALMOST REAL" PEOPLE: THE BIBLICAL AND ARCHAEOLOGICAL EVIDENCE

In general, the persons listed in the box at the top of p. 50 of the March/April 2014 issue of *BAR* exclude persons in two categories. The first category includes those about whom we know so little that we cannot even approach a firm identification with anyone named in an inscription. One example is "Shalman" in Hosea 10:14. This name almost certainly refers to a historical person, but variations of this name were common in the ancient Near East, and modern lack of information on the biblical Shalman makes it difficult to assign it to a particular historical situation or ruler, Assyrian or otherwise. See Francis I. Andersen and David Noel Freedman, *Hosea* (The Anchor Bible, vol. 24; Garden City, N.Y.: Doubleday, 1980), pp. 570–571. A second example is "Osnappar" (=Asnapper) in Ezra 4:10, who is not called a king, and for whom the traditional identification has no basis for singling out any particular ruler. See Jacob M. Myers,

Ezra-Nehemiah (The Anchor Bible. vol. 14; Garden City, N.Y.: Doubleday, 1981), p. 333.

The second category of excluded identifications comes from the distinction between inscriptions that are dug up after many centuries and texts that have been copied and recopied through the course of many centuries. The latter include the books of the Bible itself, as well as other writings, notably those of Flavius Josephus in the first century C.E. His reference to Ethbaal (='Ittoba'al ='Ithoba'al), the father of Jezebel (1 Kings 16:31). is not included in this article, because Josephus' writings do not come to us from archaeology. See *IBP*, p. 238 n. 90; cf. *Raging Torrent*, pp. 30, 115–116 (p. 133 refers to an Ethbaal appointed king of Sidon by Sennacherib, therefore he must have lived a century later than Jezebel's father).

Ammon

Person #1 | Balaam son of Beor, fl. ca. 13th century (some prefer late 15th century), Numbers 22:5

In a wall inscription on plaster dated to 700 B.C.E. (*COS*, vol. 2, pp. 140–145). It was discovered at Tell Deir ʿAllā, in the same Transjordanian geographical area in which the Bible places Balaam's activity. Many scholars assume or conclude that the Balaam and Beor of the inscription are the same as the biblical pair and belong to the same folk tradition, which is not necessarily historical. See P. Kyle McCarter, Jr., "The Balaam Texts from Deir ʿAllā: The First Combination," *BASOR* 239 (1980): pp. 49–60; Jo Ann Hackett, *The Balaam Text from Deir ʿAllā* (Chico, Calif.: Scholars Press, 1984), pp. 27, 33–34; idem, "Some Observations on the Balaam Tradition at Deir ʿAllā," *Biblical Archaeologist* 49 (1986), p. 216. Mykytiuk at first listed these two identifications under a strong classification in *IBP*, p. 236, but because the inscription does not reveal a time period for Balaam and Beor, he later corrected that to a "not-quite-firmly identified" classification in "Corrections," pp. 111–113, no. 29 and 30, and in "Sixteen," p. 53.

Appendix: Evidence for Biblical figures

Although it contains three identifying marks (traits) of both father and son, this inscription is dated to ca. 700 B.C.E., several centuries after the period in which the Bible places Balaam. Speaking with no particular reference to this inscription, some scholars, such as Frendo and Kofoed, argue that lengthy gaps between a particular writing and the things to which it refers are not *automatically* to be considered refutations of historical claims (Anthony J. Frendo, *Pre-Exilic Israel, the Hebrew Bible, and Archaeology: Integrating Text and Artefact* [New York: T&T Clark, 2011], p. 98; Jens B. Kofoed, *Text and History: Historiography and the Study of the Biblical Text* [Winona Lake, Ind.: Eisenbrauns, 2005], pp. 83–104, esp. p, 42). There might easily have been intervening sources which transmitted the information from generation to generation but as centuries passed, were lost.

PERSON # 2 | BAALIS, KING OF THE AMMONITES, R. EARLY 6TH CENTURY, JEREMIAH 40:14

In an Ammonite seal impression on the larger, fairly flat end of a ceramic cone (perhaps a bottle-stopper?) from Tell el-Umeiri, in what was the land of the ancient Ammonites. The seal impression reveals only two marks (traits) of an individual, so it is not quite firm. See Larry G. Herr, "The Servant of Baalis," *Biblical Archaeologist* 48 (1985): pp. 169–172; *WSS*, p. 322 no. 860; *COS*, p. 201; *IBP*, p. 242 no. (77); "Sixteen Strong," p. 52. The differences between the king's name in this seal impression and the biblical version can be understood as slightly different renderings of the same name in different dialects; see bibliography in Michael O'Connor, "The Ammonite Onomasticon: Semantic Problems," *Andrews University Seminary Studies* 25 (1987): p. 62 paragraph (3), supplemented by Lawrence T. Geraty, "Back to Egypt: An Illustration of How an Archaeological Find May Illumine a Biblical Passage," *Reformed Review* 47 (1994): p. 222; Emile Puech, "L'inscription de la statue d'Amman et la paleographie ammonite," *Revue biblique* 92 (1985): pp. 5–24.

Northern Arabia

Person #3 | Geshem (= Gashmu) the Arabian, r. mid-5th century, Nehemiah 2:10

In an Aramaic inscription on a silver bowl discovered at Tell el-Maskhuta, Egypt, in the eastern delta of the Nile, that mentions "Qainu, son of Geshem [or Gashmu], king of Qedar," an ancient kingdom in northwest Arabia. This bowl is now in the Brooklyn Museum. See Isaac Rabinowitz, "Aramaic Inscriptions of the Fifth Century B.C.E. from a North-Arab Shrine in Egypt," *Journal of the Near Eastern Studies* 15 (1956): pp. 1–9, Pl. 6–7; William J. Dumbrell, "The Tell el-Maskhuta Bowls and the 'Kingdom' of Qedar in the Persian Period," *BASOR* 203 (October 1971): pp. 35–44; *OROT*, pp. 74–75, 518 n. 26; *Raging Torrent*, p. 55. Despite thorough analyses of the Qainu bowl and its correspondences pointing to the biblical Geshem, there is at least one other viable candidate for identification with the biblical Geshem: Gashm or Jasm, son of Shahr, of Dedan. On him, see Frederick V. Winnett and William L. Reed, *Ancient Records from North Arabia* (University of Toronto Press, 1970), pp. 115–117; *OROT*, pp. 75. 518 n. 26. Thus the existence of two viable candidates would seem to render the case for each not quite firm (*COS*, vol. 2, p. 176).

Southern Kingdom of Judah

Person #4 | Shebna, the overseer of the palace, fl. ca. 726–697/696, Isaiah 22:15–19 (probably also the scribe of 2 Kings 18:18, etc., before being promoted to palace overseer)

In an inscription at the entrance to a rock-cut tomb in Silwan, near Jerusalem. There are only two marks (traits) of an individual, and these do not include his complete name, so this identification, though tempting, is not quite firm. See Nahman Avigad, "Epitaph of a Royal Steward from Siloam Village," *IEJ* 3 (1953): pp. 137–152; David Ussishkin, *The Village of Silwan* (Jerusalem: Israel Exploration

Society, 1993), pp. 247–250; *IBP*, pp. 223, 225; "Sixteen Strong," pp. 51–52.

PERSON #5 | HANANIAH AND HIS FATHER, AZZUR, FROM GIBEON, FL. EARLY 6TH AND LATE 7TH CENTURIES, RESPECTIVELY, JEREMIAH 28:1, ETC.,

In a personal seal carved from blue stone, 20 mm. long and 17 mm. wide, inscribed "belonging to Hananyahu, son of 'Azaryahu" and surrounded by a pomegranate-garland border, and (*WSS*, p. 100, no. 165). This seal reveals only two marks (traits) of an individual, the names of father and son, therefore the identification it provides can be no more than a reasonable hypothesis (*IBP*, pp. 73–77, as amended by "Corrections," pp. 56–57). One must keep in mind that there were probably many people in Judah during that time named Hananiah/Hananyahu, and quite a few of them could have had a father named 'Azariah/'Azaryahu, or 'Azzur for short. (Therefore, it would take a third identifying mark of an individual to establish a strong, virtually certain identification of the Biblical father and/or son, such as mention of the town of Gibeon or Hananyahu being a prophet.)

Because the shapes of the letters of the Hebrew alphabet gradually changed over the centuries, using examples discovered at different stratigraphic levels of earth, we can now date ancient Hebrew inscriptions on the basis of paleography (letter shapes and the direction and order of the strokes). This seal was published during the 19th century (in 1883 by Charles Clermont-Ganneau), when no one, neither scholars nor forgers, knew the correct shapes of Hebrew letters for the late seventh to early sixth centuries (the time of Jeremiah). We now know that all the letter shapes in this seal are chronologically consistent with each other and are the appropriate letter shapes for late seventh–century to early sixth–century Hebrew script—the time of Jeremiah. This date is indicated especially by the Hebrew letter *nun* (n) and—though the photographs are not completely clear, possibly by the Hebrew letter *he'* (h), as well.

Because the letter shapes could not have been correctly forged, yet they turned out to be correct, it is safe to presume that this stone seal is genuine, even though its origin (provenance) is unknown. Normally, materials from the antiquities market are not to be trusted, because they have been bought, rather than excavated, and could be forged. But the exception is inscriptions purchased during the 19th century that turn out to have what we now know are the correct letter shapes, all of which are appropriate for the same century or part of a century (*IBP*, p. 41, paragraph 2) up to the word "Also," pp. 154 and 160 both under the subheading "Authenticity," p. 219, notes 23 and 24).

Also, the letters are written in Hebrew script, which is discernably different from the scripts of neighboring kingdoms. The only Hebrew kingdom still standing when this inscription was written was Judah. Because this seal is authentic and is from the kingdom of Judah during the time of Jeremiah, it matches the setting of the Hananiah, the son of Azzur in Jeremiah 28.

Comparing the identifying marks of individuals in the inscription and in the Bible, the seal owner's name and his father's name inscribed in the seal match the name of the false prophet and his father in Jeremiah 28, giving us two matching marks of an individual. That is not enough for a firm identification, but it is enough for a reasonable hypothesis.

PERSON #6 | GEDALIAH THE GOVERNOR, SON OF AHIKAM, FL. CA. 585, 2 KINGS 25:22

In the bulla from Tell ed-Duweir (ancient Lachish) that reads, "Belonging to Gedalyahu, the overseer of the palace." The Babylonian practice was to appoint indigenous governors over conquered populations. It is safe to assume that as conquerors of Jerusalem in 586 B.C.E., they would have chosen the highest-ranking Judahite perceived as "pro-Babylonian" to be their governor over Judah. The palace overseer had great authority and knowledge of the inner workings of government at the highest level, sometimes serving as vice-regent for the king; see S. H. Hooke, "A Scarab and Sealing

From Tell Duweir," *Palestine Exploration Fund Quarterly Statement* 67 (1935): pp. 195–197; J. L. Starkey, "Lachish as Illustrating Bible History," *Palestine Exploration Fund Quarterly Statement* 69 (1937): pp. 171–174; some publications listed in *WSS*, p. 172 no. 405. The palace overseer at the time of the Babylonian conquest, whose bulla we have, would be the most likely choice for governor, *if* they saw him as pro-Babylonian. Of the two prime candidates named Gedaliah (= Gedalyahu)—assuming both survived the conquest— Gedaliah the son of Pashhur clearly did not have the title "overseer of the palace" (Jeremiah 38:1), and he was clearly an enemy of the Babylonians (Jeremiah 38:4–6). But, though we lack irrefutable evidence, Gedaliah the son of Ahikam is quite likely to have been palace overseer. His prestigious family, the descendants of Shaphan, had been "key players" in crucial situations at the highest levels of the government of Judah for three generations. As for his being perceived as pro-Babylonian, his father Ahikam had protected the prophet Jeremiah (Jeremiah 26:24; cf. 39:11–14), who urged surrender to the Babylonian army (Jeremiah 38:1–3).

The preceding argument is a strengthening step beyond "Corrections," pp. 103–104, which upgrades the strength of the identification from its original level in *IBP*, p. 235, responding to the difficulty expressed in Oded Lipschits, *The Fall and Rise of Jerusalem: Judah under Babylonian Rule* (Winona Lake, Ind.: Eisenbrauns, 2005), p. 86 n. 186.

PERSON #7 | JAAZANIAH (= JEZANIAH), FL. EARLY 6TH CENTURY, 2 KINGS 25:23

In the Tell en-Naṣbeh (ancient Mizpah) stone seal inscribed: "Belonging to Ya'azanyahu, the king's minister." It is unclear whether the title "king's minister" in the seal might have some relationship with the biblical phrase "the officers (Hebrew: *sarîm*) of the troops," which included the biblical Jaazaniah (2 Kings 25: 23). There are, then, only two identifying marks of an individual that clearly connect the seal's Jaazaniah with the biblical one: the seal owner's name and the fact that it was discovered at the city where the biblical "Jaazaniah, the son of the Maacathite," died. See William F. Badè, "The Seal of Jaazaniah," *Zeitschrift für die alttestamentlishe Wissenschaft* 51 (1933): pp. 150–156; *WSS*, p. 52 no. 8; *IBP*, p. 235; "Sixteen Strong," p. 52.

Person # 8 | Hezir (Ḥezîr), founding father of a priestly division in the First Temple in Jerusalem, early tenth century, 1 Chronicles 24:15

In an epitaph over a large tomb complex on the western slope of the Mount of Olives, facing the site of the Temple in Jerusalem. First the epitaph names some of Ḥezîr's prominent descendants, and then it presents Ḥezîr by name in the final phrase, which refers to his descendants, who are named before that, as "priests, of (*min*, literally "from") the sons of Ḥezîr." This particular way of saying it recognizes him as the head of that priestly family. See *CIIP*, vol. 1: Jerusalem, Part 1, pp. 178–181, no. 137.

Also, among the burial places inside that same tomb complex, lying broken into fragments was an inscribed, square stone plate that had been used to seal a burial. This plate originally told whose bones they were and the name of that person's father: "'Ovadiyah, the son of G...,'" but a break prevents us from knowing the rest of the father's name and what might have been written after that. Immediately after the break, the inscription ends with the name "Ḥezîr." Placement at the end, as in the epitaph over the entire tomb complex, is consistent with proper location of the name of the founding ancestor of the family. See *CIIP*, vol. 1, Part 1, p. 182, no. 138.

As for the date of Ḥezîr in the inscriptions, to be sure, Ḥezîr lived at least four generations earlier than the inscribing of the epitaph over the complex, and possibly many more generations (*CIIP*, vol. 1, Part 1:179–180, no. 137). Still, it is not possible to assign any date (or even a century) to the Ḥezîr named in the epitaph above the tomb complex, nor to the Ḥezîr named on the square stone plate, therefore this identification has no "airtight" proof or strong case. The date of the engraving itself does not help answer the question of this identification, because the stone was quarried no earlier than the second century B.C.E. (*CIIP*, Part 1, p.179, no. 137–138).

Appendix: Evidence for Biblical figures

Nevertheless, it is still a *reasonable* identification, as supported by the following facts:

- Clearly in the epitaph over the tomb complex, and possibly in the square stone plate inscription, the Ḥezîr named in the epitaph is placed last in recognition of his being the head, that is, the progenitor or "founding father" of the priestly family whose members are buried there.

- This manner of presenting Ḥezîr in the epitaph suggests that he dates back to the founding of this branch of the priestly family. (This suggestion may be pursued independently of whether the family was founded in Davidic times as 1 Chronicles 24 states.)

- Because there is no mention of earlier ancestors, one may observe that the author(s) of the inscriptions anchored these genealogies in the names of the progenitors. It seems that the authors fully expected that the names of the founders of these 24 priestly families would be recognized as such, presumably by Jewish readers. In at least some inscriptions of ancient Israel, it appears that patronymic phrases that use a preposition such as *min*, followed by the plural of the word *son*, as in the epitaph over the tomb complex, "from the sons of Ḥezîr," functioned in much the same way as virtual surnames. The assumption would have been that they were common knowledge. If one accepts that Israel relied on these particular priestly families to perform priestly duties for centuries, then such an expectation makes sense. To accept the reasonableness of this identification is a way of acknowledging the continuity of Hebrew tradition, which certainly seems unquenchable.

See the published dissertation, L. J. Mykytiuk, *Identifying Biblical Persons in Northwest Semitic Inscriptions of 1200–539 B.C.E.* (Atlanta: Society of Biblical Literature, 2004), p. 214, note 2, for 19th and 20th century bibliography on the Ḥezîr family epitaph.

Person # 9 | Jakim (Yakîm), founding father of a priestly division in the First Temple in Jerusalem, early tenth century, 1 Chronicles 24:12

On an inscribed ossuary ("bone box") of the first or second century C.E. discovered in a burial chamber just outside Jerusalem on the western slope of the Mount of Olives, facing the site of the Temple. The three-line inscription reads: "Menahem, from (*min*) the sons of Yakîm, (a) priest." See *CIIP*, vol. 1, Part 1, pp. 217–218, no. 183, burial chamber 299, ossuary 83.

As with the epitaph over the tomb complex of Ḥezîr, this inscription presents Yakîm as the founder of this priestly family. And as with Ḥezîr in the preceding case, no strong case can be made for this identification, because the inscriptional Yakîm lacks a clear date (and indeed, has no clear century). Nevertheless, it is reasonable to identify Yakîm with the Jakim in 1 Chronicles 24 for essentially the same three reasons as Ḥezîr immediately above.

Person # 10 | Maaziah (Maʿaziah = Maazyahu = Maʿazyahu), founding father of a priestly division in the First Temple in Jerusalem, early 10th century, 1 Chronicles 24:18

On an inscribed ossuary ("bone box") of the late first century B.C.E. or the first century C.E. Its one-line inscription reads, "Miriam daughter of Yeshuaʿ son of Caiaphas, priest from Maʿaziah, from Beth ʿImri."

The inscription is in Aramaic, which was the language spoken by Jews in first-century Palestine for day-to-day living. The Hebrew personal name Miriam and the Yahwistic ending –iah on Maʿaziah, which refers to the name of Israel's God, also attest to a Jewish context.

This inscription's most significant difficulty is that its origin is unknown (it is unprovenanced). Therefore, the Israel Antiquities Authority at first considered it a potential forgery. Zissu and Goren's subsequent scientific examination, particularly of the patina (a coating left by age), however, has upheld its authenticity. Thus the

Appendix: Evidence for Biblical figures

inscribed ossuary is demonstrably authentic, and it suits the Jewish setting of the priestly descendants of Ma'aziah in the Second Temple period.

Now that we have the authenticity and the Jewish setting of the inscription, we can count the identifying marks of an individual to see how strong a case there is for the Ma'azyahu of the Bible and the Ma'aziah being the same person: 1) Ma'azyahu and Ma'aziah are simply spelling variants of the very same name. 2) Ma'aziah's occupation was priest, because he was the ancestor of a priest. 3) Ma'aziah's place in the family is mentioned in a way that anchors the genealogy in him as the founder of the family. (The inscription adds mention of 'Imri as the father of a subset, a "father's house" within Ma'aziah's larger family.)

Normally, if the person in the Bible and the person in the inscription have the same three identifying marks of an individual, and if all other factors are right, one can say the identification (confirmation) of the Biblical person in the inscription is virtually certain. But not all other factors are right. A setting (even in literature) consists of time and place. To be sure, the social "place" is a Jewish family of priests, both for the Biblical Ma'azyahu and for the inscriptional Ma'aziah. But the time setting of the Biblical Ma'azyahu during the reign of David is not matched by any time setting at all for the inscriptional Ma'aziah. We do not even know which century the inscriptional Ma'aziah lived in. He could have been a later descendant of the Biblical Ma'azyahu.

Therefore, as with Ḥezîr and as with Yakîm above, we cannot claim a clear, strong identification that would be an archaeological confirmation of the biblical Ma'azyahu. We only have a reasonable hypothesis, a tentative identification that is certainly not proven, but reasonable—for essentially the same three reasons as with Ḥezîr above.

See Boaz Zissu and Yuval Goren, "The Ossuary of 'Miriam Daughter of Yeshua Son of Caiaphas, Priests [of] Ma'aziah from Beth 'Imri'," *Israel Exploration Journal* 61 (2011), pp. 74–95; Christopher A. Rollston, "'Priests' or 'Priest' in the Mariam (Miriam) Ossuary, and the Language of the Inscription," Rollston Epigraphy (blog), July 14, 2011, www.rollstonepigraphy.com/?p=275, accessed October 10, 2016; Richard Bauckham, "The Caiaphas Family," *Journal for the Study of the Historical Jesus* 10 (2012), pp. 3–31.

Symbols & Abbreviations

ANEHST Mark W. Chavalas, ed., *The Ancient Near East: Historical Sources in Translation* (Blackwell Sources in Ancient History; Victoria, Australia: Blackwell, 2006).

ABC A. Kirk Grayson, *Assyrian and Babylonian Chronicles* (Winona Lake, Ind.: Eisenbrauns, 2000).

ANET James B. Pritchard, ed., *Ancient Near Eastern Texts Relating to the Old Testament*, 3rd ed. (Princeton, N.J.: Princeton University Press, 1969).

B.C.E. before the common era, used as an equivalent to B.C.

BASOR *Bulletin of the American Schools of Oriental Research*

c. century (all are B.C.E.)

ca. circa, a Latin word meaning "around"

cf. compare

CAH John Boardman et al., eds., *The Cambridge Ancient History* (2nd ed.; New York: Cambridge University Press, 1970).

CIIP Hanna M. Cotton et al., eds., *Corpus Inscriptionum Iudaeae/Palaestinae*, vol. 1: Jerusalem, Part 1 (Berlin and Boston: De Gruyter, 2010). Vol. 1 consists of two separately bound Parts, each a physical "book."

"Corrections" Lawrence J. Mykytiuk, "Corrections and Updates to 'Identifying Biblical Persons in Northwest Semitic Inscriptions of 1200–539 B.C.E.," *Maarav* 16 (2009), pp. 49–132, free online at docs.lib.purdue.edu/lib_research/129/.

COS William W. Hallo and K. Lawson Younger, eds., *The Context of Scripture*, vol. 2: *Archival Documents from the Biblical World* (Boston: Brill, 2000). Dearman, *Studies* J. Andrew Dearman, ed., *Studies in the Mesha Inscription and Moab* (Atlanta: Scholars Press, 1989).

esp. especially

fl. flourished

IBP Lawrence J. Mykytiuk, *Identifying Biblical Persons in Northwest Semitic Inscriptions of 1200–539 B.C.E.* (Atlanta: Society of Biblical Literature, 2004). This book is a revised Ph.D. dissertation in Hebrew and Semitic Studies, University of Wisconsin-Madison, 1998, which began with a 1992 graduate seminar paper. Most of ***IBP*** is available on the Google Books web site: www.google.com/search?tbo=p&tbm=bks&q=mykytiuk+identifying&num=10

ibid. (Latin) "the same thing," meaning the same publication as the one mentioned immediately before

idem (Latin) "the same one(s)," meaning "the same person or persons," used for referring to the author(s) mentioned immediately before.

IEJ *Israel Exploration Journal*

ITP Hayim Tadmor, *The Inscriptions of Tiglath-pileser III, King of Assyria* (Fontes ad Res Judaicas Spectantes; Jerusalem: Israel Academy of Sciences and Humanities, 2nd 2007 printing with addenda et corrigenda, 1994).

n. note (a footnote or endnote)

no. number (of an item, usually on a page)

OROT Kenneth A. Kitchen, *On the Reliability of the Old Testament* (Grand Rapids, Mich.: Eerdmans, 2003).

P&B Edwin M. Yamauchi, *Persia and the Bible* (Grand Rapids, Mich.: Baker, 1990).

Pl. plate(s) (a page of photos or drawings in a scholarly publication, normally unnumbered,)

r. reigned

Raging Torrent Mordechai Cogan, *The Raging Torrent: Historical Inscriptions from Assyria and Babylonia Relating to Ancient Israel* (A Carta Handbook; Jerusalem: Carta, 2008).

RlA *Reallexikon der Assyriologie und Vorderasiatischen Archäologie* (New York, Berlin: de Gruyter, ©1932, 1971).

RIMA a series of books: *The Royal Inscriptions of Mesopotamia: Assyrian Periods*

RIMA 3 A. Kirk Grayson, *Assyrian Rulers of the Early First Millennium BC, II (858–745 BC)* (RIMA, no. 3; Buffalo, N.Y.: University of Toronto Press, 1996).

"Sixteen" Lawrence J. Mykytiuk, "Sixteen Strong Identifications of Biblical Persons (Plus Nine Other Identifications) in Authentic Northwest Semitic Inscriptions from before 539 B.C.E.," pp. 35–58 in Meir Lubetski and Edith Lubetski, eds., *New Inscriptions and Seals Relating to the Biblical World* (Atlanta: Society of Biblical Literature, 2012), free online at docs.lib.purdue.edu/lib_research/150/.

Third Kenneth A. Kitchen, *The Third Intermediate Period in Egypt (1100–650 B.C.)* (2nd rev. ed. with supplement; Warminster, England: Aris & Phillips, 1986).

WSS Nahman Avigad and Benjamin Sass, *Corpus of West Semitic Stamp Seals* (Jerusalem: The Israel Academy of Sciences and Humanities, Israel Exploration Society, and The Hebrew University of Jerusalem, The Institute of Archaeology, 1997).

References

Kenneth A. Kitchen, *The Third Intermediate Period in Egypt (1100–650 B.C.)* (2nd rev. ed. with supplement; Warminster, England: Aris & Phillips, 1986), pp. 466–468.

Wayne T. Pitard, *Ancient Damascus: A Historical Study of the Syrian City-State from Earliest Times until its Fall to the Assyrians in 732 B.C.E.* (Winona Lake, Ind.: Eisenbrauns, 1987), pp. 138–144, 189.

Gershon Galil, *The Chronology of the Kings of Israel and Judah* (SHCANE 9; New York: Brill, 1996), p. 147.

A. Kirk Grayson, *Assyrian Rulers of the Early First Millennium BC, II (858–745 BC)* (RIMA 3; Buffalo, N.Y.: University of Toronto Press, 1996), p. vii; idem, "Assyria: Ashur-dan II to Ashur-nirari V (934–745 B.C.)," in *CAH*, vol. III, part I, pp. 238–281; idem, "Assyria: Tiglath-pileser III to Sargon II (744–705 B.C.)," in *CAH*, vol. III, part II, pp. 71–102; idem, "Assyria: Sennacherib and Esarhaddon (704–669 B.C.)," in *CAH*, vol. III, part II, pp. 103–141; idem, "Assyria 668–635 B.C.: The Reign of Ashurbanipal," in *CAH*, vol. III, part II, pp. 142–161.

Donald J. Wiseman, "Babylonia 605–539 B.C." in *CAH*, vol. III, part II, pp. 229–251.

Pierre Briant, *From Cyrus to Alexander: A History of the Persian Empire* (Winona Lake, Ind.: Eisenbrauns, 2002), "Index of Personal Names," pp. 1149–1160.

An Invitation to Participate in a Grand Adventure

Sooner or later, all school times end. Academicians call the graduation exercises that take place at the end of class work *commencement* for a good reason: It's because once the lessons have been completed, the time comes for the theoretical to become the practical. Serious life must now begin. Training exercises fade into memories, and the purpose for those lessons becomes manifest.

This study in the remarkable trustworthiness of the Scriptures is like those class lessons. Our examination is a theoretical exercise. But for us to allow these studies to remain theoretical exercises only is to waste—perhaps eternally—the opportunity and potential presented to us through those lessons. In much the same way, the pain and suffering of life should be allowed to bear their proper fruit. And so the necessity of putting the theoretical to work in the realm of the practical brings up the common question asked on so many levels of sincerity by those who are skeptical about the claims of Jesus recorded in the Gospels. The question usually runs something like this:

> *If the claims of Jesus of Nazareth to be God incarnate are true, what proof can you present of the practical reality of God's love being demonstrated through him?*

In essence, the question is "If God exists, prove it." Or better yet, the question is: "So what? How can this possibly matter to *me*?" The answers to questions like these are *anything* but theoretical.

The main thing is this: the Bible makes it clear that everyone will have questions like those articulated above answered with undeniable certainty at the end of days. *Everyone* gets the opportunity to confront God with their objections to life. But there will be surprises. Most notably, most of humanity will discover that the accusers will become the accused. As the New Testament phrases things, we all have an appointment to appear before the judgment seat of the Messiah. As Jesus put it, "All judgment has been given to the Son of Man."

At that time, the stage play we call "real life" will be over, and the Director will come on stage to reward all of the players according to their works. That day will not be the time to choose which side to serve. It will be the time to demonstrate what side has already been chosen.

And so I pose this question: What shall we do when that focus of our deepest hunger and yearnings (or, perhaps, the object of our greatest fears and terrors…) comes undeniably and unavoidably close, enveloped in light unbearable and full of glory, holiness, and righteousness? What shall we do when heaven and earth fly away from the presence of the Lamb? What is to be our response when our greatest fear or our greatest hope invades us and our self-centered tranquility and separateness from all that is truly eternal? In a word, will we be *prepared*? Will we be caught:

- *Settled down in our contentment apart from God, or*
- *Suffering in the miseries created for us by those who have oppressed us, or*
- *Full of anger because of harvests reaped by us through the consequences of our own unwise choices in life, or*
- *Faithful and content, having been reconciled to absolute holiness by the one who claimed that he came to redeem his elect when we come face-to-face with a real-time experience of sovereign holiness, righteousness, and unconquerable power?*

Better yet, what will the response be to us from God himself, when he meets us face-to-face at that last day? Will he respond to us as he did to Job, when that long-suffering servant finally had the opportunity to confront God about the troubles which had afflicted him? In Job 38:1-3:

> [1] *The* LORD *responded to Job from the whirlwind and said:*
> [2] *"Who is this who keeps darkening my counsel without knowing what he's talking about?*
> [3] *Stand up like a man!*
> *I'll ask you some questions,*
> *and you give me some answers!"*

Or shall God respond to us, not with questions such as the above, but with an approving comment? Perhaps as the Master responded to his faithful followers in the parable told by Jesus in Matthew 25:21: "Well done, good and trustworthy servant!"

The importance of preparing for eternity should not be overlooked by the Christian community, either. We Christians address Jesus the Messiah by the term "Lord," but all too often we ignore the implications of how that term should affect our day-to-day responses to life and circumstances. As a famous inscription located on a painting inside the Lübeck Cathedral (German: *Dom zu Lübeck*, or colloquially *Lübecker Dom*) in Lübeck, Germany phrases our obligations to Jesus the Messiah:

This Ye Call Me

Ye call Me Eternal, then seek Me not.

Ye call Me Fair, then love Me not.

Ye call Me Gracious, then trust Me not.

Ye call Me Just, then fear Me not.

Ye call Me Life, then choose Me not.

Ye call Me Light, then see Me not.

Ye call Me Lord, then respect Me not.

Ye call Me Master, then obey Me not.

Ye call Me Merciful, then thank Me not.

Ye call Me Mighty, then honor Me not.

Ye call Me Noble, then serve Me not.

Ye call Me Rich, then ask Me not.

Ye call Me Savior, then praise Me not.

Ye call Me Shepherd, then follow Me not.

Ye call Me Way, then walk with Me not.

Ye call Me Wise, then heed Me not.

Ye call Me Son of God, then worship Me not.

When I condemn you, then blame Me not.

To those who haven't yet met Jesus of Nazareth in his post-resurrection fullness, I ask you this respectful question: Are you looking for proof that God exists, and that he intervenes sovereignly to his greater glory and your great good? If so, you cannot do much better than to invite him to reveal himself to you. To prepare you for

An Invitation to Participate in a Grand Adventure

this meeting, I invite you to read through the material below, which you can use to begin your journey on what Chuck Missler calls the Grand Adventure, and by which you can discover from firsthand experience that when Jesus said "I am the light of the world," He meant *precisely* what He claimed.

How to Meet the Most Amazing Man who ever Lived …

If you're ready to meet the most amazing man who ever walked the face of the earth, it's best to begin with the basics. In Matthew 5:3-11, you'll find the basic instructions you need to meet him set forth in remarkable simplicity and succinctness within the opening phrases of the first public statement that Jesus the Messiah made before a large group of people.

Step 1: Admit your Spiritual Poverty

This is what He told the crowd that had assembled to listen to him:

> ³*"How blessed are those who are destitute in spirit,*
> *because the kingdom from heaven belongs to them!*

In making this statement, Jesus of Nazareth informs us that the riches of God's kingdom belong only to the bankrupt in spirit. The first step to meeting God in the person of Jesus the Messiah is to admit that your own personal positive characteristics have no value when it comes to meeting God's requirements. Human beauty, wealth, wisdom, intellect, abilities, cleverness, and anything else that qualifies us to be a part of the merely human condition are useless criteria by which to define our eligibility to enter the Kingdom of God.

Step 2: Begin to Mourn

If coming to God in the midst of spiritual poverty and bankruptcy is your first step to spiritual redemption, please be advised that taking this first step will immediately take you to your second step: you will begin to experience deep grief.

> ⁴ *"How blessed are those who mourn,*
> *because it is they who will be comforted!*

"The truth will set you free," Jesus once promised his followers, but before it does that, it's going to make you miserable for a short season. God will use your personal poverty of spirit to draw you to Himself, and the clearest proof that this drawing process is underway will be that you begin to mourn. You'll grieve over how your behavior and attitudes toward life have offended God and have resulted in endless lost opportunities to enjoy what could have been. Maybe you'll also grieve about those whom you have hurt, betrayed, defrauded, or sinned against.

STEP 3: BE BROUGHT TO A STATE OF HUMILITY

One of the most immediate results of this mourning will be that it causes you to see your true state before him.

> ⁵ *"How blessed are those who are humble,*
> *because it is they who will inherit the earth!*

You will be made humble, which comes about by beginning to know Jesus the Messiah well enough that you see yourself in perspective. In taking this third step toward salvation, you will be made qualified to inherit your place that God made you to enjoy for the rest of eternity.

STEP 4: BEGIN TO HUNGER TO KNOW HIM

After you've realized your own poverty of spirit, after you've begun to mourn because of what has been lost, and after you've begun to see yourself in perspective, compared to His pristine purity and holiness, you will begin to hunger to be like Him with respect to righteousness:

> ⁶ *"How blessed are those who are hungry and thirsty for*
> *righteousness, because it is they who will be satisfied!*

You will begin to want to spend time getting acquainted with God's word, the Bible, because within that book you'll find a road map to personal maturity. You'll seek out the company of like-minded Christian believers, and you'll look for a local church that can encourage you in your new Christian life.

Step 5: Treat Others the Way Jesus has Treated You

God will begin to work deep within you, creating a righteous state before him in which you will take your seat as God continues his work of directing every detail of your life to come. That ongoing process of personal growth will express itself in how you treat others:

> ⁷*"How blessed are those who are merciful,*
> *because it is they who will receive mercy!*

You will have been shown mercy, and as a result, you'll begin to show mercy to others after you've realized your own poverty of spirit, after you've begun to mourn because of what has been lost, and after you've begun to see yourself in perspective, compared to his pristine purity and holiness. You will begin to hunger to be like him with respect to righteousness.

Step 6: Let your Heart be Transformed from the Inside out

As God continues his work deep within you to conform your heart and mind to the image of his son, the Lord Jesus the Messiah, others around you will begin to notice the change you'll have been going through. Some of your friends and acquaintances might even tell you that there's something new about you. Maybe they won't exactly have the words to describe what they see, but see it they will. The truth is, they'll be seeing your purity of heart that has been rooted deep within you:

> ⁸*"How blessed are those who are pure in heart,*
> *because it is they who will see God!*

And you'll begin to see God at work, using you to bring a testimony of how God can change the lives of anyone who comes to him, bringing salvation from sin, deliverance from all sorts of bondage, and hope to the hopeless. Jesus the Messiah will have transformed your life, and now you'll see Him at work changing others.

Step 7: Let your Life begin to be Productive for God's Glory

You will become a peacemaker. That is, you'll begin to be known as one who brings peace and security to the lives of those who have neither of these valuable qualities. You'll be given wisdom, whenever you ask for it, to fashion peace out of conflict, serenity out of confrontation, and tranquility out of disruptive relationships.

*⁹ "How blessed are those who make peace,
because it is they who will be called God's children!*

Some of those to whom you minister will begin to tell you that they've finally met one of God's genuine children. "Finally, a true Christian!" could well be what they say about you.

Step 8: Watch Some People Hate you for your New Life

Be prepared, though, and forewarned: some people will react with animosity, anger, and hatred. The reason for this is that most people are opposed, not only to their own salvation, but to the salvation of others. Not wanting to know God, they won't want you to know him, either, and so you'll find yourself being opposed.

¹⁰ "How blessed are those who are persecuted for righteousness' sake, because the kingdom from heaven belongs to them!

Be prepared for it, because people like this will surely come into your life, and you'll need to learn how to give an answer to these people whom you will find opposing you.

Step 9: View Yourself in Light of Eternity, not Present Circumstances

Keep in mind as you begin your new relationship with God that you aren't the first person who chooses to follow Jesus of Nazareth and then comes into a world of trouble:

> ¹¹*"How blessed are you whenever people insult you, persecute you, and say all sorts of evil things against you falsely because of me!* ¹²*Rejoice and be extremely glad, because your reward in heaven is great! That's how they persecuted the prophets who came before you."*

How to Begin to Recognize your own Poverty of Spirit

You have broken God's holy Law. Realizing that this is true is the first step to learning the true state of your standing before God, which is that of spiritual bankruptcy in his perfect, holy, and righteous presence.

You don't think so?

"I'm not so bad," you tell yourself.

Really?

Ask yourself some questions:

- *Have you ever lied? Yes, you have. You've broken the ninth commandment.*

- *Have you ever stolen anything? Yes, you have. You've broken the eighth commandment.*

- *Have you ever committed adultery? Yes, you have, because Jesus said that to even lust after someone is the same as committing adultery. So you've broken the seventh commandment.*

My friend, you have broken three out of ten of God's commandments. And by desiring her or him in the first place, you are coveting someone's wife or daughter, or husband or son. So you've broken the tenth commandment. So far, you've broken four out of ten.

Shall we try for five out of ten? Jesus said to hate someone is to commit the sin of murder in your heart. And that's where sin starts. So you've broken the sixth commandment.

Now let's check the balance sheet: You have admitted that you are a lying, thieving, covetous, murdering, adulterer—and we've only looked at five of the ten.

Shall we go for six? By doing all these things, you have dishonored your father and mother. My friend, you've broken the fifth commandment. Now you've broken six out of the Ten Commandments.

If you will be honest with yourself, you have broken all the others, too. And these are just a summary of God's holy Law.

You've got a problem, my friend.

And it's a serious problem, because the penalty for breaking God's Law is severe indeed. But it's not just your problem. In fact, it's everybody's problem.

The penalty is death, and not just physical death. The penalty is eternal death, separation from God in a place that you really don't want to go to.

But there's some good news. In fact, it's great news. That eternal penalty has already been paid. God Himself paid it and paved the road for our salvation through Jesus Christ. Jesus Christ is the *only* road, the only means by which we may be saved. Why? Because his sinless life and his death at Calvary are the perfect substitute for you, satisfying the demands of a holy God.

The road to salvation through Jesus Christ is clearly presented in the New Testament. The Apostle Paul's letter to the Romans teaches us some principles about this that will help solve the problem we all face.

1. ALL PEOPLE ARE BORN SINNERS

We are all unrighteous people.

As it is written, "Not even one person is righteous. No one understands. No one searches for God. All have turned away. Together they have become completely worthless."

Romans 3:10-12

This means that no one is righteous before God and, in fact, no one is even searching for Him.

2. All People Sin

Our best efforts will never measure up.

… since all have sinned and continue to fall short of God's glory.

Romans 3:23

This means that *you* have sinned. You have not earned, and do not deserve, eternal life. There are two things you need to know to be saved: *First*, you need to know that you are a sinner who has violated God's laws. *Second*, you need to know that there is a terrible and eternal price for sin.

3. The Price of Sin is Death

Adam sinned and gave Satan a foothold in the world. By nature, we are all separated from God.

Just as sin entered the world through one man, and death from sin, therefore everyone dies, because everyone has sinned.

Romans 5:12

We are all born in sin. We deserve death and hell.

4. Jesus Paid Your Debt

He did this by dying in your place.

For the wages of sin is death, but the free gift of God is eternal life in union with the Messiah Jesus our Lord.

Romans 6:23

5. You Have Earned Death, not Eternal Life

So Jesus, in effect, went to the "Bank of Heaven" and paid your debt for you. Jesus paid the price for you to obtain salvation and eternal life. You cannot earn this payment. Eternal life must be accepted as a free gift from God.

6. Christ Died in Your Place

He paid your price, suffering so that you would not have to suffer eternally.

*But God demonstrates his love for us by the fact that the
Messiah died for us while we were still sinners.*

Romans 5:8

Due to unconditional love, Christ died in your place, paying a debt He did not owe. We all have an unpaid debt of sin that Christ is willing to pay for us. How do we get our debts paid by Christ? If you accept His payment of your debt by receiving Him as your Lord and Savior, He will make you His child and take you to heaven when you die.

His invitation is open to anyone… even you.

"Everyone who calls on the name of the Lord will be saved."

Romans 10:13

The word "everyone" includes you. The word "saved" means to be delivered from the guilt and penalty of sin. That includes the present guilt you've incurred. One day in the next life it will include permanent deliverance from the power and presence of it. How do you "call on the name of the Lord" to be saved?

7. You Must Confess your Sin and Declare His Lordship

You declare his Lordship over your life by believing in your heart that God raised Christ from the dead.

*If you declare with your mouth that Jesus is Lord, and believe
in your heart that God raised him from the dead, you will
be saved. For one believes with his heart and is justified, and
declares with his mouth and is saved.*

Romans 10:9-10

The Bible promises us that God forgives our sin when we accept the work that Christ did for us when He died on Calvary. You can do this by praying this short, simple prayer:

"Lord, Jesus, I have broken God's holy Law. I know that I am a sinner and I need you. I know that you paid the price for my sins by dying on the cross. I ask that you forgive my sins; and I receive you as my Savior and Lord. I thank you for forgiving my sins and giving me eternal life. Take control of the throne of my life. Make me the kind of person you want me to be. Amen."

Look to God's Word for encouragement as you begin your new life in Christ. Remember these simple truths:

- *If we make it our habit to confess our sins, he is faithful and righteous to forgive us those sins and cleanse us from all unrighteousness. (1 John 1:9)*
- *The Spirit himself testifies with our spirit that we are God's children. (Romans 8:16)*
- *For by such grace you have been saved through faith. This does not come from you; it is the gift of God and not the result of works, lest anyone boast. (Ephesians 2:8)*
- *For I consider that the sufferings of this present time are not worth comparing to the glory that will be revealed to us. (Romans 8:18)*
- *I have written these things to you who believe in the name of the Son of God so that you may know that you have eternal life. (1 John 5:13)*
- *Therefore, if anyone is in Christ, he is a new creation. Old things have disappeared, and—look!—all things have become new! All of this comes from God, who has reconciled us to himself through Christ… (2 Corinthians 5:17-18a)*

Be sure to read a portion of God's Word every day and look for a local church to attend so you can be equipped to grow in your new life.

An Introduction to the Koinonia Institute

BY CHARLES W. MISSLER, PHD
FOUNDER - KOINONIA INSTITUTE

You are invited to undertake a lifelong adventure, exploring the Word of God among an international fellowship without borders — neither intellectual nor geographic. This is an opportunity to "bloom where you are planted" by studying the Bible — and related topics — in virtual classrooms on the Internet, while discovering the unique calling on your own life and preparing for the challenges which will inevitably emerge on your personal horizon.

This is not for everyone. It is designed for those who are truly committed to becoming an Ambassador for the Coming King. Here you will find flexible paths of achievement without any straitjackets of presumption or tradition. We are non-denominational, but decidedly from a conservative, traditional, evangelical perspective.

We believe that the world is heading into extremely turbulent times that will test all of our presumptions and beliefs. It is our objective to identify, encourage, and equip leadership for the challenges ahead. Pray seriously about joining us and assisting us in developing this unique Fellowship.

MISSION STATEMENT

Koinonia Institute is dedicated to training and equipping the serious Christian for ministry in today's world.

For several decades the ministry of Koinonia House has been to create, develop, and distribute educational materials for those who take the Bible seriously as the inerrant Word of God. As an affiliated ministry, the Koinonia Institute is focused on three supporting areas:

- To provide instructional programs to facilitate serious study of the Bible among thinking Christians;

- To encourage and facilitate both individual and small group weekly study programs for personal growth; and

- To research, monitor and publish information to stimulate awareness of the strategic trends which impact our times and our personal ministries and stewardships.

The Institute is committed to accomplishing these goals through a program of lifelong learning, utilizing Internet resources as a means to do this and creating and developing an intelligence network among its members. Koinonia Institute is formed around three tracks — The Berean, The Issachar, and The Koinonos, which can lead to a two and four year degree in Biblical Studies. For information about each track, please see the Student Handbook.

Visit our website at https://koinoniainstitute.org

INDEX

Symbols
1 Samuel 21:1-6 152
1 Timothy 1:3-7 33
2 Chronicles 9:1-12 161
2 Peter 2:1-3 34

A
Abel 120, 121
Able 120
Abraham 88, 143, 144, 145
Acts 8:27-35 190
Acts 28:25-27 185
Adam and Eve 70, 82, 116
Against Heresies 41
Aleppo Codex 56
Alphabet, Hebrew 22, 23, 54, 249
Alphabet, Hittite 23, 24
Alphabet, Proto-Hebrew 23

B
Bethesda Pool 44, 45
Biblical Archaeology Review .. 225

C
Cain 121
Capernaum 147
Chetubim 44, 50, 51, 152, 156
Chronicles 24:20-22 121
Circumcision 64
Creed of Athanasius 15, 19
Creed of Chalcedon 14

D
Daniel ... 127, 156, 207, 208, 209
Daniel 7:13 158
Daniel 9:24-26 127
Dan Musick 13
Darren Slade 181
Dead Sea Scrolls 179, 184
Deutero-Isaiah 179
Deuteronomy 6:4-5 104
Deuteronomy 6:10-15 107
Deuteronomy 6:16-19 108
Deuteronomy 8:1-20 105
Deuteronomy 18:18-19 84
Deuteronomy 19:15-21 109
Dr. John Piper 27, 28
Dr. Robert Dick Wilson ... 11, 12,
  69, 164, 222

E
Elijah 103, 148, 149, 168
Emergent Church. 26, 27, 28, 29,
  32
Ephesians 4:11-16 36

G
Garden of Eden 82, 224
Genesis 3:15 82
Genesis 49:10 78
Gospel of John 9, 40
Gospel of Luke 39
Gospel of Mark 38
Gospel of Matthew 37, 182

H
Hagiography 13
Hebrew Scriptures 1, 2, 7,
  43, 48, 49, 59, 76, 87, 156, 199,
  215, 216, 222

277

Heresy 31
Hosea 150, 210, 212, 213
Hosea 6:1-7 150

I

Isaac 64, 88, 143, 144
Isaiah 10, 172, 178, 179, 180, 182, 183, 196, 197, 198, 199, 200, 201, 205
Isaiah 1:9 187
Isaiah 6:1-5 180
Isaiah 6:9-10 .... 173, 186
Isaiah 9:1-2 184
Isaiah 11:10 188
Isaiah 29:13-21 198
Isaiah 40:3-5 189
Isaiah 42:1-4 194
Isaiah 53:1-2 179
Isaiah 53:1-12 191
Isaiah 53:12 200
Isaiah 54:10-14 201
Isaiah 56:6-7 202
Isaiah 62:1-3 195
Isaiah 65:1-3 195

J

Jacob 64, 78, 81, 82, 89, 143, 144
Jeremiah 5:20-31 170
Jeremiah 7:8-15 203
John 1:3 119
John 1:19-25 83
John 1:23 189
John 1:45 9
John 2:13-17 204
John 3:13-15 72
John 5:8-12 46
John 5:17-18 46
John 5:24-29 47
John 5:39-40 48
John 5:43-47 10
John 5:45-47 48

John 6:13-15 84
John 6:30-3 85
John 6:44-45 200
John 6:49 85
John 7:19 74
John 7:22 64
John 8:2-11 112
John 8:37-39 145
John 8:56-58 146
John 10:34-36 86
John 12:37-38 .... 179, 190
John 12:37-41 185
John 12:39-43 180
John 13:18-19 154
John 15:23-25 154
John the Baptizer 74, 83, 188, 214
Jonah 116, 165, 167, 168, 169, 170
Jude 3-19 34
Jude 20-2 35
Jude 24-25 35

K

Kenosis 12, 13, 20
Kenoticists 13, 15, 16, 17, 18
Kenotic (see also kenoticists) .. 15, 17
King David 81, 149, 154, 155, 156, 158, 159, 160, 234
Kings 10:1-10 161
King Solomon 160
Koiné Greek 25, 86

L

Leningrad Codex 56
Leprosy 63
Leviticus 14:1-32 60
Leviticus 19:18 104
Luke 3:4-6 188
Luke 4:3-4 105
Luke 4:5-8 107

Index

Luke 4:9-12	108	Mark 10:2-4	69
Luke 4:16-20	194	Mark 10:5-9	119
Luke 4:16-30	206	Mark 10:17-19	71
Luke 6:1-5	152	Mark 11:15-17	202
Luke 7:26-27	213	Mark 12:10-11	159
Luke 7:48-50	118	Mark 12:24-27	144
Luke 8:4-10	178	Mark 12:28-34	104
Luke 10:8-12	147	Mark 12:35-37	155
Luke 11:29-32	166	Mark 13:14-19	208
Luke 11:48-51	120	Mark 13:24-25	197
Luke 11:49-51	120	Mark 13:26	208
Luke 13:35	160	Mark 14:2	211
Luke 16:16-17	74	Mark 14:17-21	49
Luke 17:26-27	143	Mark 14:48-50	211
Luke 17:28-30	147	Mark 14:61-62	156
Luke 18:17-20	71	Masoretic Text	57, 179
Luke 18:31-33	87	Matthew 3:3	188
Luke 19:8-10	145	Matthew 4:12-14	183
Luke 19:45-46	202	Matthew 5:17-19	50
Luke 20:17-18	159, 160	Matthew 8:1-4	59
Luke 20:37	145	Matthew 8:5-12	143
Luke 21:20	125	Matthew 8:16-17	190
Luke 21:21-24	127	Matthew 10:11-15	146
Luke 22:36	200	Matthew 10:26-28	117
Luke 23:14-27	77	Matthew 10:34-36	209
Luke 23:29-31	212	Matthew 11:23-24	147
Luke 23:44-47	78	Matthew 12:1-8	150
		Matthew 12:15-21	193
M		Matthew 12:38-41	166
Malachi	7, 213, 214	Matthew 12:42	160
Manna	84, 85	Matthew 13:10-13	170
Mark 2:10	116	Matthew 13:10-15	172
Mark 2:23-28	151	Matthew 13:14-15	184
Mark 4:10-12	177	Matthew 13:53-58	205
Mark 6:1-6	205	Matthew 15:1-6	67
Mark 7:5-8	198	Matthew 15:7-9	186, 197
Mark 7:6-7	186	Matthew 16:1-4	167
Mark 7: 8-10	70	Matthew 18:15-16	108
Mark 7:11-13	70	Matthew 19:1-6	68
Mark 9:2-6	148	Matthew 19:3-6	116
Mark 9:11-12	213		

Matthew 19:7-8 69
Matthew 19:16-19 71
Matthew 21:12-13 202
Matthew 21:14-16 153
Matthew 21:42-44 158
Matthew 22:29-32 144
Matthew 22:35-40 103
Matthew 22:41-46 155
Matthew 23:1-7 87
Matthew 23:37-39 159
Matthew 24:15-18 208
Matthew 24:29 197
Matthew 24:30 211
Matthew 24:31 211
Matthew 24:36-39 142
Matthew 26:63-64 156
Micah 209, 210
Moses. 22, 44, 46, 47, 48, 59, 64, 68, 70, 72, 74, 83, 87, 119, 148, 149
Mount Sinai 67

N

Nebuchadnezzar 242, 243
Neo-Arians 15
Neviim 44
Nineveh 116, 166, 167, 168, 169
Noah 142
Numbers 21:4-9 72
Numbers 24:17-19 82

P

Pharisees 67, 68, 69, 70, 73, 83, 112, 116, 120, 146, 155, 166, 196, 198
Philippians 2:6-8 20
Protoevangelium 82
Proto-Isaiah 178, 180
Psalm 8:1-2 153
Psalm 110 155
Psalm 110:1-7 157

Q

Queen of Sheba 160, 163

R

Revelation 19:14-15 32
Robert Dick Wilson (see also Dr. Robert Dick Wilson) 11, 55, 69, 85, 164, 221, 222
Roberts Fragment 41
Romans 9:29 187
Romans 10:15-17 191
Romans 10:20 195
Romans 15:12 187

S

Samaritan Targum 80
Sennacherib.. 169, 235, 236, 240, 241, 246
Sennacherib, King (see also Sennacherib) 168
Septuagint 57, 66, 179
Shiloh 78, 89
Sodom 146, 147
Synoptic Gospels.... 71, 152, 201, 205

T

Talmud 52, 53
Tanakh 7, 12, 43, 48, 51, 64, 115, 149, 208, 220
Targum 79, 80, 82, 174, 175, 176, 188
Targum of Jonathan (see also Targum) 80, 176
Targum of Onkelos (see also Targum) 79, 176
Tel Dan inscription 149
Ten Commandments.. 26, 71, 76, 103
The Shining One 82
Timothy 3:1-6 33

Torah . 22, 44, 50, 59, 64, 66, 67, 68, 74, 213

W
War of the Jews 128

Z
Zechariah 120, 121

ABOUT THE AUTHOR

WILLIAM P. WELTY, PH.D.

Dr. Welty (http://williamwelty.com) is the Executive Director of the ISV Foundation of Bellflower, California, producers of the *Holy Bible: International Standard Version*. He is a graduate (M.Div., 1978) of Trinity Evangelical Divinity School of Deerfield, Illinois and holds a Ph.D. degree in Christian Communications (2005) from Louisiana Baptist University.

ABOUT THE HOLY BIBLE: INTERNATIONAL STANDARD VERSION

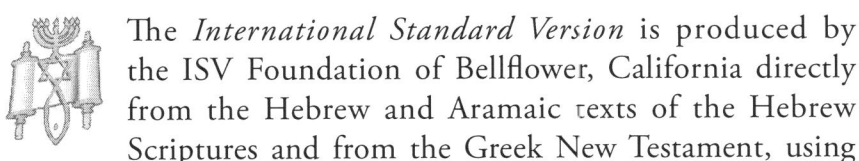

The *International Standard Version* is produced by the ISV Foundation of Bellflower, California directly from the Hebrew and Aramaic texts of the Hebrew Scriptures and from the Greek New Testament, using a team of conservative Biblical and lay scholars drawn from the international Christian community. It is published in a variety of electronic formats, including Amazon Kindle® and Barnes and Noble Nook® editions, as well as Adobe Acrobat® PDF formats and in HTML format for use by webmasters. Visit http://isv.org to learn more.

ALSO BY THE AUTHOR:

A Person of Substance: Word Studies on the Character Qualities of Christian Leadership. (Bellflower, CA: ISV Foundation, 2014)

Anselm Writes Again: A 2st Century Scholar Revisits a Christian Classic. (Bellflower, CA: ISV Foundation, 2015)

The Creation Account: Addressing the Young Earth vs. Old Earth Controversy. (Bellflower, CA: ISV Foundation, 2016)

For a Time Like This: Studies in the Life of Queen Esther. (Bellflower, CA: ISV Foundation, 2016)

How to Repent When You're Not Guilty: A Guide for God's People Who Want to Make America Great Again. (Bellflower, CA: ISV Foundation, 2016)

I, Jesus: an Autobiography. (Reporoa, New Zealand: Koinonia Institute, 2014)

On the Validity of the State of Israel. (Reporoa, New Zealand: Koinonia Institute, 2015)

Partners in God's Grand Plan: Studies in the Lives of Naomi and Ruth. (Bellflower, CA: ISV Foundation, 2016)

Since He Wrote about Me: Jesus of Nazareth speaks in his own words about the authenticity, reliability, and accuracy of the Hebrew Scriptures. (Bellflower, CA: ISV Foundation, 2016)

Surviving God's Discipline of a Nation. (Bellflower, CA: ISV Founda-tion, 2015)

Mary: Ten Test Questions for the World's Finest Woman. (Coeur d'Alene, ID: Koinonia House, 2016)

The Messiah's Manifesto: Studies in the Sermon on the Mount. (Bellflower, CA: ISV Foundation, 2016)

Ministry for the Senior Saint: The Book of Deuteronomy and its Lessons from the Life of Moses. (Bellflower, CA: ISV Foundation, 2017)

A User's Manual for the Bible: A Simple and Practical Answer to the Chal-lenge Faced by the Church from the Emergent Church Heresy. (Bell-flower, CA: ISV Foundation, 2014)

What to Expect when You Go to Court: A Case Study in Politically Motivated State Persecution. (Bellflower, CA: ISV Foundation, 2017)

The World's Last Emperor: Jesus of Nazareth Speaks about the End of the World and How he will Make it Happen. (Bellflower, CA: ISV Foun-dation, 2015)

As Contributing Author and/or Editor

A Harmony of the Gospels from the International Standard Version. Edited by William Welty. (Toluca Lake, CA: Davidson Press, 2013)

Between Christ and Muhammad: The Irreconcilable Differences of Christianity and Islam. (Yorba Linda, CA: Davidson Press, 2002)

Encyclopedia of Bible Difficulties. By Dr. Gleason L. Archer. Contributing researcher: William Welty. (Zondervan Publishing, 1982)

Golgotha: The Search for the True Location of Christ's Crucifixion. By Dr. Robert Cornuke. Contributing editor: William Welty. (Coeur d'Alene, ID: Koinonia House: 2016)

Holy Bible: International Standard Version. Associate Editor: William Welty. (Bellflower, CA: ISV Foundation 1996-2016)

How to Be a People Helper. By Dr. Gary R. Collins. Contributing researcher: William Welty. (Vision House: 1976)

Ministry, Finance, and Ethics. (Irvine, CA: Fieldstead Institute, 1984)

Secret History: An Eyewitness Account of the Rise of Mormonism. Translated from John Ahmanson's original Danish edition by Dr. Gleason L. Archer; edited by William Welty. (Chicago: Moody Press, 1984)

See www.williamwelty.com to learn more.